THE
LITTLE
HISTORY
OF
ENGLAND

JONATHAN
McGOVERN

For my parents

First published 2024

The History Press
97 St George's Place, Cheltenham,
Gloucestershire, GL50 3QB
www.thehistorypress.co.uk

British Library Cataloguing in Publication Data.
A catalogue record for this book is available from the British Library.

ISBN 978 1 80399 466 6

Typesetting and origination by The History Press.
Printed and bound in Great Britain by TJ Books Limited, Padstow, Cornwall.

Trees for Life

CONTENTS

England in the late ninth century.

The United Kingdom and Ireland in the present day.

PREFATORY NOTE

This book is a super-concentrated history of England. I have tried to make the narrative as simple as possible without dumbing the material down. If this has meant occasionally having to state the obvious, I can only ask readers to take it in good part. I wanted this book to be accessible, dependable and, above all, useful.

1

IN THE BEGINNING

England is not really very old. There was no kingdom of England until the tenth century AD, no kingdom of Great Britain until 1707 and no United Kingdom of Great Britain and Ireland until 1801. The universe, by contrast, started to expand 13.8 billion years ago, and the earth was formed out of a whirling cloud of dust and gas about 9.3 billion years later. The landmass of Britain took shape over millions of years as a result of massive geological events such as the closure of oceans and the collision of continents.

Dinosaurs roamed parts of the country until their extinction at the end of the Cretaceous, about 66 million years ago, due to the fallout from an asteroid colliding with the earth. The landmass of Britain began to resemble its current shape during the Tertiary Period, which ended 2.6 million years ago. Britain's climate during the Tertiary was largely subtropical, the coasts arrayed with palm trees and the swamps infested with crocodiles.

Britain's prehistory was influenced by wave upon wave of human migration. Bipedal hominins of the genus *Homo* evolved in Africa 2.3 million years ago and may have first found their way to Britain as early as 900,000 BC, during the Early Pleistocene epoch, when Britain's climate cycled between congenial warmth and icy cold. For an unimaginable length of time, successive waves of hunter-gatherer hominins made Britain their home, including communities of heavy-browed Neanderthals. Hominins travelled to Britain via Doggerland, an area of land that once connected south-east Britain to the continent. They fashioned rudimentary tools and weapons from natural materials like flint, hunted the woolly rhinoceros and the mammoth, and wore skins to stay warm. They were absent from Britain from around 180,000 BC because the climate had become inhospitably cold. During the

Eemian interglacial (130,000–115,000 BC), Doggerland was submerged under water due to rising temperatures and sea levels. It re-emerged as a narrower land bridge when temperatures began to cool again, forming an entry point for hominins to trickle back into Britain from around 60,000 BC.

HOMO SAPIENS

Homo sapiens, the best and worst of creatures, evolved in Africa 200,000 years ago and first arrived in Britain in about 40,000 BC (Upper Palaeolithic period). Early *Homo sapiens* populated Britain for tens of thousands of years. They organized themselves into nomadic kinship groups and practised cave and rock painting. Eventually, they displaced their hominin cousins. The most famous early *Homo sapiens* specimen from Britain is Cheddar Man, dating from the eighth millennium BC (Mesolithic period), whose remains were discovered in a subterranean waterway in Somerset at the turn of the twentieth century.

A new, comparatively advanced type of *Homo sapiens* reached Britain's shores from the Mediterranean in around 4000 BC (Neolithic Period), crossing over on rafts because Doggerland was now permanently submerged. The country that welcomed the Neolithic settlers would have been a magical place to modern eyes, covered in forests that had sprung up since the melting of the Pleistocene ice. These settlers introduced farming to Britain, lived in villages and were well organized and technical. Though their lives were hard – with atrocious levels of infant mortality – they probably 'worked fewer hours per year than a modern man or woman'.[1] Their outstanding legacy is Stonehenge, which they built over the course of several centuries in what is now Wiltshire, with the iconic circle of sarsen stones erected between 2600 and 2400 BC. The purpose of Stonehenge is still debated, but it was probably some kind of temple. For reasons now unknown, possibly genocide or perhaps just disease, the Neolithic settlers were displaced in around 2400 BC by yet another wave of migrants, named the Beaker People because of the bell-shaped beakers they buried in the graves of their dead. The Beaker People were descended from the Yamnaya peoples of the Eurasian Steppe, a belt of grassland stretching from Central Europe to East Asia.

CELTIC MIGRATION

The last great prehistoric migration to Britain began in the Bronze Age. In around 1000 BC, there was an influx of settlers from what is now France, who brought with them Celtic culture and languages. This is about the time that Britain was ruled, according to legend, by a Trojan descendant of Aeneas called Brute, who is said have rid the land of giants. Fanciful chronicles, such as Geoffrey of Monmouth's twelfth-century *History of the Kings of Britain*, record that Brute was the ancestor of King Leir and other legendary kings. Centuries after the arrival of the Beaker People and the Celtic migrants, their descendants could plausibly consider themselves indigenous Britons because the details would likely have passed out of memory by then. It is hard to know how far the two groups intermingled, or to what extent their numbers were boosted by continuing Celtic migration. These genetically and culturally diverse peoples are commonly referred to as the Celts or Britons. They got on with their simple lives while great civilizations were growing up elsewhere in the world. The ascendant Roman Republic proved its growing might in 202 BC, when a Roman army defeated the Carthaginian general Hannibal.

The population of Britain in the first century BC was possibly as large as 2 million, equivalent to about a fifth of the population of modern London. These 2 million people were divided into more than thirty tribes, each with their own customs and chieftains (sometimes called kings and queens). There were the Parisi in what is now the East Riding of Yorkshire, the Demetae and Silures in South Wales and the Dumnonii in the West Country. The Romans called the whole island 'Britannia' because some of its inhabitants were known as the Pritani. According to Roman testimony, each tribe had two governing classes: a knightly class, who served as military leaders, and a priestly class called druids, who arranged religious ceremonies, settled legal disputes, divined the future and even organized human sacrifices, possibly using the terrible Wicker Man. The Greek geographer Strabo observed that the Britons were taller and darker-haired than the Gauls, or French Celts, but also more barbaric. Not so barbaric, though: they knew the arts of metalwork, pottery, glass production and horsemanship and they traded with their neighbours, regularly providing tin to enterprising Phoenician merchants. Some Britons lived in basic towns that were connected to each other by a network of roads. Like their ancestors, they dwelt in roundhouses: primitive structures built of stone or other materials, with conical thatched roofs.

ROMAN BRITAIN

Great empires invariably conquer, absorb, bully or at the very least meddle in the affairs of less developed states. This is done to protect imperial interests, certainly, but there is more to it than that: empires reach out, probe and expand as if by some law of nature. Britain's history was to be shaped forever when her elites came into direct conflict with the Roman Empire. Julius Caesar, then Roman governor of Illyricum and Cisalpine Gaul, invaded Britain in 55 and 54 BC (Late Iron Age). The first invasion was really a reconnaissance mission, while the second was a display of military strength, with Caesar accompanied by five legions. His immediate aim was to stop Britain from aiding the enemies of Rome during the Gallic Wars, so his interventions were modest: he made treaties, established a few Roman puppets as British chieftains, and took a few token hostages, before returning his attention to the main objective, the conquest of Transalpine Gaul. He later described the ways of the Britons in his *Commentaries on the Gallic War*: the men shaved all their body hair, saving only their moustaches and the hair on their heads, and daubed themselves with war-paint to enhance their fearsomeness in battle. He also claimed that the Celts practised polyandry. Caesar's *Gallic War*, however, is not exactly a reliable guide to prehistoric Britain: modern archaeologists have shown that his comments on British agriculture are grossly inaccurate.

About a century after Caesar's departure, Emperor Claudius, the fourth emperor since the end of the Roman Republic, authorized a more ambitious invasion of Britain. Rome was alarmed by the spread of anti-imperial sentiment on the island, particularly on the part of two kings of the Catuvellauni tribe, the brothers Caratacus and Togodumnus, who ruled territory that now falls within London, Essex and Hampshire. These brothers attacked a Roman ally named Verica, king of the Atrebates tribe, which furnished a good pretext for Roman intervention. Claudius also coveted Britain's rich mineral resources: gold, silver, tin and lead. Four Roman legions under the command of Aulus Plautius landed in Britain in around May AD 43, probably at Richborough on the east coast of Kent. Some British chieftains resisted the arrival of the Claudian invaders, while others put up little to no defence, signing up as client kings under the protection and authority of Rome.

Togodumnus was slain in battle, while his brother evaded capture for a few more years and the invaders seized the strategically important town of Camulodunum (Colchester) from the Catuvellauni tribe. They set it up as their capital, intending to extend Roman dominion over the whole island. Emperor Claudius himself arrived in Britain in August with war elephants and a portion of the Praetorian Guard – an elite unit of imperial bodyguards – though he stayed no longer than a couple of weeks. When Plautius was recalled to Rome in AD 47, Publius Ostorius Scapula succeeded him as governor. Ostorius Scapula and his successors established hundreds of military sites in Britain, ranging from small forts and stores bases to full legionary fortresses. Imperial Rome maintained overseas territories in part for military-strategic reasons: the emperor needed the support of a large army, and it was politically safer to have such an army spread out across the world rather than concentrated in one place.

BOUDICCA'S REBELLION

The Britons eventually revolted, as the subjugated inevitably do, in AD 60, under the leadership of Queen Boudicca from the East Anglian Iceni tribe. According to the Roman historian Cassius Dio, Boudicca exhorted her men to oppose the 'imported despotism' and to return to their 'ancestral mode of life', for it was better to be poor and free than wealthy and enslaved.[2] The rebels sacked Colchester and other towns, slaughtering tens of thousands of Roman citizens, but the rebellion was eventually crushed by the fifth Roman governor, Gaius Suetonius Paulinus, whose men reportedly slew 80,000 Britons in battle. With their immense resources and knowledge, the Romans seemed like creatures from another world. They were to remain Britain's overlords for more than three centuries.

Successive Roman governors extended imperial dominion over the island, conquering Wales in the reign of Emperor Flavius (AD 69–79), but they failed to subdue Scotland or Ireland. Although the governor Gnaeus Julius Agricola won a significant victory over the tribes of Scotland at the Battle of the Graupian Hill (AD 83), his successors failed to follow up on this achievement. The Romans evacuated southern Scotland in the reigns of Trajan and Hadrian, and Hadrian's Wall was built in 122 across what is now Cumbria and Northumberland to guard against incursions by the Caledonians, a Celtic tribe. This policy of retreat was briefly reversed during the reign of Emperor Antoninus Pius (138–61), first of the so-called Good Emperors. In Antoninus' reign, Hadrian's Wall was temporarily abandoned, and a new turf wall called the Antonine Wall was built further north, west of the Firth of Forth. However, Hadrian's Wall came back into service in around 154. After fighting a wasteful war on the northern border, the Romans abandoned their ambition of conquering Scotland. The best and most fertile land, in any case, was to be found in lowland Britain.

WHAT THE ROMANS DID FOR US

There were two kinds of Roman province: senatorial provinces, governed by annually appointed proconsuls, and imperial provinces, run by long-term governors accountable directly to the emperor. Roman Britain was an imperial province, run with the aid of a complex bureaucracy. The governor's staff was headed by a centurion, who was assisted by other officeholders such as adjutants and registrars. Taxes were collected by procurators, who operated semi-independently of the governor and received an annual salary of 200,000 sesterces. Britain's client kings were left undisturbed at first so long as they supported the Roman administration, but one after another their kingdoms fell under the direct governance of Rome.

The Romans founded new towns across Britain, recognizing that urbanization was the foundation of civility, and these towns served as administrative centres. The Romans were the first to recognize a piece of land north of the Thames as prime real estate, where they founded the great city of Londinium. Roman London was graced with a forum, a basilica, an amphitheatre, temples and bathhouses. The conquerors also laid at least 8,000 miles of layered road in Britain. Two of the great Roman roads were Watling Street, which ran north-west from Dover all the way to Chester, and the Fosse Way, which connected London to York. The British gradually succumbed to the allure of urban civilization, with all its creature comforts. Their elites built villas for themselves in the Roman style, especially in the south, with timber frames, mosaic floors and underfloor heating. They became rather fond of sipping imported wine from red Samian ware cups. However, Britain remained very much a country under occupation, with over 50,000 troops stationed there by the mid-second century. The governors exercised absolute authority over everyone living in Britain except Roman citizens, who had the right to appeal to Rome.

Emperor Septimius Severus (reigned 193–211), a despot who had to be carried in a litter on account of illness, arrived in Britain in 208 accompanied by his family and a section of the Praetorian Guard. He directed a campaign against the Caledonians in Scotland and put down a rising of the Maetae, another Celtic tribe living south of the Caledonians, in 210. During his reign, Severus split Britain into two provinces, Britannia Superior in the south and Britannia Inferior in the north, with Londinium and Eboracum (York) chosen as the respective capitals. The administrative geography of Britain would thus remain unchanged until 296, when the co-emperor Diocletian divided Britain into four provinces, administered from London, York, Cirencester and Lincoln. After facing three years of guerrilla warfare in the north, Severus died at York in 211.

The third century was a time of great political insecurity for the Roman Empire, which was troubled by coups and countercoups, and emperors being assassinated seemingly every other year. This inevitably led to increasing militarization in Britain. In around 286, the Roman naval commander Carausius pulled off a coup to establish himself as 'emperor' of an independent territory that included Britain and part of France, but was eventually assassinated by his own finance minister, and Britain was reconquered by the co-emperor Constantius I in 296. The Roman army, newly conscious of its enormous power, was at this time in the habit of appointing emperors on its own authority, choosing whichever men happened to offer its soldiers the most money, termed a 'donative'. The army did not hesitate to remove its chosen emperors if they failed to pay up, or if some other candidate came along and offered more. For instance, Constantine the Great (reigned 312–37) was proclaimed emperor by the army at York in 306.

CHRISTIANITY AND COLLAPSE

The Roman Empire had always been polytheistic, but for three centuries the monotheistic Christian faith had been radiating out from its point of origin in Palestine, then a Roman province. In a decision that would have momentous consequences for world history, Emperor Constantine converted to Christianity because he believed that the Christian God had blessed his efforts at the critical Battle of Milvian Bridge on 28 October 312. Constantine's conversion, and the later promotion of Christianity as the Roman state religion under Emperor Theodosius (reigned 379–92), placed all the might of the Roman Empire behind what had once been a peripheral and persecuted religion. Bishops were introduced in Britain by 314, and by the late fourth century Christianity was widespread. Among the British Christians were Pelagius, branded a heretic for denying the doctrine of original sin, and Patrick, who served as Bishop of Ireland and later became her patron saint. The fourth century was a veritable golden age for Roman Britain, a time of prosperity and commercial expansion. The Romans were keen to maintain peace and order on the island, which indicates that it had become an important source of revenue.

The eventual decline of Roman power in Britain was closely connected to the general decline of the Roman Empire. The Roman army in Britain removed to Gaul in 407 on the orders of the lowborn usurper Emperor Constantine III, and there was a native British revolt against Roman rule in 409. In the following year, Alaric, king of the Germanic tribe known as the Visigoths, sacked the City of Rome itself. From this date, the Romans were too troubled with internal crises to care much about a rainswept isle where neither olive nor vine could prosper. They stopped demanding taxation from Britain, and over the following couple of decades, Roman infrastructure in Britain disintegrated. The collapse of Roman Britain positively invited invasion. The Britons faced immediate incursions from Picts (tribesmen from what is now Scotland) and Scots (tribesmen from what is now Ireland). They appealed to Emperor Honorius for help in around 410, but he advised them 'to take precautions on their own behalf'.[3] The Roman administration and army were leaving for good. Britain was on her own.

2

THE ANGLO-SAXONS
(426–1066)

There is scant evidence about the nature of British government immediately after the Roman withdrawal. It has been suggested that emergency power might have been wielded by the council of the *civitates*, a formerly ceremonial body composed of representatives of the towns. Alternatively, British petty emperors may have emerged to fill the power vacuum. All former Roman provinces experienced 'radical material simplifications', and many technologies requiring large-scale organization fell into abeyance.[1] However, some Roman infrastructure survived. The British citizens of Verulamium (near St Albans) continued to maintain their town's plumbing network after the departure of their erstwhile masters, while a Roman bath-house in Bath was still open for business a century later.

The events that followed are described in an epistle by the sixth-century British writer Gildas. Titled *On the Ruin and Conquest of Britain*, this epistle tells a compelling, if rather simplified, story. In 426, a generation after the Romans had left, a man named Vortigern established himself as king of the Britons. Vortigern is said to have invited Germanic mercenaries into the country to defend its inhabitants from barbarian incursions. Gildas simply called the mercenaries Saxons, but later sources identified them as Angles, Saxons and Jutes (and sometimes Frisians), hailing from territories now in northern Germany, the Netherlands and Denmark. They were promised land grants in return for their help, a typically Roman strategy, which suggests that Vortigern may have been a member of the Romano-British elite.

The mercenaries were led, according to tradition, by two brothers called Hengest and Horsa. Vortigern's short-sighted policy was to have disastrous consequences for the Britons, as the newcomers are said to have mutinied and claimed large swathes of territory for themselves and their kin. A period of protracted warfare ensued between the natives and the Germanic warriors, whose descendants became known as the Anglo-Saxons, or English. This narrative is roughly consistent with the best modern research, though geneticists have proved that continental northern Europeans had already begun to arrive in Britain in substantial numbers before the Roman withdrawal. The three centuries following the fall of the Western Roman Empire in 476 are known as the Migration Period for good reason; wandering and dislocated tribes, mostly from northern Europe, moved into former Roman territories in droves in search of opportunity.

KING ARTHUR

Legend has it that the Britons were led to victory by King Arthur, son of Uther Pendragon. Arthur is not mentioned in any documents until the ninth century, apart from a solitary reference in a Welsh poem, *The Gododdin*, which was written in around 600 but carries little weight because the relevant passage may have been interpolated by an even later scribe. Many of the details now associated with Arthur – the magicians Merlin and Morgaine, the sword in the stone and the knights of the round table – were probably invented by later writers, though it is not impossible that they were passed down from an earlier, oral tradition. There was certainly a British military triumph in around the year 500 at Mount Badon, probably located somewhere in southern England, which may have been the work of a king named Arthur.

However glorious, the British victory was short-lived, for the Anglo-Saxons later regained the upper hand and won a decisive victory in 571 at Bedcanford, a place that has not been located with certainty by modern historians. By the mid-seventh century, the Anglo-Saxons ruled most of what is now England, and they ultimately became the dominant (and quite possibly the majority) population. A number of British kingdoms survived, such as Cornwall, which did not come under English rule until the early ninth century. Some displaced Celts took refuge among the Welsh hills and the crags and glens of the Scottish Highlands. The triumph of the Anglo-Saxons is reflected in the fact that a version of their language is still spoken in England today. The Welsh and Cornish languages, meanwhile, are direct descendants of the Celtic tongue that was predominant in Britain: Brythonic. England's place names are also overwhelmingly of Germanic origin, though it is difficult to know how many of these are Germanic variants of earlier place names.

Anglo-Saxon communities coalesced into territorial kingdoms in the sixth century. It used to be said that there were seven kingdoms by the seventh century (The Heptarchy), but in fact the number varied, and there were other kingdoms besides the traditional seven (East Anglia, Essex, Kent, Mercia, Northumbria, Sussex and Wessex). The kings south of the River Humber submitted to overlordship – where necessary – from more powerful kindgoms, while the north-eastern kingdom of Northumbria was normally politically independent. Rival kingdoms competed for supremacy, with Kent, Northumbria, Mercia and Wessex each at one time the most powerful in the land. Northumbria was the hegemon king-dom for most of the seventh century, having gobbled up British kingdoms in the Pennines such as Elmet, but lost its position of supremacy in around 685.

Anglo-Saxon society was stratified, with kings at the top, followed by *ealdormen* and *thegns* (noblemen and gentry; the terms changed meanings over time), *ceorls* (free peasants), *laets* (the half-free) and serfs or slaves (often of 'Celtic' extraction). There were few defined constitutional limits on the power of kings, but in practice they were expected to seek advice in great assemblies, known in later times as the *witan* or *witenagemot*. The common Anglo-Saxon folk lived in little thatched cottages, while their nobles lived in long timber halls.

THE ANGLO-SAXONS FIND GOD

By the sixth century, all the British tribes and kingdoms were Christian. The pagan Anglo-Saxons began to convert to Christianity in the same century, in part because kings sought to civilize and 'Romanize' their dominions. Another attractive feature of Christianity, from a king's point of view, was the doctrine of obedience to rulers, deriving principally from Chapter 13 of St Paul's Epistle to the Romans. The Anglo-Saxon conversion was described at some length in the eighth century by the Venerable

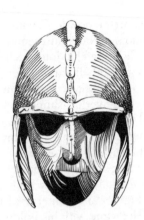

Anglo-Saxon helmet from the late sixth or early seventh century, unearthed in 1939 at Sutton Hoo, Suffolk. Made from iron and tinned copper.

Bede, a polymath who spent most of his life at Jarrow Abbey in Northumbria. The first Christian Anglo-Saxon ruler was King Æthelberht I of Kent (reigned ?560–616), who was converted to the faith by his wife and a delegation of missionaries sent to England by Pope Gregory the Great. After the Christianization of the realm, some English clerics established international reputations. Alcuin of York (d. 804) worked as a tutor in Charlemagne's household and was one of the architects of the Carolingian Renaissance, a flowering of learned culture and scholarship.

Within the Anglo-Saxon Christian church, there were at first divisions between the proponents of Roman and Celtic practices, with the central dispute concerning how to calculate the date of Easter Sunday. At the Synod of Whitby in 664, King Oswiu of Northumbria (reigned 654–70) came down in favour of the Roman date of Easter. Other kings followed suit, and so Oswiu's decision heralded the beginning of the ascendancy of Roman Catholic religion throughout the island.

MERCIA AND WESSEX

In the English kingdoms during the seventh and eighth centuries, succession crises were routine, the murder of kings was commonplace. Three kings of Northumbria were assassinated and four deposed between 765 and 796, as four noble families competed for supreme power. The kingdom of Mercia became the supreme kingdom in the eighth century, expanding its dominions to absorb neighbouring kingdoms such as Hwicce in the West Midlands. The despotic Æthelbald of Mercia (d. 757) was the mightiest king of this period, but little is known about the politics of his reign. He exercised overlordship over southern England, including London, until he was murdered in his sleep by his own bodyguards.

Mercian supremacy continued during the reign of Offa (757–96), the first Anglo-Saxon monarch to be called 'king of the English' (*'rex Anglorum'*) in charters that are definitely authentic. Offa established relations with the mighty Charlemagne, king of the Franks and emperor of the Romans, although he offended Charlemagne with his boldness in trying to negotiate an unequal marriage alliance between his son and Charlemagne's daughter. He also built Offa's Dyke to defend his kingdom from the Welsh dwelling beyond his western border. There is significant debate surrounding the purpose of this 64-mile border rampart, which may have been designed to thwart 'cattle rustlers and small-scale raiding parties' rather than armies.[2] After Offa's long reign came to an end, he was succeeded as king of the Mercians by Ecgfrith (who died of sickness a few months later), followed by Coenwulf (reigned 796–821), remembered as a powerful ruler. Meanwhile, a prince of the Kentish blood royal named Ecgberht, who had formerly been a political exile at the court of Charlemagne, won the crown of Wessex by conquest in 802. In 825, Ecgberht defeated King Beornwulf of Mercia in battle, and in 829 he conquered Essex and received the submission of the king of Northumbria. Wessex thereafter replaced Mercia as the foremost kingdom of England. Southern England has been the dominant element in the British Isles ever since.

VIKING MENACE

Beginning in the late eighth century, the kingdoms of England – along with the rest of western Europe – faced an acute threat from bands of Danish and Norse pagan warriors, known to the English of that time as *flotan*, or seamen. We know them better as the Vikings. When the first Vikings sailed to the British Isles in their enormous longships, they preferred to pick low-hanging fruit, sacking a series of secluded religious houses that they found to be basically defenceless: Lindisfarne Priory on Holy Island in 793, Jarrow Abbey in 794 and Iona Abbey in 795. Over time, their targets became more ambitious, and they held certain advantages over the English, not least the element of surprise, as well as their superior seafaring capability. A Viking ship excavated in Norway two centuries ago (the Gokstad ship) is over 76ft long and would have had the capacity to carry around thirty men.

Addicted to the marauding life, Viking bands fell into a pattern of raiding southern England practically every year. One desperate annual sally, followed by months of ease and idleness, was preferable to toiling at the plough. The most serious invasion was mounted in 865, when three brothers, Ivar the Boneless, Halfdan and Hubba, landed in East Anglia. Unlike earlier raiding parties, whose leaders had been mainly interested in looting, Ivar and his confederates sought lasting conquest. They captured York in 866, renaming it from Eoforwic to Jorvik, and their presence helped to bring unprecedented prosperity to the city. Viking armies also conquered the kingdoms of Northumbria, East Anglia and much of Mercia between 867 and 874 and came very close to conquering Wessex too. It is easy to exaggerate the barbaric nature of the Vikings, who were not without culture, but equally, it should not be forgotten that they sacrificed enemies to Odin by ripping their lungs out through their backs (a practice called 'blood eagle'). That both Anglo-Saxons and Vikings were formidable warriors may be confirmed by the fact that the all-powerful Byzantine emperors, who styled themselves Lords of the Cosmos, employed them indiscriminately as mercenaries to form their imperial bodyguard.

The fate of Wessex still hung in the balance in 871, when an energetic young nobleman by the name of Alfred succeeded his late brother, Æthelred I, as king of the West Saxons. Alfred's military skill, particularly his creation of a standing army and his establishment of naval defences and burhs (fortified settlements surrounded by earthworks), saved his kingdom from Viking domination. According to a probably apocryphal story, first recorded two or three centuries after Alfred's death, the king was forced to hide from Danish Vikings in a West Country swineherd's cottage in 878, where he was chastised by the man's wife for allowing her hearth-baked loaves to become scorched: 'Why, man, do you sit thinking there, and are too proud to turn the bread?'[3] In the same year, Alfred defeated the Danes, led by Guthrum, at the Battle of Edington. Guthrum then agreed to submit to Christian baptism and to withdraw from Wessex as two of the conditions of the Treaty of Chippenham, sometimes called the Treaty of Wedmore.

A later treaty, probably signed in 886, established the boundaries between English territory centred in the south and west and Danish territory centred in the north and east, called the Danelaw because it was administered according to Danish legal traditions. In the later years of his reign, Alfred introduced to the kingdom of Wessex a law-code called the Doom Book, which, among other things, contained the earliest English treason legislation. This code was passed with the consent of the *witan*, arguably a foretaste of the English Parliament's later legislative function. Alfred was traditionally credited with dividing England into counties and hundreds (subdivisions within each county), and while this is now known to be inaccurate, England was certainly 'shired' in the late Anglo-Saxon period. Later in his life, the king was taught to read Latin by a bishop named Asser, and he spent his mature years translating Latin prose and poetry into his native tongue.

THE UNIFICATION OF ENGLAND

Political and territorial unification was the hallmark of the later Anglo-Saxon period. Edward the Elder, king of the West Saxons from 899 to 924, survived a rebellion by his cousin Æthelwold at the very outset of his reign, and in the following decades, he succeeded in capturing most of the Danelaw, forcing the local Anglo-Danish gentry to recognize his sovereignty. He gained control of London in 911, was recognized as king of Mercia in 918 and became overlord of the fledgling kingdom of Scotland in 920. Edward's son Æthelstan (king of the West Saxons 925–939) is often regarded as the first king of England because he came to rule over Wessex, Mercia, Northumbria, Cornwall, York and the Danelaw, winning a famous victory against a coalition of Scots, Dublin Norsemen and Strathclyde Welsh at the Battle of Brunanburh (937).

After Æthelstan's death, however, his composite kingdom collapsed. In 940, King Edmund (reigned 939–46) ceded significant territories in the Midlands and Lincolnshire to Norse Vikings led by Olaf Guthfrithsson, king of Dublin.

It was not until the reign of Edgar (king of the English 959–75) that England was unified for good, 'put together out of the traditions of Mercia and Wessex under the pressure of the Vikings'.[4] The name of England is derived from the Old English name 'Ænglaland', Land of the Angles. Edgar maintained peace by running a strict and powerful government. He also oversaw a programme of monastic reform, attempting to strengthen the moral and spiritual character of monasteries and strictly enforcing the Rule of Saint Benedict, a sixth-century manual of precepts for monastic life. After his death, Edgar was succeeded by his teenage son, Edward the Martyr (reigned 975–8), whose sobriquet gives a clue as to his fate. During Edward's brief reign, two factions contended for political dominance: a royalist 'monastic' party, led by the king, and an 'anti-monastic' party that opposed the growing influence of monks, nominally headed by the king's half-brother, Æthelred. Edward was ultimately murdered by the anti-monastic party at Corfe on 18 March 978, and though Æthelred bears no blame since he was around 10 years old at the time, he was crowned king as a result.

Æthelred II of Wessex, king of England from 979 to 1013 and again from 1014 to 1016, used to be referred to as Æthelred the Unready, but this has long been recognized to be a misnomer based on his Old English nickname. Chroniclers contemptuously called him Æthelred Unræd ('Ill-counselled Æthelred'), a pun on his name implying that he should have sought better advice. Although he seems to have been a capable king in his early adulthood, Æthelred was later dominated by successive factions of powerful advisers. Under his watch, the Vikings – who had by now converted to Christianity – were newly emboldened to make incursions into English territory. At the Battle of Maldon in 991, an English army was wiped out by a host of Viking marauders who arrived on ninety ships. To make matters worse, Æthelred levied a heavy tax on his subjects called the Danegeld, used to buy off invaders and to pay renegade Danish soldiers fighting for the English. Æthelred combined incompetence with ruthlessness; in November 1002, he ordered the slaughter of all the Danes in England, a black deed known as the St Brice's Day Massacre, though how many Danes were actually killed is unknown.

THE DANISH KINGS OF ENGLAND

Swein Forkbeard, king of Denmark, invaded England in 1013, possibly in pursuit of revenge for his slain kinsmen, and forced Æthelred into exile. Though Æthelred soon managed to recapture his throne, his position remained precarious. Swein's son, Cnut, launched a massive invasion of England in 1015 with the aid of his housecarls, a company of elite soldiers, and Æthelred died of unrelated causes in the following year. Cnut defeated Æthelred's son, Edmund Ironside, at the Battle of Ashingdon in Essex in 1016, establishing himself as the first Danish king of England. According to one version of events, Edmund would have won the battle had he not been double-crossed by the Mercian *ealdorman* Eadric Streona, who falsely proclaimed the king's death in the heat of battle to dishearten the English.

Cnut cemented his new position by appointing leading Danish allies to the English aristocracy, and by marrying Æthelred's widow, Emma, in 1017. He had two wives to warm his bed despite being a Christian; the other was called Ælfgifu, literally 'Elf's Gift'. He won the approval of a national assembly held at Oxford in 1018, collecting a tribute of over £80,000 from his new subjects. Cnut built a palace on the bank of the Thames to shore up his power, which was later rebuilt by Edward the Confessor and became known as Westminster Palace. Westminster would serve as a centre of royal administration for centuries to come, and of course Parliament still meets there today. In 1019, Cnut inherited the crown of Denmark after the death of King Harald II, Swein's firstborn son, and he ruled over both kingdoms until his death in 1035.

A few years into his reign, Cnut divided England into four districts: East Anglia, Mercia, Northumbria and Wessex. Wessex was placed under the jurisdiction of the powerful Anglo-Saxon nobleman Earl Godwin, while Mercia was given to Earl Leofric, the husband of Lady Godiva. According to a story first recorded in the early thirteenth century, Lady Godiva rode naked through Coventry in 1057 to save its inhabitants from paying a toll, with her long hair covering 'the whole of her body like a veil'.[5] Cnut's appointment of earls as deputies raised the unwelcome possibility that they would become overmighty subjects, but Cnut did not really have to worry about this because he had all the power of Denmark at his disposal to keep them in line. A tale of Cnut's feigned attempt to hold back the tide was first recorded over a century after his death, and it is just as doubtful as the Godiva story. Seated on the seashore, Cnut commanded the sea not to flow over his land, and when the tide came in as usual, he declared: 'Let all men know how empty and worthless is the power of kings, for there is none worthy of the name, but He whom heaven, earth, and sea obey by eternal laws.'[6]

Two more Danes occupied the English throne after Cnut's death, his feuding sons Harold Harefoot, son of Ælfgifu (reigned 1035–40), and Harthacnut, son of Emma (reigned 1040–2), whose name literally means 'tough knot'. Though Cnut had intended for Harthacnut to be his successor, this plan failed because Harthacnut was too slow in travelling to England to receive the crown. Seizing the advantage of proximity, Harold had himself proclaimed king in Harthacnut's absence. Harthacnut waited until 1040 before he finally set sail for England to claim his inheritance by force. He defeated his brother in battle with the assistance of his half-brother, the Anglo-Saxon nobleman Edward the Confessor.

Edward the Confessor possibly served as joint-king with Harthacnut from 1040 to 1042. When Harthacnut died in 1042, Edward became king in his own right, marking the return of the crown to the Anglo-Saxon line. He ascended the throne in his late thirties and ruled for over two decades as a forceful and uncompromising king, even outlawing his own father-in-law, Earl Godwin, in 1051. The second decade of Edward's reign was a time of peace and prosperity, but instability returned in 1065 with a rebellion in Northumbria, which resulted in the king's agent, Earl Tostig, being forced into exile. Edward died soon after with no male heir, and the crown descended upon his brother-in-law, the powerful nobleman Harold Godwinson, chief of the House of Godwin.

THE FIRST ENGLISH LITERATURE

A substantial literature survives from the Anglo-Saxon period, written in both Latin and Old English, including religious works, collections of riddles and over 30,000 lines of vernacular poetry. The heroic poem *Beowulf*, the crowning glory of Old English literature, was probably written in the seventh or eighth century. Set in fifth-century Sweden and Denmark but reflecting English values, *Beowulf* narrates the eponymous hero's defeat of three successive monsters: a demon called Grendel, Grendel's mother and finally, fifty years later, a fire-breathing dragon. This poem, with its flashing swords and majestic mead-halls, gives an incomparable taste of Anglo-Saxon civilization. It was first translated into modern English in 1837, and there have been many other translations since; Seamus Heaney's (1999) is the best for general purposes. Another terrific Anglo-Saxon poem is *The Wanderer*, a lament of 115 lines in which the speaker describes the hardships he has suffered while roaming the world after the death of his lord:

> A man without country, without kin,
> Knows how cruel it is to have sorrow
> As a sole companion. No one waits
> To welcome the wanderer except the road
> Of exile itself. His reward is night-cold,
> Not a lord's rich gift of twisted gold
> Or a warm hearth and a harvest of wealth.[7]

The Victorians were fascinated by the Anglo-Saxons, believing their habits and customs to be the origin of England's democratic traditions and love of freedom. In 1896, the novelist and historian Sir Walter Besant wrote that the qualities of the Anglo-Saxons, especially masterfulness, obstinacy and restlessness, remain noticeably present in the English character. It has also been suggested that the English fondness for word games, puzzles and quizzes can be traced to the Anglo-Saxon love of riddles.[8] Few historians would endorse such ideas today, but analysis of modern DNA has been used to estimate that the present-day English population owes at least 10 per cent and possibly as much as 40 per cent of its ancestry to this redoubtable breed of scholars and conquerors.

3

THE NORMANS
(1066–1153)

Everyone knows that William the Conqueror, the bastard-born Duke of Normandy, won the crown of England by conquest at the Battle of Hastings in 1066. The rulers of the Duchy of Normandy in the eleventh century were French-speaking nobles of Viking warrior stock. Edward the Confessor, whose reign we have already described, was à friend to Normandy and had willingly appointed Normans to government posts in England. In fact, he had even gone so far as promising to name Duke William as his successor to the throne. Since England's southern coast is less than a hundred nautical miles from the tip of Normandy, the kingdom of England was a tempting prize for an ambitious Norman duke.

According to the version of events told by the Normans, the English nobleman Harold Godwinson swore in Normandy in 1064 or 1065 that he would support William's claim to the English throne. Whether or not this really happened (it probably did), Harold secretly resolved to claim the throne for himself. When Edward died, Harold was formally elected as king by the nobles of England, who needed little convincing that a Norman succession was not in their best interests. He was crowned on 6 January 1066 at the newly built Westminster Abbey. His allies announced that the late king had named Harold as his successor on his deathbed, in a last-minute change of heart. Soon after Harold's accession, what looked like a great tailed star appeared in the sky, now known to be Halley's Comet, which wise men interpreted as a fearful omen.

THE BATTLE OF HASTINGS

William must have expected Harold's double-dealing because he had been planning to invade England for at least three years. With the blessing of Pope Alexander II, he readied a fleet of ships and recruited a mixed army of Normans, Bretons and Frenchmen, who agreed to join the campaign in return for a share of any future spoils. They landed at Pevensey, an abandoned fortified settlement in East Sussex, before sunrise on 28 September 1066. King Harold had precious little time to ready his men for battle, since only three days earlier he had fought and defeated his brother Tostig and the Norwegian king Harald Hardrada – another claimant to the throne of England – at the Battle of Stamford Bridge in the East Riding of Yorkshire. Harold then marched 250 miles south to meet the Normans at a location about 6 miles from the town of Hastings, East Sussex. The main landmarks of the terrain were two hills about a mile apart (Caldbec Hill and Battle Hill) and a grand old apple tree. The English army was composed of around 7,000 men and consisted mainly of axemen fighting on foot, while the Norman army was of roughly the same size and included archers, crossbowmen and cavalry. The population of England in 1066 was around 1.75 million, so her fate was left in the hands of a tiny fraction of Englishmen.

The Battle of Hastings was fought on 14 October 1066. According to the Norman historian William of Jumièges, the Duke of Normandy reassured his supporters that King Harold's champions would be easily beaten because they were 'effeminate young men, sluggish in the art of war'.[1] The chronicle also records that the duke engaged in psychological warfare by sending a minstrel called Taillefer to dismay the English. Taillefer rode in advance of the Norman army and tauntingly juggled with his sword. When an English soldier rode forward to confront him, the Norman deftly beheaded the Englishman and held the head aloft as a trophy, a sign that providence favoured the duke's cause. The English had a favourable position on high ground, assuming formation on Battle Hill. They formed a shield wall and successfully blocked the first Norman cavalry charge.

However, the Normans may then have used a feigned retreat, tricking some of the English to pursue them and fall into a trap. The Normans attacked the English lines again, killing King Harold

Scene from the Bayeux Tapestry depicting the death of King Harold in 1066.

(possibly with an arrow through the eye) and his two younger brothers. Demoralized, the English took to flight and many were cut down by the pursuing Normans. After his victory at Hastings, William proceeded to capture Canterbury, Winchester and London. The Norman triumph was later depicted in the Bayeux Tapestry, a linen embroidery stitched in Canterbury, measuring over 200ft. The English were understandably less jubilant; a native chronicler alleged that God had permitted William's victory as punishment 'for the people's sins'.[2] The real reasons were somewhat more mundane, including the superiority of Norman military technology. For example, the Anglo-Saxons had built no castles worthy of the name.

WILLIAM THE CONQUEROR

On Christmas Day 1066 King William I was crowned at Westminster Abbey, marking the beginning of his twenty-one-year reign. He had a harsh and commanding voice, coupled with the strength befitting a warrior king. His height was reasonably impressive for his time, 5ft 10in, and though his body was altered by obesity in his later years, he retained an aura of majesty. A monk who knew him personally testified to his capacity for hard work, his moderation in drinking and his religiosity. His contemporaries noted that he was far more powerful than any previous king of England, and that under his watch, the realm became more secure and orderly. Others, however, emphasized his cruelty and avarice. Anglo-Saxon critics complained about his draconian Forest Law, which seemed to prove that he was more interested in preserving game than in securing the welfare of his own subjects.

A new Norman elite, marked by different customs and personal names, replaced the Anglo-Saxon nobility within the decade after 1066. There was now a language barrier between rulers and ruled, the former speaking French and the latter Old English, a situation that often results in relatively light government. England's new masters retained many native institutions, such as the office of sheriff, or shire reeve, which had been around for at least a century. But they also innovated, for instance by introducing the French system of military feudalism, a hierarchical system of vassalage under which noblemen held lands of the king in return for armed service. This was to have far-reaching consequences for English law and society. If a knight wished to avoid military service, he had to pay a fee called scutage, or shield money, with which the king could hire a mercenary instead. As well as being nominal owner of all the land in England, King William also retained about 17 per cent as his own personal estate. Over time, the hierarchy of the titled lay elites would stabilize as a series of graded ranks: dukes, marquesses, earls, viscounts and barons.

The combination of strong native kingship with continental-style feudalism eventually enabled the government of Norman and Angevin England to become 'the most effective and wide-reaching central government of the time', although the French monarchy would overtake England's in strength by the late thirteenth century.[3] The Normans built castles throughout the country that served both as practical defences and symbols of conquest. One fine example of a surviving Norman keep is at Castle Rising in

Norfolk, constructed in around 1140. Over time, the differences between Anglo-Saxons and Normans became blurred by intermarriage and cultural assimilation – the monastic historian William of Malmesbury, born in around 1090, claimed to have both Saxon and Norman heritage. Nevertheless, the aristocracy of England would remain Norman in language, culture, and to a large extent in blood, for centuries to come.

RESISTANCE AND REPRISALS

The English majority did not much care for the Norman yoke. There were uprisings in Kent in 1067 and Exeter in 1068, followed by a much more serious northern rebellion in 1069. The Northern rebels, supported by King Swein II of Denmark and Malcolm Canmore, king of Scots, besieged York and killed the castellan. William violently repressed the rebellions before spending Christmas in York (normally a lovely place for it, but an ungodly warzone in 1069). After these macabre festivities, he launched a series of infamous campaigns collectively referred to as the Harrying of the North (1069–70), destroying men and crops and plunging the north of England into famine, to the extent that a third of the land in Yorkshire was still classified as waste sixteen years later. Harrying had also been practised as retribution for misbehaviour by the Anglo-Saxon kings. Another attempted northern rebellion in 1075, which involved a coalition of English, Danish, Breton and Norman interests, was likewise unsuccessful. While consolidating their authority in England, the Normans made incursions westward, permanently acquiring significant territories in South Wales. From the 1070s to the 1090s, William also fought intermittently with the king of Scots, who sought to aggressively expand his own frontiers.

William spent over three-quarters of his time in Normandy from 1072 to 1087, returning to England only when necessary. In his absence, government was conducted by regents, including his half-brother Odo, Bishop of Bayeux (eventually imprisoned for his overweening ambition) and Lanfranc, Archbishop of Canterbury.

In 1085, hoping to augment the Crown's tax revenues, William ordered his servants to survey the entire country to gather details about land and property ownership in each shire. The project was completed efficiently in around a year, no doubt reflecting a fear of the king's displeasure, and the result was the monumental Domesday Book, so-called because its records were considered to be as definitive as the day of judgment. The Domesday Book recorded the name, size, ownership and value of every manor in England – one of the greatest logistical feats in English history.

During a campaign in France in 1087, the king fell ill, either because he was thrown from his horse or because of an intestinal problem. He died in the priory of Saint-Gervais near Rouen, surrounded by his family and courtiers. Possibly acting under pressure from his advisers, he bequeathed the Duchy of Normandy to his eldest son, Robert (nicknamed 'Curthose', or 'short-stockings'), while the kingdom of England fell to his second son, William Rufus, 'the Red' – this epithet referred either to his red hair or to his ruddy complexion. William's third and final surviving son, Henry, got no lands but did receive £5,000 in treasure. This settlement was quite in keeping with Norman customary law. William I's body was treated dishonourably after his death, robbed by his own servants and abandoned by the magnates in their scramble to secure the succession.

WILLIAM'S FEUDING SONS

William Rufus, whose eyes were of different colours, ruled England from 1087 to 1100. A contemporary report offers a glimpse of his tough character, claiming that he 'feared God too little, and man not at all'.[4] He successfully consolidated Norman rule and crushed the most serious revolt of the Norman period, the barons' rebellion of 1088. The barons' main grievance was the partition of England and Normandy, which had complicated their affairs and put them into the awkward and dangerous position of serving two masters. Their plan was to install Robert, Duke of Normandy as king of England, so as to reunite the two realms. While most of the great landowners in England joined the rebellion – chief among them Bishop Odo – many Englishmen outside of the political elite supported Rufus. Robert tried to send the rebels help by sea but his forces were driven back, and Rufus captured Odo after a six-week siege of Pevensey Castle, newly refortified by the Normans. The other rebels surrendered at Rochester, leaving Rufus as undisputed king of England, although he did head off another brief baronial rebellion in 1095.

A decade after the barons' rebellion, in February 1096, Robert of Normandy decided to go on crusade. He agreed to lease the Duchy of Normandy to his brother and former enemy, William Rufus, for three years. Rufus proved to be an effective custodian of Normandy, winning back the province of Maine (formerly lost by Robert) in the summer of 1098. Rufus's reconquest of Maine was achieved with the help of the military expert Robert de Bellême, an alleged sadist who was said to enjoy torturing his prisoners. In the mid-1090s, Rufus appointed a low-born genius named Ranulf Flambard ('Ranulf the Torch') as chief minister in England, and he rose to the challenge of increasing the royal revenue by improving the mechanisms of tax collection.

As for ecclesiastical affairs, Rufus had a fraught relationship with Anselm, Archbishop of Canterbury, who often squabbled with the king over the rights of the Church, particularly in the see of Canterbury, and who voluntarily went into exile in Rome in October 1097. Anselm is remembered for formulating the 'ontological argument' to prove the existence of God. The argument runs as follows:

It is possible to imagine a being which is greater than any other conceivable being. If such a being did not exist in reality, then it would be possible to imagine a still greater being, which existed in both theory and reality. Since nothing can be greater than a being than which no greater can be conceived, God must exist both in theory and in reality.

This wonderfully mind-bending argument has left many scratching their heads in the centuries since it was formulated.

KING HENRY I

Rufus was shot dead by a stray arrow while hunting in the New Forest on 2 August 1100. His brother Henry, now 32, acted quickly to secure the throne, having himself crowned only three days later and seizing control of the royal treasury. He was fortunate in that Robert of Normandy, who had a better claim to the throne, was out of the country. King Henry I actively courted his subjects' approval. First, he issued a coronation charter that promised to reform the supposedly rapacious behaviour of his predecessor. Then, on 11 November 1100, he married the Scottish Anglo-Saxon princess Edith (given the Norman name 'Matilda'), who was the great-great-granddaughter of Æthelred Unræd. This union was cleverly designed to win Anglo-Saxon support for Henry and his heirs by ensuring that future kings would share a dose of the blood of England's majority population. Matilda was a competent queen to whom her husband normally entrusted the direction of affairs when he was out of the country. A contemporary story gives a hint regarding her character. Once, her brother stumbled across her washing and kissing the feet of lepers. When he said that Henry would never kiss her again if he heard about it, Matilda replied: 'Everyone knows that the feet of the eternal king are to be preferred to the lips of a mortal one.'[5]

The former minister Ranulf, now in disgrace, was imprisoned in the Tower of London, but the plump man managed to escape using a rope that his allies smuggled into his cell inside a cask of wine. With Ranulf's support, Robert, who had now reassumed control of Normandy, invaded England on 20 July 1101 to challenge King Henry. Two great armies stood ready to fight at Alton in Hampshire, but the brothers saved bloodshed for the time being by agreeing to terms. Robert was offered a cash pension and the eventual succession to the throne if the king failed to father a legitimate son. Robert broke this treaty in 1106 and was defeated at the Battle of Tinchebray on 28 September (the fortieth anniversary of William the Conqueror's landing in England), after which Henry gained possession of Normandy. England and Normandy were thus reunited by accident rather than design. The deposed Duke Robert spent the final three decades of his life in comfortable imprisonment in England.

SCHOLAR AND PHILANDERER

Henry was in many ways a successful king and duke. He later put down a succession of Norman rebellions that sought to install Robert's son William Clito as Duke of Normandy. On 20 August 1119, he defeated the king of the Franks, Louis the Fat, at the Battle of Brémule. However, in order to secure a peace treaty, he agreed to pay homage to Louis, thus implicitly acknowledging that he held the duchy of Normandy as a fief under Louis's overlordship. Henry flaunted his fine education and became known centuries later as Henry Beauclerc, meaning 'Good Scholar'. However, his life was not all books and papers, for he fathered at least twenty-two bastards with different mistresses, probably a royal record. William of Malmesbury defended him on this score, unconvincingly arguing that he entertained mistresses not because of 'fleshly lusts' but because of his 'love of begetting children'.[6]

Henry's government made important contributions to administrative efficiency. For instance, the Exchequer (named after a chequered cloth used to make calculations) emerged as a revenue department with clearly defined procedures, probably having evolved from an Anglo-Saxon institution called 'the Tallies'. Henry also kept a strict watch on the affairs of the Church: one royal writ he supposedly issued for the election of a bishop has gone down in history as an amusing example of illusory free choice: 'I order you to hold a free election, but nevertheless I forbid you to elect anyone except Richard, my clerk, the archdeacon of Poitiers.'[7]

Henry I fathered only two legitimate children. The first was William the Ætheling, who perished in a shipwreck in 1120 at the age of about 17, when a vessel named the *White Ship* sank in the English Channel with the cream of the royal household on board. Both passengers and crew had treated the short trip as an alcohol-fuelled pleasure voyage, and the ship had struck a rock just off Barfleur. Henry's second legitimate child was a daughter called Matilda. She was married to the Holy Roman Emperor from 1114 to 1125 and retained the title of empress after his death. Henry named Matilda as his heir in 1126, a year before she remarried. The rub was that England had never had a queen regnant, and there were many who preferred to keep it that way. At a conference with his leading barons early in 1127, Henry persuaded them that

Empress Matilda was the best choice and extracted oaths of support for her future claim. Oath-taking was rather more serious in an age where oath-breaking was thought to be a mortal sin carrying the penalty of eternal hellfire, so Henry and Matilda might have considered the succession to be relatively secure – but of course it was not as simple as that.

KING STEPHEN

When Henry died in the winter of 1135, practical politics and self-interest won the day, and the barons acted as if they had made no sworn promises. The most powerful landowner who held estates in England was Stephen of Blois, Henry I's nephew and William the Conqueror's grandson. Although he was in Boulogne on the day of the king's death, Stephen perceived that this was a singular opportunity to seize the crown for himself. He arrived in England four days later, where he was greeted by an epic thunderstorm which seemed to presage some future danger to the state. Received with acclamation by the citizens of London, Stephen quickly won over most of the Anglo-Norman aristocracy. His younger brother Henry, now bishop of Winchester, also managed to win the Church's endorsement of Stephen's claim to the throne. With such a broad base of support, Stephen was crowned with little opposition on 26 December 1135, at the age of about 43. An official story was fabricated that Henry I had granted the crown to Stephen on his deathbed. This made the whole affair look less like a coup.

Stephen's easy rise to the throne suggests that he was well liked at first, but he might only have been preferred because of a widespread fear of Angevin control over England represented by Matilda's claim (the empress was now married to the Count of Anjou). Stephen was reportedly kind and gentle – not exactly the qualities that best fitted a man to rule in the cutthroat world of twelfth-century politics. William of Malmesbury described him as 'a man of energy but little judgement, active in war, of extraordinary spirit in undertaking any difficult task, lenient to his enemies and easily appeased'.[8] He faced a series of revolts from the outset of his reign, significantly Hugh Bigod's uprising in 1136 (involving the capture of Norwich Castle) and Baldwin de Redvers's capture of Exeter in the same year, which the rebels eventually surrendered after a three-month siege. Stephen also experienced serious trouble in Wales, where he lost control of Ceredigion in 1137, and in Scotland. The Scottish king, David I, who had been educated at the Anglo-Norman court, seized Carlisle and Newcastle in 1136. Despite defeating the Scots at the Battle of the Standard in Yorkshire on 22 August 1138, Stephen found it difficult to expel them from the north; in fact, he basically conceded Northumbria and part of Cumbria to the Scots.

Just after Whitsuntide 1138, one of the king's principal supporters, Robert of Gloucester, renounced his homage to the king in a formal feudal process known as *diffidatio*, and declared his support for Matilda. Gloucester was prompted to take this drastic step by the apparent breakdown of royal order in the Welsh marches, where he held vast estates and therefore had much to lose. Gloucester's disobedience proved to be contagious, as more and more rebellions began to spring up around the country. Matilda was expected to invade England at any moment. At a council in Oxford in June 1139, Stephen made a surprise arrest of two political rivals and suspected traitors, the bishops of Lincoln and Salisbury. Matilda landed at Arundel, West Sussex, on 30 September 1139, which is usually considered to be the beginning of the Anarchy (1139–54), a period of protracted civil war. Stephen had Matilda surrounded on her arrival, but for some unknown reason (it is tempting to suggest chivalry) he allowed her to travel unmolested to her power base. The king's fortunes took a turn for the worse in February 1141, when he was captured by Matilda's men during an unsuccessful siege of Lincoln Castle and transported to Bristol to be held under close guard.

THE ANARCHY

Matilda hurried to the City of London, planning to have herself crowned with no further delay. However, according to the chronicler Henry of Huntingdon, she 'alienated nearly all hearts by her intolerable pride'.[9] She came up against the formidable political skill of Stephen's wife, also called Matilda, who canvassed loyalist support in the capital. The Londoners, bearing as they did

a residual loyalty to the king, drove the haughty empress out of the city on 24 June 1141, the date of her intended coronation. She fled to Oxford and then Winchester, until she was smoked out and forced to retreat to Gloucester. The rebel Robert of Gloucester was captured shortly afterwards during a failed siege of Winchester Castle. There followed a high-stakes prisoner exchange, with King Stephen released in return for Robert's freedom. Stephen was re-crowned at Canterbury, and yet there could be no denying that his authority had suffered a battering. Matilda was nearly captured at Oxford in the winter of 1142, but she managed to escape across the snow in camouflage by wearing a white cloak, crossing the frozen-over River Isis on foot.

The stalemate that followed is vividly illustrated by the coinage of the period. After 1141, Stephen and Matilda struck coins in their own names, as did David of Scotland, who supported Matilda's claim. The absence of central royal authority led to widespread oppression by petty tyrants and mob bosses, and it is no wonder that many contemporaries thought this England's darkest hour. Magnate after magnate fortified castles against the king – at least forty new ones were built – which ultimately became, according to chroniclers, places of wickedness, torture and unspeakable atrocities. Prisoners were allegedly subjected to all manner of awful torments: suffocated with smoke, hung up by their thumbs, consigned to dungeons full of snakes and so on. Nevertheless, since rival monarchs generally maintained order within their spheres of influence, the period might be best described as one of divided rule. No fewer than 171 religious houses were established during Stephen's reign, which could hardly have been achieved in conditions of total anarchy, though it is exactly the sort of thing one would expect to happen at a time of weak central authority.

Empress Matilda changed the political calculus in 1148 by leaving the realm, for she recognized that her son, Henry, had the best chance of establishing Angevin rule in England. Stephen's own son, William, had no great desire to become king, so the way was open for compromise. In 1153, after Henry landed in England, the two factions agreed on a deal, the Treaty of Winchester, which stipulated that he would become king after Stephen's death. Stephen obligingly passed away the next year, whereupon Henry was elevated to the throne. The 'Anarchy' was over, and the period of Angevin rule – a name derived from the House of Anjou – had begun.

4

THE ANGEVINS
(1153–1216)

King Henry II's accession in 1153 was a first in many respects. He was the first Angevin king of England, tracing his descent from the House of Anjou on his father's side and from William the Conqueror on his mother's side (Henry I was his maternal grandfather). He was also the first Plantagenet king of England, broadly defined – a name derived from the French for common broom, *plante à genêt*, because his father wore a sprig of this yellow shrub in his helmet. Moreover, Henry was the first post-Conquest king to have a significant measure of Anglo-Saxon blood, which he derived from his Scottish maternal grandmother, Queen Matilda. Crowned at the age of 21, Henry restored much-needed leadership to a country that had seen fifteen years of divided rule. According to the statesman and scholar Peter of Blois, who knew the king personally, he was red-haired and of average height, with a broad chest and the arms of a boxer. He had superhuman energy, enjoyed martial sports and disdained to wear gloves in the winter, but he also loved reading and shone in polite company.

THE ANGEVIN EMPIRE

At the time of his accession, Henry already held sway over an extensive territory. As the son of Geoffrey of Anjou, he was Count of Anjou and Duke of Normandy, and as the husband of the famous beauty Eleanor of Aquitaine, he was Duke of Aquitaine (also called Gascony), a region in south-western France. In Normandy, he recovered the important fortress of Gisors and a borderland called the Norman Vexin from King Louis, to whom they had been conceded by Geoffrey of Anjou, Empress Matilda's husband. Henry also expanded the bounds of his dominions into Wales, aided by internal divisions among his enemies, and recaptured the northern English counties that had been seized by King David of Scotland. He laid claim to Ireland, where the Angevins capitalized on superior military knowledge and established an area of dominion around Dublin later referred to as the Pale. Chief among the conquerors of Ireland was Richard fitz Gilbert de Clare, 2nd Earl of Pembroke, also known as Strongbow. The king's dominions, often called the Angevin Empire, remained perhaps the most important political entity in western Europe for five decades. In England, Henry sought to reverse the effects of the Anarchy by ordering the demolition of unlicensed castles, issuing a new, uniform coinage, and restoring the collection of royal revenue.

TURBULENT PRIEST

Henry's relationships with the Church and churchmen were sometimes fraught. The historian Gerald of Wales recounted a story where the monks of St Swithun's Priory in Winchester prostrated themselves before the king to complain about the cruelty of their bishop, who had cut the number of dishes on their table from thirteen to ten. The king replied that he himself was content with three dishes at court, and he urged the bishop to reduce the monks' diet to the same frugal level. More famously, Henry had a troubled relationship with Thomas Becket, who served as royal chancellor until 1162 and after that as Archbishop of Canterbury. The king originally sponsored Becket's election and enthronement as archbishop in the hopes that he would support royal interests, but he seems to have underestimated the man's independence and attachment to the Church. King and archbishop clashed over issues such as church property and clerical immunity. In one letter, Becket told Henry that since 'kings receive their power from the church', they 'do not have the power to command bishops to obey'.[1] After opposing the Constitutions of Clarendon (1164), which sought to restrict church privileges, Becket was forced to escape the king's wrath by fleeing to France and hiding away in the Abbey of St Columba, where he remained from 1166 to 1170.

When Becket returned to England in 1170, the king, residing in Normandy, reportedly hinted that he wished the archbishop dead: 'What miserable drones and traitors have I nurtured and promoted in my household, who allow their lord to be shamefully contemned by a low-born cleric?' This version of the quotation, translated from Latin, was recorded by a monastic eyewitness of Becket's death called Edward Grim, but the phrase is more often remembered as 'Will no one rid me of this turbulent priest?', a version invented in 1740.[2] Four of the king's knights obeyed this oblique command by travelling to Canterbury and murdering Becket in cold blood inside the cathedral in December 1170. Henry received absolution from papal legates for his complicity in the assassination, but not until he had submitted to a whipping.

THE GREAT REBELLION

Henry faced a series of rebellions throughout his reign, many involving his own family members. His brother Geoffrey raised a revolt in Anjou in 1155 to try to force Henry to hand over his possessions in Anjou, Maine and Touraine, as directed by their father's will, but Henry bought his brother off with an annual pension. In 1173 came the Great Rebellion, which pitted Henry against the kings of France and Scotland, the counts of Boulogne and Flanders, many of his own English barons and even his own wife and sons, who were frustrated about their exclusion from power. Eleanor, now an ageing beauty, was possibly also angered by the king's secret affair with the young Rosamund Clifford. Henry triumphed against all odds, thanks to a combination of political skill and the devil's luck. The count of Boulogne died in a freak crossbow accident in the summer of 1173, and Eleanor was captured in the same year, despite having disguised herself as a man to evade detection. Henry quickly forgave his rebellious sons, perhaps recognizing in them his own ambitious spirit. Eleanor remained incarcerated for the remainder of Henry's reign, although she was treated more leniently in the later years, being allowed frequent leaves of absence. As punishment for his own part in the rebellion, King William of Scotland had to surrender five royal castles, including Berwick and Edinburgh, to the English.

Henry's reign witnessed the birth of the common law, a set of legal principles applied equally over the entire realm, which was later exported around the world, from North America to Hong Kong. Many early common law principles were recorded in a legal treatise known as *Glanvill*, which, despite the name, may not have been written by the justiciar Ranulf de Glanvill. The common law was administered by the king's courts at Westminster Hall, a magnificent venue which Henry ordered to be refurbished. Henry sponsored large-scale building projects throughout the realm, constructing magnificent castles, bridges and hospitals (charitable institutions with various purposes), which served as tangible signs of kingly might and prosperity. He also strengthened England's system of military feudalism, commissioning a document called the Assize of Arms (1181) that laid down rules about the military equipment and service required of different classes of freemen. He faced more family trouble in the last years of his reign when one of his two surviving sons, Richard, allied himself with King Philip II of France to force Henry to recognize him as his heir. Henry agreed to their terms – he had little choice – and shortly afterwards he died in sad isolation at Chinon in Normandy.

RICHARD THE LIONHEART

King Richard I, commonly named Richard the Lionheart, ruled England from 1189 to 1199, but he was away from the realm for all but six months of his reign. His Spanish wife, Berengaria of Navarre, never even set foot in England. In the historical romance *Ivanhoe* (1819), Sir Walter Scott described Richard's reign as 'like the course of a brilliant and rapid meteor... his feats of chivalry furnishing themes for bards and minstrels, but affording none of those solid benefits to his country on which history loves to pause'.[3] Richard earned a reputation for mismanagement with his willingness to sell off Crown lands and royal offices to the highest bidder. Scotland was released from English subjection for the relatively low price of 10,000 marks (about £6,700), which one chronicler scornfully described as 'a price not worth naming'. On one occasion, Richard joked: 'I would sell London if I could find a buyer.'[4]

In December 1189, the king set out for the Holy Land to participate in the Third Crusade (1189–92), which placed the polity under strain because no king of England had ever travelled so far away. In his absence, Richard appointed a regency council of five men, including the two chief justiciars, to govern the realm. But this scheme proved unworkable, and in March 1190, William de Longchamp, Bishop of Ely was confirmed as sole chief justiciar, essentially the king's supreme deputy. Longchamp was arrogant and unpopular – one chronicler explained that his arrogance stemmed from insecurity about his short stature – and he ended up facing a rebellion led by the king's brother Count John (later King John) in 1191. Longchamp's enemies told a bizarre story about his fruitless attempt to flee England disguised in women's clothes after the rebellion. While trying to find a ship that would afford him passage, he was said to have been groped by a 'half-naked fisherman who was wet and cold from the sea and who thought that the bishop was the sort of woman who might warm him up… Suddenly pulling up the gown, he plunged unblushingly in – only to be confronted with the irrefutable evidence that the woman was a man.'[5]

England had not participated meaningfully in the successful First Crusade (1096–9), planned by Pope Urban II, which had led to the Christian conquest of Jerusalem. Nor had she contributed much to the Second Crusade (1147–9), except to send around 200 ships to help expel the Moors from Lisbon. The immediate cause of the Third Crusade was the reconquest of Jerusalem by the great Saladin, Sultan of Egypt and Syria. The crusaders ultimately failed to take back Jerusalem, although a treaty was agreed that allowed continued Christian access to the city. Conflict between East and West intensified the popularity of the Islamic notion of *jihad*. Islamic scholars have identified two kinds of *jihad*: the greater *jihad* (each believer's spiritual struggle) and the lesser *jihad* (military struggle against infidels), and both kinds can be traced to the earliest days of Islam. During the crusades, the concept of *jihad* served as a propaganda weapon against the European militants.

The first stop on Richard's crusade was Norman-ruled Sicily, where he managed to settle a dispute over his sister's dowry by capturing the city of Messina. After wintering in Sicily, Richard proceeded to conquer Cyprus in the spring of 1191. During the Cyprian campaign, Richard promised not to put Isaac Comnenus, the Orthodox Christian Emperor of Cyprus, in irons. When Isaac was captured, the king kept the letter but not the spirit of his promise by having the petty emperor bound in chains of silver. Cyprus provided a money supply and a base from which to launch further crusading activity. In June, Richard arrived at Acre, which had been the most significant port city of the Christian kingdom of Jerusalem, and which was now in Saladin's hands. Richard besieged the city alongside Philip II of France, forcing its surrender to the crusaders on 12 July and mercilessly executed 3,000 prisoners-of-war. Although the crusaders failed to recapture the city of Jerusalem, they won fame for their martial exploits.

A KING'S RANSOM

Richard intended to return to England in 1192. He arrived at Corfu by mid-November, and from there he planned to cross unnoticed through eastern Germany because a complicated diplomatic situation compelled him to avoid passing through French territory. Unfortunately, however, Duke Leopold V of Austria harboured a grudge against the English king because of a petty dispute that had occurred between the two men during the Siege of Acre. Leopold gleefully arrested his royal enemy and delivered him to Heinrich VI, Holy Roman Emperor, in January 1193. The emperor demanded the payment of 150,000 silver marks (about £100,000) to secure the king's release. This money was raised by heavy taxes on the English people and by the appropriation of church goods. Richard arrived back in England on 13 March 1194, but only three months later, he departed from the land that had bankrolled his misadventures, never to return. The remainder of his life was taken up with a painful war of attrition in France, during which he defended his possessions in Normandy and constructed a great castle named Château Gaillard at Les Andelys on the Seine. He was wounded by a crossbow bolt at Châlus in March 1199 while trying to put down a minor rebellion, and died a month later when the wound became infected.

Perhaps the most remarkable character of Richard's reign was Hubert Walter, the king's straight man, who served as justiciar and Archbishop of Canterbury. Not only was he one of the most intelligent and creative English crusaders, but he also led the negotiations for Richard's release and organized the collection of revenue to pay for it. Less exciting than his exploits abroad, but ultimately more important, were the administrative reforms he introduced to English government. For example, he introduced a system of eyres, by which royal justices travelled on circuit to hear legal cases around the country; these would later be succeeded by the biannual assizes, operating on a similar principle. Hubert also invented a type of legal document called the tripartite final concord, by which agreements between parties at law were recorded in triplicate, with the third copy (or 'foot') remaining in the archive of the king's court; reforms such as these brought greater stability to the judicial system. These technical achievements are just as noteworthy, in their own way, as the romantic exploits of Richard *Cœur de Lion*.

BAD KING JOHN

The barons were divided over whether Richard should be succeeded by his 12-year-old nephew, Arthur of Brittany (designated as successor by Richard himself) or by Richard's brother, the erstwhile rebel Count John. Although Hubert Walter reportedly warned that John would be an appalling king, he had the advantage of adulthood on his side. John managed to secure the support of Normandy and to have himself crowned on 27 May 1199, only two days after arriving in England. King John was the last medieval king of England to be chosen by election, which would thereafter make way for primogeniture, or the hereditary principle, which tends to stabilize monarchical systems in the long run. John's reputation can be illustrated by his two unflattering nicknames: Lackland, because he began life as the portionless fifth son of Henry II, and Softsword (*Mollegladium* in Latin), an obvious double entendre which also implied that the king was a coward.

From the very outset of his reign, John came into conflict with his feudal overlord, Philip II of France. This was not a conflict of nations but rather a dynastic conflict between the competing Angevin and Capetian royal houses. Philip was annoyed that John had not sought his formal permission to occupy the Duchy of Normandy, and he demanded that Anjou, Maine and Touraine should be surrendered to Arthur of Brittany, which would have dismembered the Angevin Empire. Rather than submitting to these imperious demands, John declared war on Philip in the autumn of 1199. At first, luck was on his side, for his army quickly captured Arthur and forced the French king to flee from Maine. However, Arthur subsequently escaped, and French baronial support for John began to dissolve.

THE CAPETIAN CONQUEST

A peace treaty was agreed with France in January 1200, but hostilities resumed only two years later, after John broke his promise to attend an interview with Philip regarding his irregular second marriage to Isabella of Angoulême. Philip promptly declared all John's Norman possessions forfeit. Once again, John enjoyed early successes, recapturing Arthur at Mirebeau in August and probably having him murdered. However, by 1205 he had lost Anjou, Normandy and Gascony. These territorial losses began to cut England loose from continental ties and allowed her to develop along peculiarly national lines, but at the time they were ruinous for Anglo-Norman barons who held land in Normandy as well as England. There were early hopes that John might recover his losses. He set out on an expedition to do just that in 1206, but soon resorted to making a truce with Philip because success seemed so unlikely. After a conclusive English defeat at the Battle of Bouvines (1214), Capetian France was unquestionably supreme in western Europe, and it was clear that the reconquest of Anjou and Normandy was a pipe dream. The magnates grew ever more restless.

While he faced catastrophe on the continent, John enjoyed considerable successes closer to home, for instance securing possession of the fortified town of Cardigan on the Welsh coast. During these years, he made heavy financial demands on his subjects, still hoping to accumulate enough capital to challenge King Philip. Those who could not pay became the king's debtors: it has been calculated that 'magnate indebtedness to the Crown increased by 380 per cent' between 1199 and 1208, so the ultimate rebellion against the king can be seen as 'a rebellion of the king's debtors'.[6] Many other aspects of John's government alienated baronial opinion. For example, his opposition to Stephen Langton's appointment as Archbishop of Canterbury in 1208 provoked the pope to impose a six-year interdict on the whole realm, an 'ecclesiastical strike' that meant no church services could be celebrated except baptism and extreme unction.[7] There was also the king's cruel treatment of political enemies, such as his decision to allow the rebellious Marcher baron William de Braose's wife and children to starve to death as retribution for William's flight to France to escape punishment. The greatest humiliation to the barons, however, was the fact that John apparently enjoyed interfering with their wives and daughters.

MAGNA CARTA

Though some magnates remained loyal to the king, a large contingent formally rebelled on 5 May 1215. They tried to pressure John to renew Henry I's Charter of Liberties (1100), drawn up a century earlier to uphold the rule of law in the face of royal overreach and to regulate the relationship between king and barons. This crisis could probably have been resolved with some low-key negotiations followed by a reissue of Henry's charter, but the rebel barons deliberately stepped over the point of no return on 17 May by capturing London. In June, two weeks into a truce, the barons set up camp in a sleepy meadow called Runnymede, situated between Windsor and Staines. John rode from Windsor Castle to negotiate with them, ultimately authorizing a great charter of liberties called Magna Carta by affixing the great seal on 15 June 1215. This charter was a miscellaneous set of concessions, originally divided into sixty-three 'chapters', or short clauses. Some of these would prove to be of great importance in the future, such as the celebrated Chapter 39 against arbitrary imprisonment: 'No freeman shall be seized or imprisoned... except by the legal judgment of his peers, or by the laws of the land', while others were technical provisions: 'No Constable... shall distrain any knight to give money for castle guard.'[8] The king repudiated the charter with the pope's support only a few weeks later, to which the barons responded by renewing hostilities. The French king invaded England on 21 May 1216, entering London to great acclaim, and the barons gladly supported the candidacy of his son, Louis the Lion, for the throne of England. On 19 October, around a year and four months after the charter had been sealed, and while civil war was still ravaging the country, the unhappy king died of dysentery. The crown descended upon his son, Henry.

The Great Charter has become a byword for the liberties of English subjects. From the date of its issue there began a period of strenuous constitutional experimentation, in which the nobles tried to limit the independent authority of English kings without sacrificing the advantages of a strong monarchy. This period culminated in the deposal of King Richard II in 1399, to be described later. Magna Carta was reissued in 1216, 1217 and 1225, with the text varying each time. The 1225 charter was a lasting compromise and considerably less radical than the original charter. It was not until the seventeenth century that Magna Carta began to enjoy its modern reputation as a cornerstone of the constitution: the jurist Sir Edward Coke pronounced in 1605 that the charter is 'worthy to be written in letters of gold'.[9] History looks less kindly upon King John, whose poor reputation is one reason why there has never been a John II, for the name consequently became an unpopular choice for princes of the blood royal. Historians of the twentieth century attempted to rehabilitate his reputation on the basis of painstaking studies of administrative records, and it has been shown that John was a more capable military strategist than the loss of Normandy may lead us to believe. To many, however, he will always be remembered as Bad King John.

5

THE EARLY PLANTAGENETS (1216–1327)

King Henry III was only 9 years old when he succeeded his father. Since John had lost most of the Angevin empire, including Anjou itself, historians generally refer to Henry and later members of his dynasty as Plantagenets rather than Angevins, even though the royal line continued unbroken. Henry reigned for fifty-six years (1216–72). He began his reign as the second child king in English history, and his accession was opposed by nineteen rebel barons, who – as already mentioned – supported the claim of Louis the Lion. One key supporter of the king was his aged guardian William Marshal, Earl of Pembroke, who proclaimed that he would sooner carry the boy around in foreign lands, begging for bread, than abandon him. When Louis's allies were defeated at the Battle of Lincoln on 20 May 1217, Louis himself was paid 10,000 marks to scuttle quietly away.

The loyal Marshal was initially appointed as regent, but when he died in 1219, possibly of bowel cancer, the protection of the child king and the governance of the realm fell to a triumvirate: the Italian Cardinal Pandulf Verraccio (first counsellor), Hubert de Burgh (justiciar) and Peter des Roches (royal tutor). By 1221, however, Hubert had outmanoeuvred the other two and established himself as sole protector. A skilful administrator, Hubert governed the country capably for a decade. The king formally began his majority rule in January 1227, at the age of 19, but in reality, affairs remained under Hubert's close control until 1231, when he was supplanted by his old rival, the Frenchman Peter des Roches, who had sworn to bring Hubert down 'if it cost him all he had'.[1] Peter had been away on the Sixth Crusade, but he returned a hero and quickly won Henry's confidence. He made grand promises to increase the royal revenue and managed to have Hubert removed as justiciar in the summer of 1232. Many of Peter's allies were also appointed to office, effectively replacing one political faction with another. His administration got off to a good start, managing to convince a Great Council of magnates to vote for a significant tax in September. However, Peter proved to be high-handed and increasingly unpopular, and found himself dismissed by the king in 1234.

THE RISE OF PARLIAMENT

After Peter's removal, Henry III assumed personal control of the government from 1236 until 1258. During the king's personal rule, the Parliament of England began to emerge as an identifiable institution, with roughly stable membership and business. The Latin word *parliamentum* started appearing in official records in 1236, but it was not a precise constitutional term until later. By the early fourteenth century, Parliament would be a well-defined institution taking a prominent role in national affairs. The king is also remembered for his building projects. Starting in 1245, he rebuilt Westminster Abbey in the Gothic style, in which it can still be seen today in all its glory. His reign also marked the end of Plantagenet continental ambitions: the king's territorial losses in France were finally written off in the name of peace with the Capetian dynasty, and Henry's attempts to establish his son Edmund as king of Sicily were an utter failure. In the religious domain, one important development was the arrival of the Franciscan Friars, a mendicant order founded by the Italian Francis of Assisi, and the Dominican Friars, a preaching order founded by the Spaniard Dominic de Guzmán.

At court, the 1230s witnessed the rise of a charismatic courtier called Simon de Montfort, a Frenchman of about the same age as the king. Simon arrived in England in 1230 and initially enjoyed the king's good graces. He married Henry's sister without permission and successfully claimed the Earldom of Leicester, which had formerly been held by his uncle. King and earl soon began to quarrel frequently. In 1248, Simon was appointed as the king's vicegerent in Gascony, a dominion lost by King John and recaptured by the English in 1225, but the Gascons complained that he was an oppressive overlord. After a Gascon rebellion against Simon's supposedly tyrannical behaviour broke out in the 1250s, Henry took the rebels' side, and summoned Simon to Parliament to answer charges of misconduct. The king even travelled to Gascony in person to pacify the rebellion by offering generous terms, which fuelled growing discontent over his capricious style of government. There was also factionalism at court between two rival groups of French courtiers: the 'Lusignans', or king's party, and the 'Savoyards', or queen's party.

THE PROVISIONS OF OXFORD

Henry's barons attended upon the king in full armour in 1258 and forced him to agree that reform was needed. In April, the king convened a Parliament at Oxford because he was desperately in need of revenue, which became known as the Mad Parliament. The barons agreed to vote him a money grant on the condition that he accept a schedule of demands called the Provisions of Oxford. These Provisions forced a council of fifteen men on the king to counsel him and govern the realm, reducing him to a glorified figurehead. They also required that Parliament should be summoned three times a year (normally it met at the king's will), and made other seemingly trivial demands, including that an usher of the buttery, a department of the king's household for the storage of ale, should be dismissed. Soon afterwards, the Lusignan faction was expelled from England. The Provisions of Oxford were the first episode in the Baronial Reform Movement of 1258–67, a campaign to curb the arbitrary power of the monarch that has been described as 'a political revolution far more radical than Magna Carta'.[2] The greatest intelligence behind the Provisions was Simon de Montfort, who was in turn inspired by Aristotelian theories of tyranny and just kingship, which had been refined by the theologian Robert Grosseteste, Bishop of Lincoln.

The Provisions were a humiliation to the king. Two years after accepting them, he declared his intention to resume supreme authority in England, and he managed to win back control of his

Chancery. Simon was put on trial for various charges, including speaking against royal interests at Parliament while the king was away in France. But he persuasively answered them all, arguing that he had acted only for the common good, and ultimately the trial was postponed because the king needed Simon's military expertise in a war against the Welsh. In July 1263, the barons reimposed the Provisions of Oxford on the king, prompting the outbreak of full-scale civil war in the following year. Decisive military engagement took place in the form of the Battle of Lewes on 14 May 1264, during which the king and his son Edward were captured in Sussex. *The Song of Lewes*, a long Latin poem written shortly after the battle, celebrated the baronial victory in high-flown terms: 'The deceivers fled, and Truth prevailed.'[3]

Both sides agreed on the Mise of Lewes, a settlement that reaffirmed the Provisions of Oxford. For a brief period, Simon de Montfort assumed control of the government at the head of a council of nine, while the king remained in captivity and was forced to rubber-stamp Simon's decisions. Though he attracted incredible support among the populace, Simon could not retain the support of the magnates, a decisive flaw. He was defeated and killed at the Battle of Evesham on 4 August 1265. He found dignity in death, marching fearlessly on the enemy and refusing sanctuary by declaring, 'Churches are for chaplains, the field is for knights!'[4] Henry resumed his personal rule in 1265, though he suffered from poor health for the remainder of his life. In the spring of 1272, Norwich Cathedral was burned down by rioters, and on 16 November, while yet more riots were flaring up in London, the king expired at the age of 65.

THE REIGN OF EDWARD I

King Edward I, commonly known as Edward Longshanks on account of his height (6ft 2in), was the first king since 1066 to have an English rather than a Norman name. He began his reign *in absentia* because he was in Italy when the throne fell vacant. In 1270, at the age of 31, he had joined Louis IX's Eighth Crusade and set out for Palestine. Edward's own life hung in the balance in June 1272, when he was wounded by a Saracen's poison blade during a private interview at Acre, but according to one story, his wife saved him by sucking out the poison. It has been estimated that this crusade cost the Crown £100,000, about twice its annual income. Traditionally, a man was not king of England until he had been crowned, but when Henry died in November 1272, the barons proclaimed Edward Longshanks king and swore fealty to him in his absence. Thus began the practice of dating a monarch's reign from the day of the old king's death, rather than from the new king's coronation, a principle of continuity encapsulated in the mantra, 'The king is dead. Long live the king.'

Stories of Edward's youthful prowess abound. At a tournament in Châlons-sur-Marne in 1273, the count of Châlons, after failing to defeat the English by superiority of numbers, attempted to pull the king from his horse by the neck, but the taller and stronger Edward threw him into the dust. He also had a violent temper: it is said that he once raged against the Dean of St Paul's so furiously that the poor man died instantly from shock.

HAMMER OF THE SCOTS

Edward Longshanks was given the epithet 'Hammer of the Scots' (*Scotorum malleus*), inscribed in Latin on his tomb at Westminster Abbey. Starting in 1290, there was a Scottish succession crisis known as The Great Cause, with thirteen claimants to the vacant throne, including Robert the Bruce and John Balliol. As overlord of Scotland, Edward arbitrated between the claimants and declared John Balliol king. But his relations with Balliol later broke down, and he invaded Scotland in March 1296. In less than six months, he conquered the country, removed its king and seized the Stone of Destiny at Scone, an ancient block of sandstone weighing over 150kg that was used in Scottish coronations. Though Balliol was spared execution, Edward humiliated him by having the royal arms of Scotland publicly torn off his surcoat. There was a Scottish interregnum from 1296 to 1306, during which the English military elite attempted to consolidate Edward's grip over Scotland but faced major resistance, including a 1297 revolt led by William Wallace and Robert the Bruce. The Scottish monarchy was restored in 1306. At the same time, there was major resistance in England to Edward's high taxation, both from the gentry and from the spirituality. The king skilfully won his opponents over by promising to confirm Magna Carta and to demand no future taxes without the consent of Parliament.

THE CONQUEST OF WALES

Edward Longshanks could equally have been described as the Hammer of the Welsh, for his conquest of Wales was far more successful than his Scottish campaigns. The Norman and Angevin kings had made forays into Wales but had never managed to conquer it. Edward I invaded Wales in 1277 after declaring Llywelyn ap Gruffudd, Prince of Wales, to be a rebel. The two rulers agreed to a treaty called the Peace of Aberconwy, by which Llywelyn paid tribute to the English king and was permitted to retain his princely title. He was also fined £50,000, 'which was tantamount to saying that Llywelyn was at [the king's] mercy, as he could never find such a sum'.[5] This compromise broke down five years later when Llywelyn's brother David stirred up a revolt on 21 March 1282, which has been described as 'the last serious struggle for Welsh independence' – although this title should probably go to the Glendower rebellion a century later.[6]

Llywelyn himself joined the rebels rather than opposing his own brother, but he was cut down in battle by a commander from Shropshire called Stephen of Langton, who had no idea of the identity of the man he had just killed. The rebel host, disheartened by the death of the prince, surrendered on 25 April 1283, and David was executed. Edward assumed control of Llywelyn's princely lands and in 1284 he issued the Statute of Wales, which introduced English criminal law in Wales and established sheriffs, the chief administrative officers of the Crown, in six Welsh counties. The king of England was now truly master of Wales. Between 1277 and 1287, Edward began work on building ten royal castles in north Wales, including in Snowdonia and Anglesey, and at the Lincoln Parliament of 1301, he named his 16-year-old son Prince of Wales. This was done principally to channel revenue to his son, but it became a tradition for the king's heir apparent to be invested with the same title.

THE ENGLISH JUSTINIAN

Edward Longshanks was also an important legal reformer. In 1604, Edward Coke described him as 'our Justinian', drawing a parallel with the sixth-century Byzantine emperor who oversaw the codification of Roman law.[7] The parallel is imperfect because Edward did not codify a body of existing legal principles, but rather issued a series of great statutes designed to modify existing law. For example, the statute *Quia Emptores* (1290) was issued to check the practice of subinfeudation, whereby tenants became petty lords by subletting their lands. Edward also attempted to clamp down on private legal jurisdictions by issuing writs of *quo warranto*, which compelled subjects to demonstrate in court 'by what warrant' they exercised lucrative feudal rights and privileges to the king's loss. This campaign ruffled many feathers; it is said that the nobleman John de Warenne, who was ordered to show by what warrant he held certain privileges, responded by drawing a rusty sword and crying, 'Behold, my warrant!'[8] The implication was that his Norman ancestors had earned the privileges with their blood. Not only was the *quo warranto* campaign unpopular, but it was also mostly ineffectual.

During Edward's reign, the constitutional development of Parliament continued at pace. To the so-called Model Parliament of 1295, the king summoned nobles, representatives of counties and towns, and higher and lower clergy. Similar developments happened across the Channel at about the same time: in 1302, the king of France convened the first representative assembly known as the Estates-General, composed of lay magnates, church magnates and commons. From 1325, no English Parliament 'met without local representatives'.[9] Edward was also the first king of England to levy regular customs duties, and his reign witnessed the rise of justices of the peace (JPs), panels of gentlemen in each county who would play a leading role in local administration and justice for centuries to come.

EXPULSION OF THE JEWS

The blackest mark on Edward's balance sheet is his maltreatment of the Jews. Jews had first arrived in England in significant numbers in the Norman period, and in the late thirteenth century there were probably about 3,000 English Jews. By law they were royal chattels, meaning in essence that the king could treat them as he pleased; usually he relied on them heavily when he needed to borrow money. Though English Christians and Jews co-existed in relative harmony, there were flashpoints of trouble. Infamously, in 1189, a group of over a hundred beleaguered Jews harbouring in the Castle of York resorted to mass suicide. Antisemitism has a complex history that cannot be explored here, but one cause of conflict was that Jewish financiers lent money at interest, a practice forbidden between fellow Christians. Everyone liked moneylenders when they needed to secure a loan, but these warm feelings tended to dissipate when it was time to pay the money back with interest.

England also had a recurrent problem with coin-clipping – the criminal practice of shaving off precious metal from coins – which contributed to inflation, and Jewish merchants were believed to be chiefly responsible. In October 1278, an order went out for the arrest of all the Jews of England, some of whom were later executed on the findings of a royal commission. In 1290, Parliament voted to grant money to the king if he agreed to expel all Jews from England. Edward accepted these terms and issued a royal edict to the same effect on 18 July. Unconverted Jews remained forbidden from living in England for centuries, though Jewish migration did later resume in limited numbers and under the radar. Oliver Cromwell unofficially loosened the prohibition in the 1650s, but he did not 'invite the Jews back' in the simplistic sense that the story is sometimes told. As for King Edward I, he died from a combination of dysentery and other illnesses on 7 July 1307.

Edward Longshanks

THE TROUBLES OF EDWARD II

The life and reign of King Edward II appeared to confirm the English superstition that between the reigns of two great kings there invariably comes the reign of a lesser man. Edward was a curious character who relished the company of labourers and dedicated his time to farming, horse breeding, rowing, thatching and other unkinglike pursuits. The Victorian historian William Stubbs opined that Edward was blessed with 'the skilful hand rather than the thoughtful head'.[10] The king also had a penchant for seafood, which seemed unusual enough for contemporaries to remark upon. Before his accession to the throne, Edward had exasperated his father by spending excessive time with male 'favourites', especially the Gascon soldier Piers Gaveston. We do not know for sure that the relationship was sexual, but it was widely believed that Gaveston exercised too great an influence over the prince, and in early 1307 he was ordered to abjure the realm. However, when the old king died a few months later, the newly crowned Edward II immediately recalled his old playmate, who was honoured with the Earldom of Cornwall and a large bequest of lands. The barons simmered with resentment for Gaveston, their feelings driven both by jealousy of an upstart and by legitimate opposition to the king's self-centred decision-making.

At his coronation on 25 February 1308, the king was compelled to swear a modified oath that bound him to keep 'the rightful laws and customs which the community of the realm shall have determined', effectively signing a political blank cheque.[11] At a Parliament held in London shortly thereafter, the magnates drew up a declaration that distinguished between the Crown and the person of the king: while the former was inviolable, the latter could be forcibly removed for the good of the realm. The same declaration required Gaveston to abjure England once more, a demand he had no choice but to obey, although he returned the very next year. In 1311, a panel of twenty-one earls, prelates and barons forced a set of Ordinances on the king, which re-exiled Gaveston and asserted the barons' right to select royal councillors. The framers of these Ordinances, led by the king's stupendously wealthy cousin, Thomas, 2nd Earl of Lancaster, are known as the Ordainers or Lords Ordainer. Gaveston failed to comply with the terms of the exile, and he was beheaded by the Ordainers in Warwickshire in 1312. His execution 'had little of the character of a judicial execution, and more that of a public lynching'.[12]

IF AT FIRST YOU DON'T SUCCEED

There were also security issues on the northern border. In command of over 2,000 cavalry and 11,000 infantry, Edward personally faced the Scottish king Robert the Bruce on the battlefield at Bannockburn in 1314. According to a legend first recorded centuries after his death, Robert had learned persistence from watching a spider successfully spinning a web in a cave after many failed attempts. Spiders or no spiders, he was certainly a master of persistence. The battle, fought on 23 and 24 June, was a terrible English defeat. On the Scottish side, even the army cooks and servants joined in the fighting with whatever makeshift weapons they could lay their hands on. Edward escaped with an escort of close supporters but one of his captains, a Norman knight named Giles d'Argentan, charged alone into the Scottish lines, choosing to be hacked to pieces rather than to partake in the ignominious retreat. This was a far cry from the easy conquest of Scotland that had taken place less than two decades earlier. The king's defeat did nothing to improve his poor relations with the great men of the realm, seeming rather to confirm that they were right to check his power.

At a Parliament in York in 1314, the king was once again forced to confirm the Ordinances. The Ordainers consolidated their position by replacing pro-Edward royal officials both at court and in the regions. However, the Ordainers' policy of restricting the king's authority 'was more successful in its negative side of ruining the royal autocracy, than in its positive side of supplying an alternative system of efficient government'.[13] Furthermore, the Earl of Lancaster was unlucky in that he had to deal with unprecedentedly poor harvests and all their attendant problems – including a great famine between 1315 and 1317. He resigned as head of the king's council in April 1316, having formally held this position for only a few months. Although he and the king were reconciled in 1318, he was not readmitted to the council. Edward and Lancaster served side by side at the Siege of Berwick in 1319, producing inevitable conflict. Someone told Lancaster that the king had made a thinly veiled threat: 'When this wretched business is over, we will turn our hands to other matters. For I have not yet forgotten what was done to my brother Piers.'[14]

A new group of royal favourites emerged around this time, including Hugh Despenser the younger and Hugh Despenser the elder, provoking opposition from hard-headed politicians like the Earl of Pembroke. The Despensers were exiled at a summer Parliament in 1321, nicknamed the Parliament of the White Bend because the king's opponents wore green coats with a white 'bend', or diagonal stripe. But the baronial victory proved to be fleeting. Lancaster was defeated at the Battle of Boroughbridge on 16 March 1322 and was summarily executed on his own turf at Pontefract a few days later, after spectators pelted him with snowballs. (The world was just entering the Little Ice Age, so heavy snow in March was not unusual.) Instead of exercising cautious moderation in the wake of his lucky victory at Boroughbridge, the king decided to pass the bold Statute of York (1322). This not only repealed the Ordinances, but also declared that any future attempts to restrict royal authority 'shall be void and of no Avail or Force whatever'.[15]

EDWARD II DEPOSED

Edward's apparent drift towards absolutism alienated would-be supporters. What was more, the Despenser administration was grasping and unpopular, all too willing to employ the dark arts of coercion and blackmail. In France, a group of exiles carefully laid plans to oppose the king. They were joined in 1323 by the king's prisoner Roger Mortimer, who escaped from the Tower of London with a rope ladder after the guards were drugged with a soporific. Even the king's French wife, Queen Isabella, betrayed him: when she was sent to her homeland in 1325 to negotiate a peace, she refused to return to England, possibly because Edward was having an affair with his niece Eleanor, the wife of Despenser the younger. Under the romantic spell of Paris, Isabella was tempted into an affair of her own with the warlike Roger Mortimer. Taking the lead of the English exiles, Isabella and Mortimer invaded England in 1326 with an army of around 1,500 men. The Despenser administration made only a feeble effort to save itself. The estates of the realm, summoned in the king's name, denounced Edward for succumbing to evil counsel, disregarding the rule of law and abandoning his kingdom, and sent a delegation urging him to resign the crown. He was formally deposed on 20 January, something which had never happened before in England, although the pope had been known to depose rulers on the continent. Edward's kingly staff was broken in twain, and his eldest son, the 14-year-old Prince Edward, was crowned in his stead on 1 February 1327.

The deposed king was initially imprisoned in Berkeley Castle in Gloucestershire, but after repeated attempts to break him out, it became obvious that his existence was politically dangerous. He was probably murdered on 21 September 1327 by three hired assassins – John Maltravers, William Ogle and Thomas Gurney. There is a touching scene in Christopher Marlowe's Elizabethan play *Edward II* (1594), where the king naively speaks to his assassin as if he were a friend, though his instincts tell him to be on guard: 'Something still buzzeth in mine eares, And tells me, if I sleepe I never wake.'[16] According to the best-known rumour, he was killed with a red-hot poker thrust into the anus, or, as one writer has delicately put it, 'driven into the royal body by way of the fundament'.[17] This method would have been designed to avoid any visible sign of injury. Alternatively, it is possible that Edward was murdered by suffocation with a mattress. His heart was embalmed and encased in a silver vase, which was placed in Isabella's own tomb after her death. There were continual rumours that Edward was not really dead. According to one contemporary story, a murdered porter took the king's place, and Edward himself fled to the north of Italy to live out the rest of his days in safe obscurity – an intriguing possibility. The deposal of 1327 seemed to bode ill for the future of monarchical authority in England, but Edward's son was to turn the Crown's fortunes around by proving to be everything that his father was not.

6

THE FOURTEENTH CENTURY (1327–1400)

After Edward II's deposal and murder, the queen dowager Isabella assumed control of the government along with her lover, Roger Mortimer, and the teenage King Edward III was set up as a figurehead. This state of affairs was very fragile, for while the barons had been perfectly happy about the removal of Edward II, they disliked the proud couple who had plucked him down. Since Mortimer held no formal office, he was not properly accountable for his actions, despite his immense political power. As for Isabella, she arranged for her son to grant her enough lands to raise her annual income to 20,000 marks (about £13,000), which her enemies seized upon as evidence of greed. Edward III came into his majority in 1330, a few weeks before his 18th birthday. He issued a proclamation that set the tone of his new regime by stressing the importance of fair and consensual government: 'All matters which touch us and the estate of our realm are to be disposed of by the common council of all the magnates of the realm.'[1]

One of the king's first acts was to move against Isabella and Mortimer, who were holed up in the Castle of Nottingham. A company of the king's loyal supporters stole into the castle through a secret passage at nightfall and stormed the queen's apartments. Isabella and Mortimer were arrested, while a couple of unlucky servants were cut down in the fray. This coup was probably planned by the king's household officer William Montagu, who sagely observed that 'it is better to eat the dog than to have the dog eat you'.[2] Mortimer was tried and condemned to death by the Lords in Parliament, while the king's mother was allocated a generous pension but forced to retire from public life. By taking strong action against a political clique, Edward and his counsellors signified their respect for the political community. Throughout his reign, Edward strived to restore the trust of his barons and led his country to a series of celebrated military victories. His wife, Queen Philippa of Hainault, was happy to confine her life to the domestic sphere and won the approval of the political community, although she did enjoy the finer things in life and earned a reputation for extravagance.

Edward's earliest military interventions were in Scotland, at that time troubled by an acrimonious dispute between two political factions, one centred around the child king David II (last of the House of Bruce) and the other centred around the challenger Edward Balliol. The Davidian party sought to preserve Scotland's independence, while Balliol thought that agreeing to have Scotland carved up and further subordinated to England was a price worth paying to gain the crown. Edward III gave secret support to a 'war of private enterprise' led by Henry Beaumont and other English lords, who beat the Scottish 'nationalists' in battle at Dupplin Moor near Perth on 11 August 1332.[3] Balliol was crowned as king in September, and Edward began to support him openly, moving his central administration to York in 1333 to better support the war effort. Balliol invaded Scotland with English support in March, laying siege to the town of Berwick. Edward himself joined the siege in May, and in July he defeated a Scottish army around twice the size of his own at Halidon Hill, 2 miles from Berwick. The chief citizens of Berwick then surrendered to the English. Balliol seemed to have triumphed, but in fact he would never consolidate his authority over the whole of Scotland, and he was to face resistance and conspiracy for the rest of his life.

CLAIMING FRANCE

Throughout the Scottish conflict, the Davidian party had enjoyed the support of King Philip VI of France. Direct hostilities between England and France broke out in 1337 when Philip confiscated the Duchy of Gascony, one of England's last remaining continental possessions, in retaliation for Edward's failure to swear fealty to his overlord. The Hundred Years' War, a name invented in the eighteenth century, consisted of a series of short-term territorial

conflicts between the Houses of Plantagenet and Valois, extending
from 1337 to 1453, when Gascony was permanently annexed to
France. In 1338, the French king made a series of lightning raids
on southern England, sacking Southampton in October. Edward,
in turn, laid claim to the throne of France, symbolizing his claim
by quartering the arms of France – that is, dividing his royal coat
of arms into quarters, with the traditional lions, or 'leopards', in
two of the quarters to represent England, and a field of *fleurs-de-
lis* in the other two to represent France. In the field, he wore a
surcoat over his armour embroidered with these arms, while his
scholars and lawyers cobbled together some spurious theories to
support his claim to the French throne. Edward won a great naval
victory against the French at the Battle of Sluys on 24 June 1340, in
which around 15,000 French soldiers perished, an early portent of
England's later mastery of the seas. The first phase of the French war
concluded with a truce agreed in September 1340, which allowed
both sides to regroup.

During this intermission, Edward had to grapple with the problem of finance. He had funded the war effort with hefty taxes,
including levies on the wool trade, but there was still a serious
deficit. A scapegoat had to be found, and the blame fell on the
unfortunate Robert Stratford, chancellor and first minister, who was
removed in a winter purge. This was the prelude to a public dispute
between the king and Robert's brother John Stratford, Archbishop
of Canterbury, which historians used to interpret as 'one of the
great set pieces of English
constitutional history', since
the principle of royal account-
ability seemed to be at stake.[4]
The two men eventually
overcame their differences in
Parliament in 1341. The king
then headed a brief military
campaign in Brittany from
1342 to 1343. On the journey
back to England, he almost
died in a storm that was said
to have been stirred up by the
French queen's necromancers.

THE BATTLE OF CRÉCY

Edward's most celebrated military victory was against Philip VI at the Battle of Crécy (26 August 1346). After landing in Normandy with a great armada in July, the English launched a *chevauchée*, a raiding expedition in which soldiers laid waste to towns and villages to weaken and depress the enemy. Battle was then joined at Crécy, an arbitrary location chosen to give the English an advantageous position on high ground with a forest at their back. The French fought under the banner of the Oriflamme, a yellow flame on a red background, while the English fought under a dragon banner, just as Harold's forces had at the Battle of Hastings. Some credit for the victory must go to the martial courage of the common Englishman: as a Cornish clerk wrote a few decades later, the English were accustomed to winning every fight unless betrayed by traitors.[5]

The real secret of the English victory, however, was their methodical employment of English and Welsh longbowmen, who fought side-by-side with knights in disregard of social conventions. The French nobility, who charged on horseback, cut a finer figure but paid dearly for it. As one chronicler wrote, their illustrious cavalry charged into a hail of English arrows, 'tumbling over each other like a vast litter of pigs'.[6] This was also the first pitched battle in which the English used guns. Guns did not arrive in Europe until the late thirteenth century, though the Chinese had invented a precursor called the fire lance in around the year 1000. In all, over 1,500 French noblemen and knights lost their lives at Crécy. By contrast, it seems that no more than 300 English knights and esquires were killed. In the aftermath of the battle, Philip retreated to Amiens with a small contingent of soldiers. Back in England, the king's forces won a victory against the Scots at Durham, at the Battle of Neville's Cross.

Edward decided to capitalize on his victory at Crécy by laying siege to Calais, where he planned to establish a permanent English garrison. Since the town was strongly fortified and well provisioned, a siege would take time; cannon was only just coming onto the scene in western Europe and was still fairly primitive. The English king decided to play the long game. He built a temporary wooden town called Villeneuve-la-Hardie to house his soldiers, complete with viewing galleries for distinguished gentlemen and ladies to take in the siege. An influx of new recruits from England swelled the army ranks to around 25,000 men by the summer of 1347. Calais finally surrendered on 2 August. It would remain an English territory for over two centuries, until it was lost by Philip and Mary in 1558. Edward commemorated the victory at Crécy by founding the Most Noble Order of the Garter, an exclusive chivalric order typically composed of twenty-four favoured knights. The French motto of the Garter, *Honi soit qui mal y pense* ('Shame on him who thinks evil of it'), is found on the royal coat of arms to this day.

THE BLACK DEATH

The celebrations did not last long. In the late 1340s, England was brought to her knees by a global pandemic, the Black Death, which was possibly caused by a bacterial infection that originated in Central Asia. England had its first cases of the plague in the summer of 1348, with the infection spreading from rats to humans via fleas. According to modern estimates, between a third and one half of England's population died in the following eighteen months, cutting down the total population to perhaps around 2.5 million. To many contemporaries, it seemed that this disease heralded the end of the human species. John Clynn, an Irish monastic chronicler from Kilkenny, left some space at the end of his chronicle to be filled if 'anyone should still be alive in the future'.[7] The worst of the pestilence had passed by the end of 1349, although new cases cropped up intermittently on a smaller scale. There were fresh outbreaks in 1361 and 1368, the first of which was followed by St Maurus's Wind, one of the most devastating hurricanes in English history.

The tragedy of the Black Death had at least one positive side effect: the mass fatalities created a shortage of labour, which indirectly led to higher wages and better working conditions for labourers. However, any advantages reaped were partially negated by the effects of price rises, whilst the well-heeled men of Parliament passed self-serving labour laws to prevent workers from making the most of their bargaining position, including the 1351 Statute of Labourers. After the 1361 plague outbreak, 'employers grew obsessed with the notion that the labouring classes were taking advantage of the newly competitive market to press for easy terms and unreasonably high wages'.[8] The reign of Edward III saw the rise of the Commons in Parliament: elected representatives began to sit as a separate House to discuss the king's business, and in the penultimate Parliament of Edward's reign, known as the Good Parliament (1376), the Commons were represented by a Speaker for the first time.

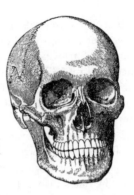

THE BLACK PRINCE

The truce with France had held since 1347, mainly because rulers were loath to raise armies at a time of plague. By 1355, however, Edward was becoming restless, and once again sought to make good his claim to the kingdom of France. In the winter of this year, his son Edward of Woodstock raided the south of France, flattening at least a dozen walled towns. Contemporaries knew this man as the Prince of Wales and Aquitaine, but today he is popularly called the Black Prince, a name which was apparently invented in the Tudor period. Though its meaning is uncertain, this name probably refers to the fact that Prince Edward's livery was black – that is, his household servants and retainers wore black. It has been said that the name refers to the prince's black armour, but it was not uncommon for nobles and knights to wear unpolished armour, which in those days was always black. At the Battle of Poitiers on 19 September 1356, the Black Prince led an army of Englishmen and Gascons to defeat a French army about twice the size of his own. King Jean II was captured and transported to London and was not released until the signing of the Treaty of Brétigny (1360), by which the French agreed to pay 3 million gold crowns into the English treasury. For the first time in over twenty years, England was at peace.

But after a relatively uneventful decade, war broke out again in 1369, and England was not to be so successful this time around. The following eight years were 'an unrelieved tale of military retreat, financial corruption, court faction, and parliamentary opposition'.[9] Charles V, king of France since 1364, entered into a secret alliance with three Gascon lords, who reneged on their loyalty to the Black Prince after a dispute about taxation. Before war was formally declared, Charles began to move against Edward's territories in France, and by 1372 he had conquered most of the northern part of the Duchy of Aquitaine. By this stage, both King Edward and the Black Prince were incapacitated, and the king's third son, John of Gaunt, had taken effective control of the domestic administration. A one-year truce with France was brokered by the pope in late June 1375, but England's fortunes continued to decline. By 1380, England had no French territories left except Calais and a strip of lands in the south. The Black Prince died on 7 June 1376, and Edward III died at Sheen Palace on 21 June 1377. The crown passed, at this miserable moment, to the Black Prince's surviving son, Richard.

THE REIGN OF RICHARD II

King Richard II was 10 years old when he inherited the throne. On 15 July 1377, the day before his coronation, he entered London with great pomp. Crowds braved the extreme heat to greet their new boy king, encouraged no doubt by the fact that the water in the two conduits of Cheapside had been replaced with free red and white wine, as was normal practice around coronation time. Parliament appointed a council to rule England during the royal minority, composed originally of the great officers of state and nine others selected by the magnates. Between 1377 and 1381, members of Parliament consented to a number of poll taxes to fund the continuing war with France. These hated impositions were the primary cause of the Peasants' Revolt, the first major crisis of Richard's unhappy reign. When the royal commissioners tried to levy Richard's third poll tax in Essex in May 1381, they were violently resisted, triggering large-scale rebellion in Essex and Kent. The rebel leader was Wat Tyler, who probably worked as a tiler, his surname reflecting his profession. Another famous rebel was the radical preacher John Ball, who preached a sermon to his compatriots on the theme of a popular proverbial couplet, critiquing the hierarchical society in which he lived: 'When Adam delved and Eve span, / Who was then a gentleman?'[10] The rebels voiced a wide range of grievances, including opposition to the Statute of Labourers.

According to an anonymous eyewitness, a mob of 60,000 commoners arrived in Southwark on 12 June and stormed the Marshalsea Prison, releasing the debtors and felons held inside. From Southwark, they progressed across London Bridge to the city proper, where thousands of citizens joined their ranks. They left a trail of destruction, razing fine houses and palaces to the ground. The king, now 14, watched the city burn from one of the turrets of the Tower of London, where he was surrounded by a protective guard. On 14 June, he rode to Mile End in East London to hold a risky interview with the rebels, offering them pardons and charters of freedom. At a similar interview at Smithfield on the following day, he agreed too readily to their demands, promising to abolish serfdom and lordship. Wat Tyler, who refused to remove his hat in the royal presence, had an altercation with the king's officers, during which he was stabbed in the neck by the Mayor of London. The leaderless rebels thereupon found themselves surrounded by the city militia 'like sheep within a pen'.[11] They were finished.

Richard never had an official minority reign because no regent was appointed to govern the realm during his childhood, but he began to exercise independent influence in around 1381, at the age of 14. From this year, he began to select his own courtiers, and two men emerged as his clear favourites: Michael de la Pole, later Earl of Suffolk, and Robert de Vere, Earl of Oxford. Unfavourable comparisons were drawn between these delicate courtiers and the favourites of Edward II. Rightly or wrongly, the political classes distrusted the influence of the new men and resented the patronage lavished upon them. They also opposed de la Pole's general policy of seeking peace with France. The major bulwark against the power of the favourites was the influence of more experienced counsellors – at least, until the king began to dismantle the old guard. In July 1382, the middle-aged chancellor Richard Scrope was sacked, apparently for refusing to seal grants of lands that he considered would impoverish the Crown. There were also rising tensions between Richard and his uncle, John of Gaunt, whose independent power was reflected in the fact that he had 300 indentured retainers. Richard even drew his sword on his uncle at court. By the summer of 1386, the breach was complete, and Gaunt departed for Spain to lay claim to the kingdom of Castile.

THE LORDS APPELLANT

Conflict between king and nobles reached boiling point in the so-called Wonderful Parliament that opened in October 1386, about the time that Chaucer began writing *The Canterbury Tales*. Both houses of Parliament demanded the removal of Michael de la Pole, now Earl of Suffolk and royal chancellor, and two other great officers of state. The king stubbornly replied that he would not 'move the least boy of his kitchen'. According to the chronicler Henry Knighton, Richard even threatened to seek the assistance of the king of France against his own rebellious subjects.[12] Members of Parliament responded by impeaching Suffolk on grounds of corruption. Impeachment was a mechanism for trying and removing royal officers that had been invented by the Good Parliament (1376). They also forced a governing council on the 19-year-old king to direct royal policy.

Seething over this humiliation, the king procured a ruling from his judges that the provisions of the Wonderful Parliament impinged upon the royal prerogative, and that the responsible parties were traitors to the realm, deserving of death. Five leading noblemen (the Lords Appellant) responded by mustering armies and drawing up a document called an 'appeal of treason' against the king's favourites, which was a novel procedure. The five lords – Gloucester, Warwick, Arundel, Nottingham and Derby – presented this appeal at the so-called Merciless Parliament on 3 February 1388, wearing shimmering golden coats and standing arm in arm. The Lords in Parliament sentenced Suffolk and Oxford, who had fled abroad, to the loss of their lands and property, while the royal favourites still residing in England were sentenced to death. The Lords Appellant had been absolutely successful in executing their programme of reform.

EMPEROR RICHARD

Fortune's wheel turned again in 1389, when Richard, now aged 22, recovered control of the government. At a Great Council of magnates, he demanded the resignation of the replacement chancellor, Thomas Arundel, and the removal of two Lords Appellant, Gloucester and Warwick, from his council. The king then began to drift towards an exalted style of kingship that could hardly be tolerated by Englishmen. For instance, he required his subjects to kneel before him whenever the royal glance fell upon them – the sort of thing that went on in the palaces of the East. The king also began to surround himself with a retinue of Cheshire bodyguards, who wore his badge of the white hart as a symbol of their loyalty. According to Aristotle's *Politics*, a royal bodyguard was only a sign of tyranny if it was composed of foreigners – but Richard's choice of guard appeared to indicate a lack of trust in Englishmen outside his own Cheshire retinue. The greatest lesson of the study of history is that 'power tends to expand indefinitely, and will transcend all barriers, abroad and at home, until met by superior forces'.[13] What was needed at this time was for opponents to arise to check King Richard's power.

A twenty-eight-year truce with France was agreed at Paris in 1396, and Richard cemented peaceful relations with his erstwhile enemy by marrying Isabella of Valois, daughter of King Charles VI. A shameful clause was inserted into the marriage treaty that bound France to help Richard wage war on his own subjects if necessary. In 1397, secure in the peace with France, Richard decided to take belated revenge on the three senior Lords Appellant who had destroyed his favourites a decade earlier. He now had the support of John of Gaunt, with whom he had reconciled. Warwick was arrested at a specially planned feast on 10 July and thrown into the Tower of London; Arundel naively surrendered because of a false promise that he would not be harmed; and Gloucester sensibly declined the invitation to the king's treacherous banquet but was arrested anyhow on the same day. All three were ironically tried by appeal of treason, the very method they had invented a decade earlier. Arundel was executed; Gloucester died in prison; and Warwick was sentenced to life imprisonment. Another of the appellants, Henry Bolingbroke, Earl of Derby (John of Gaunt's son), was pardoned of his earlier actions and created Duke of Hereford. However, Hereford's rehabilitation came to an end when he accused a fellow nobleman, the Duke of Norfolk, of treasonable words in 1398. The dukes intended to settle this matter with a trial by combat at Coventry, but Richard stopped the duel from going ahead and sent both men into exile instead – Hereford for ten years and Norfolk for life.

UNKINGED RICHARD

When the long-sick John of Gaunt died in 1399, Richard unwisely decided to disinherit the exiled Hereford, who should have succeeded his father to the Dukedom of Lancaster. He probably feared the power of a Duke of Lancaster beyond the sea, for Lancaster was the greatest landowner in the realm besides the king and therefore also, potentially, commander of the second-largest army. However, the move was a miscalculation that turned a disgruntled but faithful magnate into an opposition frontman with nothing to lose. While King Richard was away in Ireland with his most loyal supporters, Hereford sailed for England with a small group of retainers and landed at Ravenspur in the East Riding of Yorkshire, where it is said that the entire county rallied to his cause. He eventually captured the king at Chester and rode to London, setting up a commission to arrange for the king's deposal. Richard allegedly declared his resignation of the crown on 28 September, which was confirmed by a meeting of the estates (technically not a Parliament but formally similar) that opened the next day.

Hereford was crowned King Henry IV on 13 October 1399, the first English king from the House of Lancaster, a cadet branch of the House of Plantagenet. There was a snag, however: when he had arrived in England in the summer, Hereford had sworn not to seek the throne for himself. By ignoring this oath, Henry laid himself open to charges of perjury that would dog him and his Lancastrian successors for many years to come. Richard died on around 14 February 1400, probably starved to death by his gaolers at Pontefract Castle. The fourteenth century had seen the deposal of two kings and the death of up to half the English population by plague, alongside the military glories of Edward III and the Black Prince. The next century too was witness to both glory and disaster, as the period of strong kingship that was to mark the reigns of Henry IV and Henry V would be followed by the reign of another incompetent monarch, and a protracted civil war.

7

LANCASTER AND YORK (1400–1485)

Whether they liked him or not, most fifteenth-century chroniclers agreed that Henry IV, first of the House of Lancaster, was a formidable king. It used to be argued that he restored constitutional monarchy after the tyranny of Richard II, by allowing Parliament and the council to take their full share in the government of the realm. While this theory is no longer fully credited, it is true that Henry had a more consensual relationship with his subjects than his predecessor had enjoyed, and his court attracted no unpopular favourites. After winning the crown, he immediately buttressed his position by convening parliamentary trials for the so-called Counter-Appellants, men who had acquiesced in King Richard's decision to appropriate his rightful inheritance. He also put down an early plot to assassinate him, the Epiphany Rising, and had twenty-seven ringleaders executed for treason.

THE GLENDOWER REBELLION

Members of the influential Percy family, who had helped King Henry to the throne, profited enormously from having backed the right horse. Henry Percy, Earl of Northumberland, was appointed Lord High Constable, while his son, also called Henry Percy and nicknamed Hotspur, was named warden of the East March (centred at Berwick-upon-Tweed) and justiciar of Chester. Thomas Percy, Earl of Worcester, was appointed king's lieutenant in South Wales in 1401. While Henry certainly needed to reward his key allies, it was still risky for so much power to be concentrated in a single family.

The test of their loyalty came in 1400, when an Anglo-Welsh gentle-man called Owen Glendower (Owain Glyndŵr) rose up against the authority of Henry IV and proclaimed himself Prince of Wales. This revolt would prove to be a drain on the royal revenue for another fifteen years.

The Percys initially supported the king against Glendower, but their relationship with the Crown had been soured by financial disagreements. They eventually came to realize that they had interests in common with the Welsh rebel, and in July 1403, Hotspur and the Earl of Worcester began mustering soldiers in Wales in defiance of the king. They won the willing support of men in Cheshire who had formerly been supporters of Richard II. The king faced the Percys in battle at Shrewsbury on 21 July 1403, where Hotspur was slain and Worcester captured. Prince Henry, the king's heir, was shot in the cheek with an arrow that penetrated as far as his skull, but he was later saved by the London surgeon John Bradmore. The Earl of Northumberland, who raised soldiers but did not actually participate in the battle, was forgiven but forced to surrender his offices. Glendower's rebellion eventually petered out, and its leader died in around 1416 after spending a couple of years in hiding.

PARLIAMENTARY OPPOSITION

There were eleven Parliaments during Henry IV's reign, four of which openly opposed royal policy and sought to introduce rules governing the king's finances. The most hostile was the Long Parliament of 1406, which stretched from 1 March to 22 December. A minority of the Commons in 1406 were loyal promoters of the Crown's interests (at least thirty-five men, including the Speaker), while a significant majority were opponents of the court. The king and Commons agreed on a settlement in December that established an aristocratic 'continual council' responsible for governing the realm. The settlement also introduced a sharp distinction between the council (responsible for government policy) and the court (responsible for attending on the king).

Henry, who suffered from recurrent ill health, died on 20 March 1413, at the age of 45, just a month after trying to demonstrate his vigour by announcing that he would lead a forthcoming crusade to the Holy Land. About a generation after the king's death, a story was circulating that when Henry was on his deathbed, his son carried away the crown in the mistaken belief that his father had already died. The king awoke with a start and asked him, 'How do you have any right to it [the crown], for as you well know, I never had any?' His son replied: 'You held it with your sword, my lord, and for as long as I live I shall do the same.'[1] Henry IV was buried in Canterbury Cathedral, a more appropriate final resting place than Westminster Abbey because he had ruled as a usurper.

THE GREAT KING HENRY V

There is some doubt as to the precise date of King Henry V's birth, which was not recorded carefully because he was not expected to become king, but it was probably 16 September 1386. Early chroniclers of his reign presented a 'sinner to saint' narrative: until his accession to the throne in 1413, at the age of around 26, he was a riotous reprobate, but after that, he served his country with piety and application. This picture was later popularized by Shakespeare, but the truth is that Henry had already shown an aptitude for governance and warfare as a very young man. As noted already, he had accompanied his father in battle at the age of 16, surviving an arrow to the face, and when he was 20, he had begun to serve on his father's council.

At the outset of his reign, Henry faced off a feeble Lollard uprising called the Oldcastle Revolt. The Lollards were a heretical Christian sect who promoted the teachings of the Oxford scholar John Wycliffe (d. 1384), including opposition to the papacy and rejection of the doctrine of transubstantiation. A certain knight named Sir John Oldcastle was a Lollard himself and a promoter of Lollards, which should have marked him out for immediate punishment, but he was also a soldier who had served faithfully under Prince Henry before his accession to the throne, and hence enjoyed royal favour and protection. Still, he faced a formidable opponent in the person of Thomas Arundel, Archbishop of Canterbury, who made it his life's mission to stamp out religious unorthodoxy. Arundel managed to have Oldcastle excommunicated and convicted of heresy in September 1413. A month later, Oldcastle's fellow Lollards broke him out of the Tower of London, an incredible feat that may indicate there were Lollard sympathizers among the prison guards. The king learned from his intelligence agents that Lollard rebels from around the country were planning to march on London in support of Oldcastle in early 1414. A small rout of rebels was intercepted at Clerkenwell (3 miles from Westminster), of whom sixty-nine were later convicted of treason. Oldcastle himself managed to avoid detection until 1417, when he was sighted in Hereford, captured by two Welshmen, and conveyed thence to London for execution.

Harfleur and Agincourt

Henry is best remembered for his great victories at Harfleur and Agincourt. He decided to invade France in 1415 because he had a convincing claim to the Duchy of Normandy, which had been appropriated by the Capetian dynasty two centuries earlier, and because he desired to win prestige at home. The king was further provoked, if the story is to be believed, by the insulting behaviour of the French Dauphin Louis, heir apparent to the crown of France, who sent Henry a gift of tennis balls to imply that he was fitter for sport than kingship. Rather than launching a *chevauchée* in the style of his predecessor Edward III, Henry immediately laid siege to Harfleur, a strategically located fortified town in Normandy. The town fell into English hands after a six-week siege. This early victory is dramatized in Shakespeare's play *Henry V*, where the king encourages his soldiers to storm a breach in the town wall:

> Once more unto the breach, dear friends, once more…
> And you, good yeomen,
> Whose limbs were made in England, show us here
> The mettle of your pasture…
> For there is none of you so mean and base,
> That hath not noble lustre in your eyes…
> The game's afoot:
> Follow your spirit, and upon this charge
> Cry "God for Harry, England, and Saint George!"[2]

The French then chose the location of the war's most decisive engagement. The Battle of Agincourt took place on the feast day of Saint Crispin, 25 October 1415, after a night of continuous rainfall. The English were outnumbered, it used to be thought by five or eight to one, although recent research has estimated that Henry's army was composed of 9,000 soldiers and the French army (with less certainty) numbered around 12,000. Once again, England's longbowmen, who probably composed about 80 per cent of the total army, were the key to her victory. At the start of the battle, the English and French armies were separated by two woods, between which ran a narrow lane. The English waited for the French to charge towards them through the lane, each archer planting a pointed stake in the ground to slow down the cavalry charge and to buy more time for discharging arrows. The French army advanced directly into the trap and suffered enormous casualties. The victorious Henry infamously ordered his French prisoners to be executed, a cruel but pragmatic decision taken because of a false report that enemy reinforcements had arrived.

WINNING FRANCE

Henry left France almost immediately after his victory and did not return until August 1417, when he successfully conquered Normandy and later captured Rouen in 1419. He benefitted from internal divisions in France: the Armagnac–Burgundian Civil War (1407–35), not unlike the English Wars of the Roses, pitted two noble factions against each other. Henry negotiated with both sides but found more common ground with the Burgundians, with whom he signed the Treaty of Troyes in May 1420. This treaty appointed King Henry as heir to the throne of France and regent of Charles VI (Charles the Mad), and by so doing, implicitly disinherited the Dauphin Charles. In June, Henry married Charles's daughter, Catherine of France, at Troyes. He established Rouen as his administrative capital in Normandy, restoring traditional institutions such as the *grand conseil* and the Norman estates (a representative assembly).

With significant exaggeration, chroniclers compared Henry to Alexander the Great of Macedon, who had also made his great conquests as a young man. One chronicler referred to Henry as 'another Hector', drawing a parallel with the great Trojan warrior-prince.[3] Shakespeare imagined him as a hero who loved England and inspired patriotism in his subjects. Henry was the first king of this nation since 1066 who doggedly conducted business almost entirely in English, rather than in Latin or French. The English language, now enriched with a multitude of French-origin loanwords and shorn of gendered nouns, grammatical cases and other needless complexities, had been slowly replacing French as the language of the aristocracy for about a century. But this patriot king died at the height of his glory. In the summer of 1422, Henry contracted a serious illness, possibly dysentery, and on 31 August, he died at the age of about 35. Two months later, Charles the Mad also died, and the infant Henry VI was the first and only king to succeed to the 'double monarchy' of England and France.

THE REIGN OF HENRY VI

This was the fifth royal minority in English history, and the first time a baby had inherited the throne. In the absence of an adult sovereign, the first fifteen years of King Henry VI's reign were dominated by a council. Humphrey, Duke of Gloucester, an experienced soldier and the first patron of Renaissance humanism in England, was unhappy with this arrangement. A codicil to Henry V's will had appointed Gloucester as guardian and protector of the young king, which he interpreted to mean that he should also enjoy sole governance of the realm. But his wings were clipped by wary councillors, chief among them his own uncle, Henry Beaufort, Bishop of Winchester (later Cardinal). Parliament granted Gloucester the title of Protector of the Realm and principal councillor, and a salary of 8,000 marks (about £5,000), but executive authority was to be exercised jointly by the Lords of the council. The Protector was responsible for internal and external defence, while the council was responsible for governance.

Gloucester could barely conceal his resentment, and in October 1425, he and Beaufort had an irresponsible fracas near London Bridge, probably due to a dispute over who should have the custody of the 4-year-old king. Gloucester accused Beaufort of treason at the Parliament of Bats at Leicester in 1426, so-called because its members, who had been forbidden to bring swords because tempers were running so high, came armed with bats and clubs instead. The two rivals staged a public reconciliation, and the ensuing status quo remained basically untroubled until 1432, when Gloucester arrived in London with the king and had all the Beaufort allies in the central administration dismissed, establishing himself as chief minister accountable only to the king. Beaufort was briefly removed as councillor but reinstated in 1433. There were other troubles during Henry's minority, including a Lollard uprising that began in May 1431, led by the weaver Jack Sharp. This rebellion began in London and spread to several southern counties before ending with the capture of five ringleaders at Oxford on 19 May.

TROUBLES IN FRANCE

Across the Channel, England initially consolidated her recent territorial gains in France, where Henry held Normandy by virtue of conquest and Paris by virtue of alliance with the Burgundians. John of Lancaster, Duke of Bedford, was appointed Regent of France, and governed in the king's name from the splendid Parisian Palace of Les Tournelles. In 1423, Bedford commissioned the production of a propaganda poem and genealogy to be displayed in Notre-Dame, illustrating Henry VI's claim to the French crown, and a victory at the Battle of Verneuil in 1424 confirmed English supremacy in Normandy for the time being.

Unfortunately, England thereafter faced committed resistance from her Valois rival, King Charles VII, and she was hamstrung by the fact that official mismanagement had allowed the English navy to fall into disrepair. An early sign of England's reversal of fortunes came in 1428 and 1429, when the peasant girl Joan of Arc, a visionary who wore men's clothes, led a victorious campaign to relieve the English siege of Orléans. Joan then rose to become an adviser to Charles VII himself, until her capture by the Burgundians and execution for heresy in 1430. Henry VI was crowned king of France at Notre-Dame in December 1431, but this calculated bit of propaganda was an ineffective response to growing French military capabilities. At the Congress of Arras (August 1435), England's major ally, the Duke of Burgundy, switched sides and pronounced his support for Charles VII. There followed a protracted 'cat-and-mouse game of siege and counter-siege', in which various castles changed hands between the two warring nations.[4] Paris was recaptured by Charles in 1436.

Henry VI began his majority rule in 1437, at the age of 16. He married a fiery French noblewoman named Margaret of Anjou, but the royals did not produce an heir (Prince Edward) for years, and it was rumoured among the king's enemies that this child was the progeny of some more virile man at court. According to Henry's chaplain Robert Blacman, writing after the king's death, Henry had long felt or feigned a revulsion to the nude bodies of both sexes. At one Christmas as a young king, when one of his lords had intended to treat him to a show of topless ladies dancing, he had 'angrily averted his eyes'.[5] The king's frigidity was later spun as piety, which he undoubtedly had in large measure, but there may also have been sexual problems.

Joan of Arc

LOSING FRANCE

Gloucester and Beaufort, still bitter rivals, continued to sit at the council table together during the royal majority. Gloucester's wife was imprisoned in 1441 for hiring a witch to burn a wax effigy of the king, in the hopes that this would hasten his death. Beaufort retired in around 1443, and he and Gloucester both died in 1447, leaving the way clear for William de la Pole, Duke of Suffolk, the king's chief minister since 1444, to seize total control of the administration. Suffolk was ultimately blamed for much of the disastrous foreign policy that followed. England and France agreed to the two-year Truce of Tours in 1444, and the English ceded Maine to the French four years later. By 1450, England had lost all her French possessions except Calais. The Hundred Years' War thus concluded with a drawn-out English defeat. In the recriminations that followed, Suffolk was impeached of treason. The king sentenced him only to five years' exile, but he met a worse fate on 2 May 1450, when he was subjected to a mock trial aboard a ship off Dover called *Nicholas of the Tower*, and beheaded after being sentenced to death by an unlawful tribunal.

Henry has been called 'a well-intentioned duffer' and 'a miserable failure'.[6] Weak and indecisive, he relied heavily on the more robust personalities of his chief advisers. Early in his majority rule, he founded Eton College at Windsor in 1440 and King's College, Cambridge in 1441, which are normally thought to be his finest achievements. Members of Parliament did not see the building projects in the same light, complaining that the king was a spendthrift. Henry can be readily excused for having spent his subjects' money on noble building projects, but less forgivable were his careless royal grants to all and sundry. It seemed to some onlookers, especially those excluded from the showering of blessings, that Henry's household was a corrupt elite that filled its own pockets at the expense of the realm.

JACK CADE'S REBELLION

Popular grievances over the mismanagement of royal revenue compounded discontent over the king's disastrous foreign policy. Apparent wastefulness at court was more offensive than usual because England was experiencing a major recession that lasted from the 1440s to the 1470s. As so often in history, financial discontent emboldened the disaffected to oppose government policy. Armed opposition to Henry's rule came in May 1450, when the county of Kent rose in rebellion. Rumour had it that the king held Kent collectively responsible for the maritime murder of the

Duke of Suffolk and intended to turn the entire county into a forest as retribution. The rebels consisted mainly of labourers but there was also 'middle-class' support. They elected a man named Jack Cade as their leader, whose background is unknown, but who was later described as a sorcerer and former soldier. The revolt soon spread to Surrey, Sussex, Middlesex and Essex. Petitions were drawn up that claimed the king was resolved 'to live only on his commons' – in other words, that the common people were being bled dry to support the king's spending habits. But these rebels were no Bolsheviks: they also stated that the king should seek counsel from noblemen rather than 'mean persons of lower nature'.[7] They entered the City of London on 3 July and broke out the prisoners of the Marshalsea, following the example of the peasant rebels of 1381. For the next few days, they slept in Southwark and re-entered the city across London Bridge every day for more looting and drinking. By the morning of 5 July, loyalist citizens and royal troops had finally regrouped sufficiently to resist the rebels' re-entrance into the city. There was a battle, and then a truce, followed by negotiations between the rebels and the few government officials who had not fled the capital. Most of the rebels dispersed when they were promised a royal pardon. Cade was captured by the sheriff of Kent a week later, in an arrest so heavy-handed that he died of his wounds.

THE WARS OF THE ROSES

In the aftermath of Cade's rebellion, Richard Plantagenet, 3rd Duke of York, a descendant of King Edward III, emerged as the chief aristocratic opponent of the government. So began the rivalry between two branches of the Plantagenet dynasty: the House of Lancaster (headed by the king) and the House of York (headed by the duke). The House of Lancaster was represented by a red rose, among other heraldic devices, while the House of York was represented by a white rose. At first, the Duke of York did not oppose the king per se but rather Edmund Beaufort, 1st Duke of Somerset, who had emerged as the king's principal counsellor after Suffolk's murder. To blame the king directly was out of the question: 'Politicians had been thinking that the king was an ass ever since Henry had first demonstrated his asininity over a decade previously, but the current vocabulary of politics did not enable them to give such a thought expression.'[8] Despite his unmatched territorial power, the aloof Duke of York failed to recruit a broad base of support among the political classes. At the 1450 Parliament, he oversaw a programme of anti-court reform, having twenty-nine of the king's courtiers dismissed, but this proved to be short-lived because the court party soon regained the upper hand. Finding himself increasingly isolated, York marched on London with two other great lords, but he did not manage to pull off an intended coup. Though he was pardoned, he had to swear never to bear arms again.

With his great rival humbled, Somerset's administration now seemed secure, even though the other nobles disliked his policies. The central government ran relatively smoothly until August 1453, when the king suffered a mental breakdown, from which he would not recover for another seventeen months. Faced with a power vacuum, the king's council tried to establish political consensus by inviting York and Somerset to sit at the council table together, but York revived the old feud and had his rival thrown into prison for treason. York also buttressed his power by allying himself with the Neville family and having himself appointed as Protector of the Realm. His protectorate was interrupted by the sudden recovery of the king at Christmas 1454, who immediately ordered Somerset to be released. This incensed the Yorkist faction, who forthwith absented themselves from court without the king's permission and rode to their estates in the country. All the pieces were in place, the board was set. Few could doubt now that there was going to be a civil war.

With military support from the Nevilles, the Duke of York confronted the king at the town of St Albans, north of London, on 22 May 1455 with an army of around 3,000 men – the first military engagement of the Wars of the Roses. St Albans had no protective wall and the Yorkists easily broke through its feeble defences, with most of the fighting taking place in and around the marketplace. York's forces slew the Duke of Somerset and other leading Lancastrians, before prostrating themselves at the king's feet and declaring themselves his loyal subjects. In the wake of the battle, many surviving Lancastrian lords agreed to work with the Yorkists to build unity. York was again appointed as Protector, but the king dismissed him in February 1456. Henry tried to calm residual discontent by staging a so-called Loveday at St Paul's Cathedral on 24 March 1458, a symbolic settlement between the Houses of Lancaster and York, with the bishops as mediators, but this futile exercise fooled no one.

The Duke of York staged another coup in Shropshire in October 1459, claiming to oppose the king's councillors, not the king himself, but he was forced to flee after failing to muster sufficient support. At the Parliament of Devils at Coventry, the Yorkists were condemned as traitors, which meant the forfeiture of all their possessions. This was 'the first partisan act of the Wars of the Roses, an act that broke the political habit of looking for a settlement rather than seeking provocation'. The Yorkists fled into exile, only to return less than a year later to fight another set-piece battle at Northampton on 10 July 1460, under the leadership of Richard Neville, 16th Earl of Warwick (Warwick the Kingmaker), who had started out as a loyal supporter of King Henry. During the battle, the king allegedly hid in his tent, 'more timorous than a woman'.[9] The Yorkists were wholly successful in their aims, eliminating their rivals and capturing the king. They were now England's ruling faction.

York claimed the throne for himself at a Parliament that opened at Westminster on 7 October 1460, but his supporters were unwilling to remove a long-standing king. Instead, the Lords and Commons passed the Act of Accord, by which York would succeed Henry after his death, and would govern the realm as deputy in the meantime. Though a seemingly reasonable compromise, this plan had been designed by a packed House of Commons that was not truly representative of national interests. The aggrieved Lancastrians confronted and killed York at the Battle of Wakefield in the West Riding of Yorkshire on 30 December 1460. Six weeks later, the Yorkists were defeated again at the Second Battle of St Albans, in which Queen Margaret and the Lancastrians seized the person of the king. But the Yorkists' run of bad luck was over. The Duke of York's 18-year-old son and heir, Edward, Earl of March, now declared himself king. This claim he made good at the Battle of Towton in North Yorkshire on 29 March 1461, supported by Warwick the Kingmaker. Towton was the largest battle of the Wars of the Roses, possibly involving 75,000 men in all, fought in the midst of a ferocious blizzard. Edward was then crowned at Westminster, while King Henry fled to Scotland, only to be captured by the Yorkists five years later. The House of York was wholly in the ascendant.

EDWARD IV AND THE READEPTION

King Edward IV ruled England from 1461 to 1470 and again from 1471 to 1483. Immediately after the victory at Towton, he showed leniency towards his Lancastrian enemies to a degree that attracted criticism from his own followers. Despite this clemency, he did not fail to prevent uprisings against his rule in England, Scotland and Wales. There was also a threat of war with France and rumours of an anti-English alliance: Edward believed that the leaders of western Europe wished to extinguish 'the people, the name, the tongue and the blood English of this our said realm'.[10] Edward was traditionally regarded as a lazy and indulgent king, but this picture is not entirely accurate. Many believed he was just a figurehead, and that Warwick was the intelligent force behind the throne: they joked that there were two kings of England, one called Warwick and another whose name escaped them.

As he grew older, Edward became progressively less tolerant of the man who cast such a mighty shadow over him, and their relationship completely broke down in the summer of 1467. Warwick secretly conspired with the Lancastrian party, and his retainers stirred up a rebellion in Yorkshire under the nominal leadership of a man named Robin of Redesdale. He also reconciled himself with Margaret of Anjou, wife of King Henry VI. In the spring of 1470, Warwick invaded London with his key allies, including the Welshman Jasper Tudor, whose nephew would later reign as the first Tudor monarch. King Edward fled the country and Henry VI was seated once again on the throne he had lost a decade earlier, a coup known as the Readeption. But he did not remain there for long. On 14 April 1471, Edward defeated Warwick at the Battle of Barnet (just north of London), which was fought in confusion on both sides because the battlefield was thick with fog. Then, on 4 May, Edward won a final victory by crushing Margaret of Anjou's invasion force at the Battle of Tewkesbury, in which Henry's only son was killed. Henry, who had failed in his promise to restore unity to England, was murdered in the Tower of London later that same month. Edward remained king of England for the next twelve years with comparatively little disturbance to his authority, though there were still dynastic troubles. He had his own brother, George, Duke of Clarence, executed for treason in 1478. The method of execution was most unusual – Clarence was probably drowned in a barrel of sweet malmsey wine. The king himself died rather more prosaically on 9 April 1483, possibly from a stroke. He was succeeded by his 12-year-old son, King Edward V.

THE PRINCES IN THE TOWER

Edward IV was only 40 when he died, and had carelessly failed to make a plan for the government of the realm in case he happened to die before his heir had reached adulthood. He also left behind a second son, Richard, Duke of York (aged 9). The boy-king Edward V reigned for less than three months before he was deposed by his uncle, Richard, Duke of Gloucester.

This ruthless but efficient seizure of power was achieved by stages. Firstly, at Stony Stratford in Buckinghamshire, Richard seized the body of the king from the Woodville family, a rival political faction centring around the king's mother, and rode to London, where he declared himself Protector of the Realm. He openly declared his loyalty to King Edward V to avoid alienating the political nation, but the queen dowager, suspecting his true intentions, claimed sanctuary at Westminster Abbey for herself and the young Duke of York. Richard then staged a second coup on 10 June 1483, claiming that the Woodvilles were planning to murder him and his then-ally, the Duke of Buckingham. On this pretext, he arrested Lord Hastings, who had united with the Woodvilles, and had him summarily executed for treason. Next, he duplicitously asked the queen to release the Duke of York from sanctuary, on the pretext that the little boy ought to attend his brother's coronation. But this was merely a ruse, for Richard proceeded to claim that Edward IV had been a product of his mother's adultery, meaning that Edward V was not a legitimate king. A meeting of the estates on 25 June formally requested Richard to take the throne himself, and he was crowned on 6 July.

The two young princes were locked up in the Tower of London, posing as they did an obvious dynastic threat to the newly crowned Richard III. They were spotted from time to time playing games in the Tower gardens, but after the summer of 1483 they were seen no more. It is likely that Richard arranged for the boys to be murdered – the killers were later identified as Miles Forest and John Dighton – but advocates for the king's innocence have never been wanting. What really matters is that public opinion both in England and Europe deemed him to be guilty. Even in the ruthless fifteenth century, a king believed to have murdered his own nephews would never win the love and respect of his subjects.

King Richard III

THE BATTLE OF BOSWORTH

Richard reigned for just over two years. On 7 August 1485, the rebel Henry Tudor landed at Mill Bay in Pembrokeshire with around 2,000 men. Henry was born at Pembroke Castle and prided himself on his Anglo-Welsh heritage, though in truth he spoke barely a word of Welsh. He was the son of the aristocrat Edmund Tudor, Earl of Richmond, and a distant relation of Edward III through his mother, Margaret Beaufort, albeit through a line that was legally debarred from the succession. Since the immediate Lancastrian line had become extinct with the murder of Henry VI in 1471, Henry Tudor's faint Plantagenet claim to the throne seemed at least somewhat convincing. He was also an honorary Lancastrian, being a nephew of Henry VI.

King Richard forced a battle near Bosworth Field in Leicestershire on 22 August 1485. Richard's army, nominally totalling 6–7,000 men, was led by the 1st Duke of Norfolk. Henry's army, probably numbering 4–5,000, was led by the 13th Earl of Oxford, who had fought on the Lancastrian side at Barnet fourteen years earlier. The Yorkist sympathiser Henry Percy, Earl of Northumberland, led an army to Leicestershire but decided to remain neutral, a decision that probably swung the battle in Henry's favour. Richard was killed in battle after charging at Henry Tudor, and he was buried in the Grey Friars Church in Leicester, where his body rested undiscovered until 2012.

Henry was crowned on the battlefield and then again formally at Westminster Abbey. Acts of attainder were passed in Parliament against some of his Yorkist enemies, authorizing the forfeiture of their property as traitors. But this was also a time of reconciliation. On 18 January 1486, Henry married Elizabeth of York, the 19-year-old daughter of Edward IV, thus symbolically uniting the warring Houses of Lancaster and York and fulfilling a promise he had made to his supporters. This union was symbolized in the emblem of the Tudor rose, which displayed the red rose of Lancaster 'charged' (in the heraldic jargon) with the white rose of York. Sir Francis Bacon later claimed that Henry only married Elizabeth because he had to, and that he treated her coolly for the remainder of his reign. Be that as it may, he eventually fathered eight children by her, three of whom survived to adulthood: Margaret, Henry and Mary. Both daughters would go on to become queens consort in foreign realms, Margaret in Scotland and Mary, the prettier of the two, in France. Eighty per cent of the peerage had fought in the Wars of the Roses, as had large numbers of the gentry, but only a tiny fraction of the overall population had seen any fighting. A long period of violent disorder was now to make way for the comparative stability of the Tudor dynasty.

8

THE EARLY TUDORS
(1485–1547)

Before his accession to the throne, King Henry VII had spent a decade in exile as a guest of the Duke of Brittany. Having long occupied a subordinate position in a foreign land, he now had the power to command. His long period of exile meant there were some practical difficulties to contend with, including his lack of familiarity with the great men of England; he knew personally 'very few of the important people upon whom he would have to rely'.[1] His conscientious disposition helped him along the way. While former kings such as Edward IV had been impatient with the bureaucratic responsibilities of late medieval monarchs, Henry VII was in his element when presented with a stack of paperwork; for most of his reign, he checked every single entry in the Chamber accounts, which recorded royal expenditure. With hindsight, it is clear that his reign was a period of relative stability after three decades of civil war. Still, the new king had to contend with dynastic threats from surviving Yorkists, many of whom had lost everything after his victory and could only resort to desperate measures to repair their fortunes.

PLOTS AND PRETENDERS

In the second year of Henry's reign, three Yorkist survivors of the Battle of Bosworth, Francis Lovell (1st Viscount Lovell), Sir Humphrey Stafford and his brother Thomas Stafford, stirred up a rebellion in Yorkshire and the Midlands. The king answered this challenge in the traditional way, raising a royal army and then encouraging the rebels to abandon their leaders by offering a general pardon. Lovell fled abroad, while Humphrey Stafford was dragged out of sanctuary and executed for treason. In 1487 came a more serious challenge from the pretender Lambert Simnel, the 11-year-old son of a carpenter and organ builder who had been trained by the Yorkists to play the part of Edward, Earl of Warwick. The real Earl of Warwick, the leading Yorkist claimant to the throne, was actually imprisoned in the Tower of London. Simnel easily won support in Ireland, where Anglo-Irish landowners generally supported the House of York, and he was crowned king of England at Dublin Cathedral in May. Some improvisation was required for this hastily arranged coronation: unable to find a suitable crown, ministers borrowed a gold circlet from a statue of the Virgin Mary.

The mastermind behind the Simnel scheme was John de la Pole, Earl of Lincoln, who had briefly served as a councillor to Henry VII. Henry had Warwick paraded around London to discredit the pretender, but most ordinary onlookers hadn't the foggiest which one was real. Simnel invaded England in June with around 5,000 men, a mixture of kerns (Gaelic warriors) and German and Swiss mercenaries. Some Englishmen enthusiastically joined the army of 'King Edward VI'. Battle was joined at Stoke Field on 16 June 1487, sometimes described as the final battle of the Wars of the Roses. Simnel's forces were routed by the Earl of Oxford, and Lovell, never shy about running away, managed to escape again to Scotland. Henry VII generously recognized that no blame could be apportioned to young Simnel, who was allowed to become a scullion in the royal kitchen. There was another rebellion in Yorkshire in 1489, this one motivated by tax grievances, in which the rebels murdered the king's agent, the 4th Earl of Northumberland, in his own manor house. All but five of the Yorkshire rebels were ultimately pardoned. A second pretender to the throne arose in 1491, a French-speaking teenager from the Low Countries named Pierrechon de Werbecque, anglicized as Perkin Warbeck. A group of Yorkists languishing in exile noticed this handsome, well-travelled boy selling silks in Cork and convinced him to impersonate Richard, Duke of York, one of the princes in the tower who had disappeared in 1483. Warbeck travelled to Flanders with his supporters, where he was accepted by the king's formidable opponent Margaret of York, dowager duchess of Burgundy, as her supposed nephew. Warbeck also won the support of King James IV of Scotland. He landed in Cornwall on 7 September 1497, encouraged by a recent anti-tax rebellion in that county, and raised thousands of troops of uncertain resolve, who soon changed their minds about revolting when they saw the strong response of the government. Warbeck was initially imprisoned and spared execution, but he proved to be a Houdini for skill in breaking out of any manner of confinement; Francis Bacon said he must have been made of mercury. After getting involved in further plots against the king, he met his final punishment on 23 November 1499. A little-known third pretender emerged in 1498, a tailor's son named Ralph Wilford, who impersonated the Earl of Warwick and was hanged.

EXPLORATION

Aside from pretenders and plots, Henry VII's reign also witnessed the first signs of England's global ambitions. In 1496, the king gave political backing and a small loan to the Venetian explorer John Cabot, who sought to find a north-western passage to China. During his second voyage in 1497, Cabot accidentally discovered North America, where Europeans had not set foot since the Vikings had attempted to start colonies there in the eleventh century. The first of Cabot's voyages took place in the same year that England signed the treaty *Intercursus Magnus* with the Archduke of Burgundy, restoring trade relations with the Low Countries after a punishing embargo that England had imposed to protest against Flemish support for Perkin Warbeck. No doubt Henry thought it possible that Cabot might help to establish an Anglo-Chinese trade, but he was too fond of penny-pinching to give the enterprise his full support. In Ireland, the Lord Deputy Sir Edward Poynings saw an act through the Irish Parliament of 1494–5 that became known as Poynings's Law. This subjected the Irish Parliament to greater English oversight by stipulating that Irish bills should be checked in advance by the English executive. It remained in full effect until 1782.

MONEY-GRUBBING

Henry's financial stringency opened him up to accusations of meanness and love of lucre, for he found ever more ingenious ways of extracting money from his subjects. His decision to levy an unparliamentary tax called a benevolence in 1491 was especially unpopular. Either Richard Fox, keeper of the privy seal, or John Morton, Lord Chancellor, invented a witty dilemma to defend the level of taxation, commonly called Morton's Fork. If somebody appeared rich, they could evidently afford the tax. If they appeared poor, they must have managed to save a lot of money and so could also afford to pay. In the latter part of his reign, Henry executed his financial policies through the counsellors Sir Richard Empson and Edmund Dudley, both brilliant lawyers from relatively humble origins. Though he was never knighted, Dudley was slightly higher born than Empson.

Empson and Dudley oversaw an expansion of the royal revenue, including the Crown's right to valuable feudal 'incidents' (traditional sums of money payable by the king's tenants), and they also sought to weaken potential opponents to the king. When subjects committed offences, the Crown forced them to enter into recognizances, which meant they would forfeit huge sums of money if they misbehaved again in the future. On the other hand, the king showed enormous generosity to some of his beloved courtiers, helping the Earl of Kent, for example, to avoid insolvency due to gambling debts. Perhaps Henry only claimed money that was due to him by right, and perhaps the recognizances were designed to ensure his subjects' obedience rather than to raise money, but his policies seemed like sharp practice, if not the actions of a 'calculating despot'.[2] When the king died on 21 April 1509, the crown passed peacefully to his 17-year-old son. Few mourned his passing.

THE REIGN OF HENRY VIII

King Henry VIII was over 6ft tall, and as a young man he was slim and muscular, a far cry from the grandly obese king familiar from the paintings. Fond of jousting and other manly pastimes, he had a more imposing presence than his desk-job father, and his subjects expected greatness of him from the start. He ordered the execution of the unpopular ministers Empson and Dudley, signalling new management of the realm. Only three years after his accession, he went to war against France as part of a Holy League orchestrated by the pope. France was becoming ever more dominant in western Europe, reason enough to go to war, and in any case, 'the treasury was full, the country willing, the pope calling'.[3] England declared war on France in May 1512 and set out to invade Gascony shortly thereafter. Henry himself crossed the Channel in 1513, bringing with him twelve monster cannon dubbed the Twelve Apostles because each one was cast with an image of an apostle.

The English besieged the small cathedral city of Thérouanne, successfully crushing a relief force at the Battle of the Spurs (16 August 1513). In September, they captured a greater prize: the fortified city of Tournai in modern Belgium. However, the Crown's limited funds meant that these victories could not be followed up with further conquests. The king returned home to national acclaim, though in truth the whole affair had little effect in either an English or an international context, except to establish Henry's reputation for valour. Thérouanne was unsuitable for garrisoning and not worth occupying, while Tournai was resold to France for 50,000 crowns as one of the conditions of a pan-European non-aggression pact, the 1518 Treaty of London. While the king was away, English forces also won a major victory at the Battle of Flodden in Northumberland (9 September 1513), killing King James IV of Scotland along with many of his nobles. The English forces were under the command of Thomas Howard, 1st Earl of Surrey, who received the Dukedom of Norfolk as his reward.

Shortly after his accession, Henry took a shine to a low-born but brilliant cleric named Thomas Wolsey, son of an Ipswich butcher, who was already known to the royal household as one of the king's chaplains. Wolsey emerged as Henry's chief minister in around 1514 and was appointed as cardinal and Lord Chancellor in 1515. It has even been said that 'from 1515 to 1529 Wolsey and not Henry was the effective ruler of the country', though the king himself was more active in government than is commonly thought, especially in the early years of his reign.[4] It was Wolsey who organized the Field of Cloth of Gold, an extravagant Anglo-French peace summit held at the Val d'Or near Guînes in 1520. This was a stupendous logistical feat involving the construction of a temporary palace and the transport of thousands of men across the Channel. Everything went without a hitch until Henry VIII was thrown onto his back during a friendly wrestling match with King Francis I, something that all the English eyewitnesses prudently forgot to record.

Glorious it may have been, but the Field of Cloth failed to secure lasting peace. There were further military campaigns against the French in 1522 and 1523, when an English army arrived in France under the new Earl of Surrey to support the Holy Roman Emperor Charles V against the Valois. After that, however, there was a twist of fate. The earth-shattering Habsburg victory at the Battle of Pavia in 1525 led to a reversal of alliances, as the English then allied with France against the Holy Roman Empire to restore the balance of power in Europe. Although the king was fond of him, Wolsey angered the nation by raising tax after tax to finance the wars. In 1525, when the minister tried to levy an unparliamentary loan cunningly described as an 'Amicable Grant', men in East Anglia and Kent took up arms in protest. Realizing that they were driven by honest frustration, Henry pardoned the rebels and promised to stop the loan.

A CURSED MARRIAGE

Henry took to wife the Spanish princess Catalina de Aragón y Castilla, better known in England as Catherine of Aragon. Catherine was born to the king of Aragon and the queen of Castille in 1485 in the university town of Alcalá de Henares, a sort of Spanish Oxford, which would later be the birthplace of Cervantes. She had been briefly married to Henry's elder brother Arthur, Prince of Wales, the former heir apparent who had died of an unidentified infectious disease in 1502. The pope issued a dispensation allowing Catherine to marry Henry after Arthur's death, despite an apparent prohibition in Leviticus 20:21: 'And if a man shall take his brother's wife, it is an unclean thing: he hath uncovered his brother's nakedness; they shall be childless.' Henry might have shrugged off this obscure edict, were it not for the fact that the couple faced difficulty in producing an heir, which seemed to be a fulfilment of the Bible's warning. There were many miscarriages and infant deaths: only Mary, born on 18 February 1516, survived to adulthood. It has been suggested by modern scholars that these reproductive troubles were because the king had the Kell positive blood type, but obviously the Tudors knew nothing of such things. Living in a pre-scientific age, they were liable to conclude that the royal marriage was cursed.

Inevitably, Henry started to blame Catherine for his failure to produce an heir. As well as enjoying a string of mistresses, he began to show an interest in Anne Boleyn, an attractive woman in her late 20s. He wrote her love letters in his own hand that combined the tender clichés of courtly love with oddly stiff and technical conceits: in one letter he described his pining for Anne during her absence, 'reminding us of a point in astronomy which is this: the longer the days are, the more distant is the sun, and nevertheless the hotter'.[5] Perhaps he had help from one of his scholars. In 1527, Henry resolved to seek a 'divorce' from Catherine (strictly speaking an annulment), opening a series of unpleasant negotiations that became known as the King's Great Matter.

Henry's case for divorce hinged on the claim that Catherine's first marriage to the teenage Prince Arthur had been consummated. Catherine always insisted that it had not, but the king's allies alleged that Arthur had left her bedchamber on their first night proclaiming that he had 'been this night in the midst of Spain'.[6] The vividness and quotability of this sexually charged phrase would suggest that it was chosen as a propaganda weapon to strengthen the king's case. In May 1529, Wolsey joined with an anglophile Italian Cardinal, Lorenzo Campeggio, to try the king's cause at Blackfriars Priory in London. However, Pope Clement VII scuppered his plans by removing the proceedings to Rome to be tried under papal jurisdiction. Wolsey had failed, and he was arrested in October on charges of *praemunire* (the crime of resorting to an ecclesiastical jurisdiction in a matter determinable in a royal court). Henry showed leniency towards his once-favourite minister, allowing him to retire to his archbishopric in York. However, when Wolsey continued to conduct secret communications with Rome, he was summoned to court again and died of dysentery on the way to London. The minister was gone, but Henry's Great Matter remained unresolved.

Into the political vacuum left by Wolsey's death entered a remarkable man in his mid-40s named Thomas Cromwell, son of a Putney blacksmith. Cromwell had travelled the world; he had been down and out; he had fought in the French army; he had worked as a cloth merchant; he had mastered the technicalities of the law; he had served as member of Parliament. Tradition has it that he was promoted to the king's service after a single interview with Henry in 1530, in which he put forward his plans to solve the king's marriage problem by breaking with the papacy. Cromwell did indeed win the king's confidence after a number of private interviews, and he was responsible for many of the revolutionary policies in the years that followed, including the unification of the kingdom of England with the principality of Wales in 1536 and the establishment of Henry VIII as king of Ireland in 1541, transforming the 'lordship' of colonial Ireland into a kingdom. This policy would be followed by the establishment of new English plantations in Ireland over the next century and beyond. However, Cromwell was not the only driving force behind government policy in the 1530s.

THE REFORMATION

Henry's theologians, including Thomas Cranmer, helped to convince him that he, not the pope, was the Supreme Head of the English Church – a monumental decision marking the beginning of the English Reformation. In January 1533, the king bigamously married Anne Boleyn, who was already pregnant with the future Princess Elizabeth, and in May, Cranmer (now Archbishop of Canterbury) declared void the king's marriage to Catherine, who was henceforth styled dowager princess of Wales. The king's claim to Supreme Headship was authorized by Parliament (which had been a fully bicameral legislature for some seven decades now), in the form of the Act of Supremacy (1534), a brief but highly significant piece of legislation that denied the pope's authority in England.

The government also introduced an oath of supremacy in support of Henry's claim, which had to be sworn by most men in positions of authority. English kingship was now caesaro-papal – that is, Henry was head of both Church and state. For the past twenty years, the firebrand theologian Martin Luther had been publicly criticizing the doctrines and practices of the Catholic Church. Luther was a professor at Wittenberg in northern Germany, now a picture-book university town but rather lowly and dirty at the time. Luther's teachings, once publicly excoriated by Henry himself, now provided a model for religious reforms in England, although the king was cautious about accepting many of the German's more radical claims. Some who refused to get on the train of reform, including Sir Thomas More, author of *Utopia*, met violent ends.

At the heart of the Reformation were opposing views regarding the nature of the Eucharist, the most important Christian ceremony. The orthodox Catholic doctrine of transubstantiation states that the bread and wine used in the ceremony are transformed literally and entirely into Christ's body and blood. Luther's view was that the bread and wine were literally transformed into Christ's body and blood while also retaining their original identity. This was less radical than the doctrine of the Swiss reformer Ulrich Zwingli, who argued that the bread and wine of the Eucharist were merely symbols. The Swiss position may seem the most sensible in a rational age, but for most of Christian history it was a shocking heresy. In 1536, Henry issued a book called the Ten Articles, approved by Convocation, the English Church legislature. Relatively conservative, the Ten Articles championed Luther's doctrine of the Lord's Supper.

One of the first stages of the Reformation was the dissolution of the monasteries. Monasteries had adorned the English landscape since the Anglo-Saxon period and were often a source of pride for local communities as well as having great spiritual value. Cromwell organized a survey of ecclesiastical wealth called the *Valor Ecclesiasticus* and gathered evidence of supposed monastic abuses, including homosexuality and masturbation. Parliament dissolved the lesser religious houses in 1536, arguing that they were irreparably corrupt, and stripped them of their valuables. Henry's wife Jane Seymour – he was now on his third wife out of six – implored him to reconsider his actions, but he reportedly warned her 'that the last queen [Anne Boleyn] died in consequence of meddling too much'.[7] Anne had been beheaded that same year for alleged adultery with several courtiers and gentlemen of the privy chamber, including her own brother.

THE PILGRIMAGE OF GRACE

The dissolution of the monasteries sparked popular unrest in several counties, starting with Lincolnshire. Rebels in Louth, a market town near Mablethorpe, complained about the despoiling of monasteries and argued that bad policy had been made because Cromwell and other councillors were 'persons of low birth and small reputation'.[8] The rebel demands were composed by George Stanes, a former clerk in the attorney-general's office who had connections with the king's court. Though the Lincolnshire Rising was quickly pacified, a more serious copycat rebellion followed in the north, called the Pilgrimage of Grace. Led by the lawyer Robert Aske, the rebels marched under the banner of the Five Wounds of Christ, a stylized depiction of the nail wounds on Christ's hands and feet and the spear wound made in his side during his crucifixion. They raised armies totalling some 60,000 men and made a traditionally miscellaneous range of demands, including the restoration of the monasteries.

The Pilgrimage of Grace lasted from 6 October to 8 December, when a general pardon was proclaimed. The king made a show of clemency by inviting Aske to spend Christmas with him at court, as memorably described by a Spanish chronicler resident in England:

> Then the King with a smiling face and words full of falseness, took from his neck a great chain of gold, which he had put on for the purpose, and threw it around Aske's neck, saying to him: "I promise thee, thou art wiser than anyone thinks, and from this day forward I make thee one of my Council."[9]

Aske was later implicated in further outbreaks of rebellion, and he was hanged in chains at York Castle on 12 July 1537: a cruel alternative to hanging by which someone was tied up in chains to die slowly and publicly. In the wake of the rebellion, the king's privy council emerged as the chief executive and policy-making body of the realm; never again would government be dominated by a Wolsey or a Cromwell. In October 1537, Jane Seymour secured the dubious honour of becoming Henry's favourite wife by giving birth to Prince Edward, the male heir whom the king had so ardently desired – though, tragically, she died shortly after the baby's birth.

A CHANGE OF HEART

Parliament finalized the dissolution of the monasteries in 1539, passing an act to close the greater monastic houses. Most of the property was engrossed by the king and his friends, disappointing the more enlightened reformers who had hoped to found colleges on the sites of former monasteries. Some were turned over to more noble purposes: the House of Grey Friars in London later became a hospital for the education of poor orphans. Wherever monastic sites fell into disuse, scavengers picked about in the abandoned buildings for iron, lead and other salvageable materials. At about the same time as the dissolution of the greater houses, Henry also approved the first authorized English translation of the Bible, the Great Bible. And yet, he also put the brakes on further religious reform by passing the Act of Six Articles, for 'abolishing diversity in opinions'. While this law restated that the king was Supreme Head of the Church, it backtracked on other key issues, for instance by restoring the Catholic conception of the Eucharist: 'after the consecration there remaineth no substance of bread or wine'.[10] Cromwell fell out of the king's favour in 1540 after arranging a royal marriage with the German noblewoman Anne of Cleves, whom Henry thought to be overweight and possibly not a virgin. Cromwell's passion for reform also put him at odds with an increasingly conservative king. He was arrested at a privy council meeting on 10 June and executed for supposed treason on 28 July.

Henry married twice again in his later years, both times to women named Catherine, possibly indicating a nostalgia for the stability of his first marriage. The marriage to teenager Catherine Howard provided no such stability, for she was executed in February 1542 after it transpired that she had sexually liaised with other men both before and after her marriage to the king. The widow Catherine Parr, on the other hand, proved to be a dutiful companion to the old rogue for the last three years of his life, and ultimately outlived him. War with France broke out again in 1544, when a massive English army led by the king himself successfully captured Boulogne, a city that had been unsuccessfully besieged by Henry's father in 1492. Unease and paranoia were the defining characteristics of the king's court in the final years of his reign. In January 1547, the young, popular aristocrat Henry Howard, Earl of Surrey – also a celebrated poet – was executed for treason for having appropriated the royal coat of arms, which was interpreted to mean that he had designs on the throne. Henry died at Whitehall Palace a few days later, on 28 January, and he was buried alongside the remains of Jane Seymour in St George's Chapel at Windsor Castle. Historians have long debated whether or not Henry VIII should be described as a tyrant. One answer is that he was responsible for both great deeds and terrible deeds, like all the other mighty rulers of history. He was succeeded by his young son, Edward, ushering in England's seventh royal minority.

King Henry VIII

THE LATER TUDORS
(1547–1603)

King Edward VI was only 9 years old when he inherited the crown. His father had tried to secure the stability of the realm by naming a privy council of sixteen men to govern during his son's minority, rather than a single Protector. However, all his plans came to nought when, only fifteen days after his death, this council ignored his final wishes and appointed Edward VI's uncle Edward Seymour as Protector of the Realm. Seymour was also created Duke of Somerset to give him the requisite status for such an exalted position. The king's councillors no doubt realized that few organizations can operate effectively without a principal; a quasi-republican board of equals might easily have become paralysed by disagreements. Somerset continued the process of Reformation that had been stopped in its tracks in the later years of Henry VIII's reign, purging the few remaining Catholics from the council and leaving only men committed or indifferent to religious reform. A passion for reformed religion lay behind practically all of his policies. For instance, he invaded Scotland in September 1547 because he hoped to unite the two countries as a single Protestant nation. He won a great victory at the Battle of Pinkie near Edinburgh on 10 September 1547, the major engagement of the so-called Rough Wooing (1544–8). Somerset also invited celebrity European reformers such as Pietro Martire Vermigli to settle in England, free from the fear of persecution.

The Edwardian Reformation was far more thoroughgoing than the Henrician. Somerset began by repealing the Act of Six Articles and introducing communion under both kinds for the laity. Formerly, only priests had partaken of the bread and wine at a celebration of the Eucharist, while laypeople had partaken of the bread alone, which was 'communion in one kind'. Another act of Parliament dissolved the chantries – small church foundations designed to provide educational services and masses for the dead – and allowed the expropriated goods to be distributed to servants of the Crown. In 1549 came the introduction of the First Book of Common Prayer, which set out a uniform Church liturgy to be used throughout England. The composition of the first prayer book was supervised by the second most important man in government, Thomas Cranmer, Archbishop of Canterbury. It was a moderate document designed as a temporary fix; Cranmer planned to introduce a more radical prayer book right from the start, but he followed a policy of gradualism to forestall conservative opposition. The first prayer book relied on ambiguity, calling the Eucharist 'The supper of the Lord, and the holy Communion, commonly called the Mass', a title that (as far as possible) pleased everybody.[1] The service itself contained a prayer for the descent of the Holy Spirit upon the bread and the wine, which would have sounded suspiciously similar to the Catholic sacrifice of the mass.

THE YEAR OF REBELLION

Nevertheless, the prayer book was still novel enough to provoke serious reactionary opposition. The new form of service came into effect on 9 June 1549, and on the very next day there was a riot in the village of Sampford Courtenay that spiralled into full-scale rebellion against the government. Rebels in Devon and Cornwall made six separate petitions to the king and council, urging them to reverse the religious reforms. It is often said that the rebels' rallying cry was 'Kill all the gentleman!', but this has recently been shown to be a misreading of an official indictment at the court of King's Bench; the Western rebellion was fuelled primarily by religious, not social, grievances. The government responded to the rebels' petitions with a flurry of books and manuscripts condemning sedition. As Somerset wrote, the rebels had wrongly acted 'against all order', but he preferred them to be 'persuaded [rather] than vanquished'.[2] However, these calls went unheeded, and the conflict was ultimately resolved by battle. After relieving Exeter from a rebel siege, the chief loyalist commander, Lord Russell, a man with decades of military experience, marched on the rebel camp at Sampford Courtenay with an army consisting of cavalry, county militiamen and German mercenaries. An unequal battle was forced on 17 August between a rebel army of around 2,000 men and a loyalist force around 8,000 strong, so it was small wonder that the rebels suffered a bloody defeat.

The Western rebellion was not an isolated event; there were uprisings in virtually every county in the spring and summer of 1549. The other most serious rebellion was Kett's Rebellion in Norfolk, led by the tanner Robert Kett. This rebellion, which was social and agrarian rather than religious in character, has been described as 'the closest thing Tudor England saw to a class war'.[3] Although it was more complicated than a 'class' struggle – Kett himself was a wealthy landowner and businessman – there was certainly an element of social conflict. For example, the rebels opposed engrossment, the consolidation of strips of open field by improving landlords from the gentry and yeomanry, and enclosure, the appropriation of common pasture by landowners. Enclosure increased the efficiency of sheep farming, England's main source of wealth, but it could deprive poorer farmers of their customary rights. It had long been – and was long to remain – a controversial practice, with possibly around half of England's farmland enclosed by 1600. It would culminate in the great parliamentary Enclosure Movement of 1760–1820. Another related point might be mentioned here. Capitalism in England is sometimes thought to have originated in the Tudor period, but England had already had a market economy for centuries, and would not become fully capitalized until the late seventeenth century (at the earliest), so it is hard to see that there is anything special about the sixteenth, except perhaps the rise of joint-stock companies.

The Norfolk rebels gathered on Mousehold Heath outside Norwich and drafted a set of twenty-nine demands, mostly concerning social matters. For instance, they asked for the standardization of English measures, for restrictions on pastoral farming, and for vicars to teach the rudiments of religion to poor children. The rebels successfully occupied Norwich, then the second-largest city in England, and defeated a loyalist relief force, but were subsequently driven out of the city. They confronted the army of John Dudley, Earl of Warwick, in a valley named Dussindale on 27 August. In the preceding days, a Delphic prophecy had been circulating that predicted the outcome of the battle, but could be interpreted as foretelling either a loyalist or a rebel victory:

> The country gnoffs, Hob, Dick and Hick
> With clubs and clouted shoon,
> Shall fill the vale
> Of Dussin's Dale
> With slaughtered bodies soon.[4]

A 'gnoff' was a lout, and 'clouted shoon' were patched shoes. In the event, the rebels were routed by Warwick's forces, and the survivors dispersed after the promise of a pardon. Although rebels usually garner more sympathy than loyalists, it cannot be said that Kett's men behaved entirely honourably. They tried to use their prisoners as human shields during the battle, and Kett himself fled the scene when he realized that victory was impossible. He was captured the following day and executed at Norwich Castle on 7 December.

THE WICKED DUKE

By late August, many in the political classes had grown uneasy about Somerset's government, believing that his idealism and permissiveness had fuelled the civil unrest. They were not disinterested judges, of course, having as they did a large stake in the landowning economy that Somerset wished to reform. Somerset was arrested in October and replaced by the Earl of Warwick, now a 'hero' after defeating Kett's rebellion. Warwick assumed the title of Lord President of the Council, a humbler title than Lord Protector, and he signalled his intention to rule with the consent of his fellow councillors. Somerset was restored to the council in April 1550, but his popularity among the people was worrisome, and he was arrested again in October for supposed treason. Although this charge did not stick, he was executed nonetheless for having summoned an unlawful assembly in breach of statute. At the final hour, he 'found friends among the poor and powerless... but his championship did the poor the less service because he had concentrated all the strong against them'.[5] Historians have varied greatly in their degree of sympathy for Somerset, but there can be no doubt that his own high-handedness and incompetence in public affairs were partly to blame for his downfall.

Warwick, in contrast to Somerset, governed as a champion of landowners rather than of the peasantry. He had himself created Duke of Northumberland in October 1551 and bestowed noble titles upon his supporters. Traditionally, he was portrayed as the 'wicked duke', in contrast to the 'good duke' Somerset, but this pantomime description ignores his real achievements, including his progress in resolving the issues of the day, such as a debased coinage and inflation (debasement had been used to finance Somerset's war effort). The mid-Tudor inflation, sometimes referred to as the Price Revolution, was caused principally by an influx of precious metals from the Americas into Europe. Population growth contributed further to price rises, with the population of England increasing from around 2.4 million in 1524 to around 3 million in 1560.

Religious reform also continued at pace during Somerset's administration. In 1552, the Church of England authorized the Second Book of Common Prayer, which introduced a radical Zwinglian communion service. Now the Eucharistic bread and wine were simply to be treated as symbols. The 1552 prayer book contained the following direction: 'And to take away the superstition which any person hath, or might have, in the bread and wine, it shall suffice that the bread be such as is usual to be eaten at the table with other meats.'[6] Now, eighteen years after Henry's Act of Supremacy, England had a communion service resembling that which was celebrated in Geneva by John Calvin, and Cranmer's reforms seemed unstoppable. However, in February 1553, the king fell terminally ill from tuberculosis, putting the whole edifice of reformed religion in jeopardy.

THE NINE DAYS' QUEEN

Edward and his advisers knew all too well that the Protestant Church was at risk. The next in line to the throne, according to the terms of Henry VIII's will, was Henry's Catholic daughter Princess Mary (aged 37), followed by his Protestant daughter

Princess Elizabeth (aged 19), followed by a scholarly, doctrinaire teenager steeped in Protestant lore named Lady Jane Grey (aged 15). Edward drew up a document entitled 'My device for the succession', which planned to overturn the established line and to allow Lady Jane to succeed immediately to the throne. The initiative surely came from Northumberland, who was seeking both the preservation of Protestantism and the fulfilment of his own dynastic ambitions. This is clear from the fact that he also arranged an emergency marriage between Lady Jane and his own son Guildford Dudley on 21 May 1553. If the plan had been simply to avoid a restoration of Catholicism, Elizabeth would have been chosen as Edward's successor. The new plan for the succession was declared by letters patent (a form of royal instrument issued under the great seal) on 21 June. The snag was that Parliament had established Mary as next in line to the throne in 1543. Since an act of Parliament could not be overturned by letters patent, it was impossible for Edward's 'device' to be firmly established without ratification by the king in Parliament – but of course, there was no time for that.

Edward died on 6 July 1553, and Lady Jane Grey was proclaimed queen in London four days later, her claim supported by much of the Protestant establishment. However, her puppeteers were outmanoeuvred by the rightful queen, Mary, who had sensibly withdrawn to the security of her estates in East Anglia. She had herself proclaimed queen there on 8 July, and won substantial military support from gentlemen in Oxfordshire, Buckinghamshire, Norfolk and Suffolk. Northumberland rallied troops and marched on Framlingham Castle in Suffolk, where Mary had set up her base, but in his absence, the councillors in London grew increasingly uneasy and decided to proclaim Mary as queen. On 3 August, she entered London amidst great rejoicing to assume the throne. Northumberland and Lady Jane were imprisoned in the Tower of London before being executed on 22 August 1553 and 12 February 1554, respectively. Lady Jane is popularly named the nine days' queen because she reigned for only nine days after she was proclaimed sovereign.

BLOODY MARY

Queen Mary I immediately oversaw the repeal of the religious legislation passed during the reigns of Henry VIII and Edward VI, restoring Catholic worship in England. The reign of a woman was a novelty in England that raised some tricky constitutional problems, including the status of the queen's prospective husband. In the autumn of 1553, Mary declared her intention to marry Philip of Spain, son of the Holy Roman Emperor. Some subjects, who thought the Spanish were a prideful race, believed that a foreign king would exercise undue influence over English policy. Royal propagandists tried to allay popular fears by circulating Philip's genealogy, which illustrated his descent from King Edward III of England. They wished to prove that Philip was not a 'stranger' because he had English blood, but the plan backfired because some thought that the government was promoting Philip's claim to the throne in his own right.

Disgruntled subjects began fomenting rebellion at Christmastime, in opposition to the restoration of Catholicism and the proposed Spanish marriage. There were supposed to be four simultaneous uprisings: in Herefordshire led by Sir James Croft; in Kent led by Sir Thomas Wyatt; in Devon led by Sir Peter Carew and the Earl of Devon; and in Leicestershire led by the Duke of Suffolk. This fourfold rebellion would have posed a serious threat to the regime, but only the rising in Kent got off to a successful start. Thomas Wyatt, son of the poet of the same name, managed to raise 2,500 soldiers in Kent, calling for their support as trueborn Englishmen. He also convinced hundreds of whitecoats, uniformed soldiers from London, to defect from a royal army commanded by Thomas Howard, 3rd Duke of Norfolk, a dignified old veteran who had been born in the reign of Edward IV. However, the queen assured herself of London's loyalty on 1 February, when she gave an inspiring speech at the Guildhall, asking the city elites whether she was rightful queen, whereupon they 'cried "yea, yea!" and that they would live and die with her majesty in the quarrel'.[7]

Wyatt was permitted to enter the city of London on 6 February, walking straight into a trap. There were skirmishes at Charing Cross and Temple Bar, after which Wyatt's forces were closed in from the south by the Earl of Pembroke. A herald convinced Wyatt to surrender rather than submitting his men to an inevitable massacre. He was executed on 11 April 1554. The royal marriage then went ahead without a hitch at Winchester on 25 July. The marriage produced no issue, although the queen had two distressing phantom pregnancies. In England, Mary's husband was called Philip I, but in Spain he was the 'prudent' Felipe II, who fought a bloody war with the rebellious Dutch and later sent an ill-fated Armada to invade England in 1588. During Mary's reign, Philip dragged England into a war with France (1557–9), to which she provided financial and military backing. England lost Calais to the French, a territory that had been populated by English wool exporters since the fourteenth century. Since the raw wool trade had long been in decline, with England now drawing most of her wealth from the woollen cloth trade, Calais was no longer so important to the English economy, but its loss was still a blow to the confidence of the nation.

Mary is remembered as 'Bloody Mary', a name invented in the seventeenth century, on account of her persecution of Protestants. In 1554, she restored three medieval acts of Parliament against heresy that had been repealed in the reigns of Henry VIII and Edward VI. The most famous is *De heretico comburendo* (first enacted in 1401), which permitted the authorities to burn heretics at the stake. One of the most committed persecutors was Edmund Bonner, Bishop of London, a man prone to fits of rage who held a grudge against Protestants for having imprisoned him in the Marshalsea for four years. In total, around 300 Protestants were executed. The highest-ranking victims were the Oxford Martyrs: Hugh Latimer and Nicholas Ridley, executed on 16 October 1555, and Thomas Cranmer, executed on 21 March 1556. Latimer, formerly Bishop of Worcester and a celebrated preacher, reportedly spoke the following words before his body went up in flames: 'Be of good comfort, Master Ridley, and play the man: we shall this day light such a candle by God's grace in England, as (I trust) shall never be put out.'[8] If Philip and Mary had produced a child, England might today have been a nominally Catholic country. But the queen died childless on 17 November 1558, after recognizing Princess Elizabeth as her rightful heir.

THE REIGN OF ELIZABETH I

Elizabeth I was the second undisputed queen regnant of England, and the greatest. She was a woman of paradoxes: imperious yet indecisive, aggressive yet tender, hard-headed yet desperate for love. Lytton Strachey, a member of the Bloomsbury Group and a man of keener historical instincts than many of the most meticulous scholars, even argued that there was a touch of the sinister about her, 'just enough to remind one that there was Italian blood in her veins'.[9] One of her most arresting characteristics, though little remarked upon, was her intellectual intricacy, born of a natural complexity of mind and sharpened by an excellent schooling in ancient languages and rhetoric under the guidance of the humanist Roger Ascham. She once boasted of her formidable learning in a speech to members of Parliament: 'I suppose few (that be no professors) have read more [than I have].'[10]

When she ascended the throne at the age of 25, the national priority was to restore the Protestant religion. In 1559, Parliament passed the Act of Supremacy, which declared that Elizabeth was Supreme Governor of the Church of England (not Supreme *Head*, as Henry and Edward had been, but it was a distinction without a difference). Parliament also reimposed an oath of supremacy, by which officeholders had to swear their loyalty to the queen as religious head. The 1559 Act of Uniformity imposed a form of worship similar to that prescribed in the 1552 prayer book. Though the Act of Uniformity was opposed by the bishops in the House of Lords, it passed by a narrow margin of three votes. Elizabeth was just as happy as her father had been to rid England of the papal yoke, but she was a centrist at heart. She had no great enthusiasm for the Protestant dogmas that animated so many among the ruling classes, and her instincts told her to allow freedom of conscience for Catholics as far as possible. As Sir Francis Walsingham wrote in 1590, the queen did not like 'to make windows into men's hearts and secret thoughts'.[11] Her religious policy was always in pursuit of balance and stability, not of some ideological goal.

On the first day of her reign, Elizabeth appointed William Cecil as her principal secretary. Cecil had gained administrative experience as a privy councillor in Edward VI's reign, and he had won Elizabeth's confidence by working for her in a paralegal capacity when she was a princess. Cecil, created Lord Burghley in 1571 and appointed as Lord Treasurer in 1572, was to remain a sensible, pragmatic and reliable servant of the Crown until his death in 1598, a perfect complement to the intense and changeable queen. There were other great ministers and favourites, including Robert Dudley, Earl of Leicester, possibly the queen's lover, who was suspected of murdering his wife in 1560 so that he would have a chance of marrying the queen. Nevertheless, he lived out this scandal and was appointed to the privy council in 1562. Most of the leaders of the Elizabethan regime were committed Protestants, though one of the queen's favourites, Sir Christopher Hatton, was a Catholic sympathizer.

MARY, QUEEN OF SCOTS

The most serious threat to Elizabeth's queenship was posed by Mary Stuart, Queen of Scots, about whom some backstory is in order. Mary, a great-granddaughter of Henry VII, was born in Scotland on 8 December 1542, and became queen only six days later when her father died. It was agreed that the child would be transported to France, eventually to marry the Dauphin and thereby to strengthen the alliance between England's two ancient rivals. If by birth she was a Scot, by upbringing she was a French princess, having spent her formative years (5 to 18) at the court of Henry II of France. She returned to Scotland in 1561 after the death of her husband. The problem was that Scottish noblemen had been getting along just fine without their absentee queen and had enacted a Protestant revolution in the Parliament of August 1560. This year marked a sea-change in Anglo-Scottish relations. Time out of mind, Scottish kings had allied themselves with France against England – the so-called 'auld alliance' – but from 1560 England and Scotland had an amicable working relationship underscored by a shared hatred of Catholicism. The Scottish Lords allowed Mary to return home and enjoy the freedom of private Catholic worship, but not to exercise real power.

Five years later, in the face of English opposition, Mary wed her cousin Henry Stuart, Lord Darnley. This union posed a dynastic threat to Elizabeth because both Mary and Darnley had a claim to the English throne. However, Darnley soon got involved in a rebellion against his new wife and he was murdered in February 1567, possibly but by no means certainly on Mary's orders. Only three months later, she married Lord Bothwell, who had allegedly abducted her and compelled her to marry him. These scandals shocked the Protestant Lords into action: a group of 'confederates' led by the Earl of Moray forced the queen to abdicate on 24 July, after which she fled to England. There she was no longer a problem for the confederate Lords, but she became a much greater problem for Elizabeth, for there was now a second queen in England, and though she was a state prisoner under close guard, she was also a dangerously seductive Catholic figurehead. As Cecil knew, many Englishmen agreed with her stance.

Mary, Queen of Scots

THE NORTHERN RISING

Cecil's fears seemed to be confirmed in the autumn of 1569, when two Catholic noblemen – Charles Neville, Earl of Westmorland, based at Raby Castle in County Durham, and Thomas Percy, Earl of Northumberland, based at Alnwick Castle in Northumberland – raised a rebellion against Elizabeth, the traditional option for nobles who had reached the end of their tether. Northumberland may have reflected on the fate of his ancestor, the first Earl of Northumberland, who had unsuccessfully rebelled against King Henry IV around 150 years earlier, but if so, it did nothing to weaken his resolve. Though the earls proclaimed that they were 'the queen's true and lawful subjects', government propagandists claimed that this was a coded reference to Mary: 'It is not our queen, Queen Elizabeth, that they mean.'[12]

Imitating the Pilgrims of Grace of Henry VIII's reign, the northern rebels held aloft the banner of the Five Wounds of Christ to signify their devotion to the old religion. Book burnings were staged across the north of England, with English Bibles and Protestant books cast into the flames. At this heady time, northerners eagerly whispered about prophecies foretelling the imminent succession of Mary to the throne of England. The Earl of Sussex, Lord President of the Council of the North, mustered a loyalist army but had to wait for reinforcements from the south, while the rebels successfully captured Barnard Castle and the port town of Hartlepool, both in County Durham. When the southern loyalists finally arrived in mid-December 1569, many rebels must have realized that the chances of victory were slim, or perhaps they decided that they did not want to die just before Christmas. They abandoned their leaders, who fled to Scotland. Northumberland was later captured and executed, while Westmorland lived in exile until his death. Out of the tens of thousands of rank-and-file rebels, a dozen or so were executed after being tried in a court, while around 500 were executed by martial law on Sussex's orders – an unprecedentedly merciless response.

CATHOLICS AND PURITANS

Just after the end of the rebellion, Pope Pius V issued a bull, or edict, known by the Latin title *Regnans in excelsis* ('Reigning upon high'), which excommunicated Elizabeth as a heretic and pronounced her 'deprived of her pretended title to the kingdom'.[13] Popes had claimed the right to absolve Christian subjects from their allegiance to monarchs since the reign of Pope Gregory VII (1073–85). The bull thus legitimized rebellion against the queen from the Catholic point of view, but it arrived too late to have any effect on the northern rebellion. It did help to drive a new wedge between Elizabeth's regime and English Catholics, between whom there had previously been a degree of mutual tolerance. The pope died shortly afterwards and did not live to see the consequences of his action. There followed a succession of Catholic plots to kill the queen or replace her with another:

the Ridolfi Plot in 1571, the Throckmorton Plot in 1583 and the Babington Plot in 1586. Thomas Howard, 4th Duke of Norfolk, who had earlier sought to wed Mary, Queen of Scots without Elizabeth's permission, was executed for his role in the Ridolfi Plot. The Babington Plot, a plan for six assassins to murder the queen, was infiltrated and exposed thanks to the informal espionage network of Francis Walsingham, the queen's principal secretary from 1573.

The plots against Elizabeth, coupled with an influx of Catholic missionaries into England, persuaded the queen and government to get tougher with the Catholics in their midst. A 1581 Act of Parliament made it high treason to promote the old religion and introduced large fines for recusants, men and women who refused to attend Protestant church services. In 1584, councillors drew up a document called the Bond of Association, which called upon Elizabeth's loyal subjects to avenge her death in the hypothetical event of her assassination. The association found many willing members, some of whom wore jewels inset with portraits of the queen to signal their resolve. As for Mary, Queen of Scots, her enemies finally convinced Elizabeth to sign her execution warrant in 1587 after she was implicated in the Babington Plot. When Mary was beheaded in the great hall at Fotheringay Castle, the voice of a preacher brought along for the occasion rang out: 'So perish all the queen's enemies!'[14]

If Catholics posed a threat to the Elizabethan polity from the 'right wing', puritans and Presbyterians posed a threat from the 'left wing'. Puritans were a loose grouping of Protestants who wanted to 'purify' the church of supposed errors and superstitions, while Presbyterians wanted to abolish the structure of Church government that centred around the bishops. These were overlapping terms: according to a phrase formulated in 1938 and used by several historians since, 'Presbyterians were indeed Puritans, but not all Puritans were Presbyterians.'[15] Puritans had friends in high places, including the Earl of Leicester. Some of the religious controversies seem trivial to modern eyes, such as the puritan opposition to the surplice (gown) and square cap worn by churchmen, a squabble that became known as the Vestiarian controversy. At the time, however, the controversies were treated with all seriousness by both sides and even led to conflict between the queen and some of her own bishops. Edmund Grindal, Archbishop of Canterbury, was forced to retire after refusing to denounce prophesyings, a style of grassroots preaching borrowed from Swiss Calvinism. In 1571, the government published the official doctrine of the Church of England, the Thirty-nine Articles. Ultimately, Elizabeth and her ministers managed to safeguard the official religion from both Roman Catholicism and presbyterianism.

THE SPANISH ARMADA

There were also dangers abroad. Philip II of Spain, who had previously been married to Elizabeth's sister Mary, claimed the throne of England in 1587. Sir Francis Drake launched a surprise attack on Spanish ships harbouring at Cádiz, a campaign fondly referred to as the singeing of the king of Spain's beard, which bought England more time to prepare. A fatefully named Invincible Armada was sent to England in 1588, carrying soldiers led by the Duke of Parma. In mounting a defence, the English had the advantage of lighter and more easily manoeuvrable ships; it has been said that the Spanish had failed to innovate because they were unfree and therefore uncreative. A popular story has it that when the Armada was sighted, Francis Drake was bowling with the other commanders on Plymouth Hoe, a ridge overlooking the harbour. Drake called for calm, declaring that there was 'time enough to finish the game and beat the Spaniards too'.[16] The earliest surviving reference to this game of bowls is in a pamphlet from 1624, so it might have actually happened, but most of the details appear to have been invented in the nineteenth century. The English came off the better in a naval battle off Gravelines in northern France, and a storm wind drove the remainder of the Spanish fleet towards Norway, a marvel in which many detected the hand of God.

ESSEX'S FALL

The royal court in the final decades of Elizabeth's reign was dominated by a new breed of young and dashing favourites, typified by two rivals: the Devonshire-born gentleman Sir Walter Raleigh and the higher-born Robert Devereux, 2nd Earl of Essex (Leicester's stepson). According to tradition, Raleigh once spread his new cloak over a muddy puddle so that the queen might walk across without getting wet. There is no contemporary corroboration of the tale, which was first recorded in Thomas Fuller's *Worthies of England* (1662), but this was the sort of gallantry that went on at the late-Elizabethan court, to delight an ageing queen. After his appointment to the privy council in 1593, the Earl of Essex repeatedly clashed with Burghley, in part because he favoured a more aggressive foreign policy. In 1598, he was appointed Lord Lieutenant of Ireland and sent to crush a rebellion against English expansion led by the Earl of Tyrone.

The whole affair was a debacle. Essex spent a great deal of public money in Ireland and achieved very little. When he did finally confront Tyrone in County Meath in August 1599, four months after his arrival, he agreed upon a truce without permission and then returned to England as quickly as he could. The furious Elizabeth commanded Essex to stay away from court, but he disobeyed this instruction and turned up unannounced in the queen's bedchamber at the Palace of Nonsuch on 24 September 1599, before she was fully dressed. He was placed under house arrest and, on 5 June 1600, sentenced for insubordination in Ireland. Though he was released at the end of August, he was forbidden to attend court, which meant that he was cut off from the fount of policy and patronage.

Essex was now a desperate man. On 7 February 1601, he paid the Lord Chamberlain's Men, Shakespeare's acting company, to stage a special performance of 'King Harry the 4th, and of the killing of King Richard II' at Essex House. This was probably Shakespeare's tragedy *Richard II*, first printed in 1597.[17] The implications were obvious: Essex wished to liken Elizabeth to Richard II, led astray by wicked councillors, and himself with Henry Bolingbroke, a powerful nobleman destined to set England back on the right course. Essex then ignored a series of council summonses and ultimately marched on the court with a retinue of around 300 followers, including three earls, feeling sure that he was popular enough to attract widespread support for a coup against the other councillors. He may have modelled his attempt on the successful Catholic coup staged by the Duke of Guise in Paris in 1585, which happened in much the same way. However, Londoners were merely bemused by the whole display. An armourer named William Pickering refused to provide supplies, prompting Essex's disappointed reply: 'Not for me, Pickering?'[18] The earl retreated to his house, where he was arrested. His trial followed on 19 February, with the prosecution led by the attorney-general Edward Coke, later a celebrated jurist, and Essex's former servant Francis Bacon, lawyer and polymath. He was executed six days later.

A GOLDEN AGE?

Elizabeth's reign marked the beginning of a golden age of English literature, graced with the talents of William Shakespeare, Edmund Spenser, Christopher Marlowe and Philip Sidney, though it should not be forgotten that most Elizabethan literature was 'astonishingly poor'.[19] Her reign was also an age of international discovery, led by the likes of Martin Frobisher, who directed three voyages to find a south-west passage to China; Francis Drake, who circumnavigated the globe in the *Golden Hind* between 1577 and 1580 in imitation of the voyage of the Portuguese navigator Ferdinand Magellan (1519–21); Walter Raleigh, who founded the unsuccessful Roanoke Colony in the New World in 1585; and John Hawkins, who shipped African slaves from Sierra Leone to the West Indies, angering Spanish and Portuguese slave monopolists and opening a discreditable chapter in English history. Some of Elizabeth's advisers thought that she should have done more to challenge Spain's growing dominance. After her death, Raleigh claimed that England could have 'beaten that great empire in pieces, and made their kings kings of figs and oranges, as in old times. But her Majesty did all by halves, and by petty invasions taught the Spaniard how to defend himself.'[20]

The Elizabethan age was not all gold and glory. Among the greatest social problems of the reign, and indeed of the whole early modern era, were poverty and vagrancy. There was an enduring distinction between the deserving and undeserving poor. Able-bodied men who roved the country, often displaced by social and economic changes, were thought to have no honest claim to charity. Contemporaries conflated gypsies and vagabonds with beggars and thieves and presented semi-fictionalized accounts of their customs, including a supposed dialect called rogues' cant. By contrast, the Elizabethans were comparatively open-handed when it came to widows, the disabled and the elderly. The Poor Laws of 1598 and 1601 codified a system of parish relief for the working poor and those unable to work.

In the later years of the reign, there were also worries about the succession. Although the 'Virgin Queen' had entertained willing suitors, such as the French Catholic Duke of Anjou, she never married, and she died childless on 24 March 1603. A story was publicized that on her deathbed, she had named King James VI of Scotland as her successor with the following cryptic words: 'My seat had been the seat of kings, and I will have no rascal to succeed me.' On prompting from her councillors, she impatiently spelled it out: 'Who should that be but our cousin of Scotland?'[21] Whether or not this story was concocted by Elizabeth's anxious councillors, James's succession had the full backing of the Protestant establishment, and so the crown descended peacefully upon him.

Queen Elizabeth I

THE EARLY STUARTS
(1603–1649)

James I was crowned king of England on 25 July 1603 at the age of 37, thanks to his own incessant campaigning and the support of Robert Cecil, son of Lord Burghley and Elizabeth's principal minister since 1598. James was an obvious choice. A descendant of Henry VII, he had successfully reigned in Scotland as King James VI for his entire adult life. His accession led to a de facto union of the English and Scottish crowns, although both countries retained their own laws and Parliaments and would not be formally united as one kingdom until 1707. James proclaimed himself king of Great Britain in 1604. This name was of course an allusion to ancient Britain, which was wrongly believed to have been a unified country encompassing the territories of England and Scotland prior to the Anglo-Saxon conquest. The adjective 'Great' was added because 'Bretagne' was already in use as the name of the region of Brittany. The first Union Flag was introduced in 1606, a combination of the St George's Cross and the St Andrew's Cross.

King James was a man of contradictions: though he held a stubbornly high-minded view of kingly authority, he was in practice familiar and friendly towards his new subjects. One of his first acts in government was to end Elizabeth's war with Spain, which was formally concluded by the 1604 Treaty of London. As for religion, James broadly continued the Elizabethan policy of censuring both Presbyterians and Catholics. At the Hampton Court conference of 14 January 1604, he argued that a Presbyterian church was as incompatible with a monarchy as was God with the Devil. '[T]ill you find that I grow lazy,' he declared, 'let that alone.' He summarized his opinion even more straightforwardly in the formula, 'No Bishop, no King'.[1] Catholics had entertained hopes that their new king would be more tolerant than Elizabeth had been. True, James had reigned in Scotland as a Protestant, but his heart might have been softened by the execution of his mother, Mary, Queen of Scots. However, they were disabused of any such notions as it soon transpired that James wished to continue the policies of his predecessor.

GUNPOWDER, TREASON AND PLOT

Most Catholics swallowed the bitter pill of continued disgrace, but a small band of extremists decided that the only thing for it was to annihilate the entire Protestant establishment. Their leader, Robert Catesby, hired a vault underneath the House of Lords and filled it with barrels of gunpowder, planning to ignite them in an adjoining mine on 5 November 1605, the proposed date of the reconvening of Parliament, when king, Lords and Commons would have been packed into the Painted Chamber in the Palace of Westminster. It is unclear whether the explosion would even have been sufficient to produce the desired effect. In any case, the conspirator Francis Tresham gave the game away by writing to his brother-in-law, Lord Monteagle, on 26 October, advising him not to attend the forthcoming session of Parliament. Monteagle showed this letter to Robert Cecil and the king, who ordered the cellars of the House of Lords to be searched twice. On the second search, they found a man standing by the barrels of gunpowder with a long match in his pocket, who spoke with a Yorkshire accent and identified himself as Guy Fawkes. In the wake of this sensational plot, James introduced the oath of allegiance, which obliged his subjects to swear that he was 'lawful and rightful King'.[2] This oath led to a paper war between English polemicists and their counterparts in Catholic Europe, who argued that the English government was pressuring Catholics to act against their conscience.

The discovery of the Gunpowder Plot was celebrated as clear proof of divine intervention: as Lancelot Andrewes, Dean of Westminster, declared on the first anniversary of the conspiracy, 'The Destroyer passed over our dwellings, this day.'[3] James may have won the approval of God himself, but he was not above criticism from his own subjects. His court was seen as prodigal and immoral, with excessive drinking bouts sometimes leading to vomiting. His promotion of Scottish courtiers also attracted criticism from Englishmen, who claimed that the Scots stood 'like mountains betwixt the beams of his grace and us'.[4] Another source of potential controversy was that the king seems to have been bisexual, though there was no word for this at the time. He bestowed great favour upon male favourites in a manner that might have reminded his chronicle-reading subjects of the excesses of Edward II and Richard II. James's favourite favourite was George Villiers, who began his career as a humble cupbearer in 1614 and was raised to the peerage as Duke of Buckingham in 1623. Parliament became an arena for subjects to express their discontent: for example, in the Addled Parliament of 1614, no legislation was passed because MPs spent most of the time criticizing royal policy. Nevertheless, James managed to brush off most criticisms about his morals and his favouritism, and widespread grumbling never grew into dangerous opposition to his kingship.

Crude but witty, James was a committed patron of learning and the arts. He supported poets and dramatists such as John Donne and Ben Jonson, and commissioned the production of the Authorized Version, or 'King James version', of the Bible (1611). Most of this was plagiarized from translations made by William Tyndale in the 1520s and 1530s, but it still stands out as a literary landmark. James also had a literary reputation in his own right, publishing works ranging from treatises on the theory of kingship to a pamphlet discouraging the practice of smoking tobacco. In 1597, before his accession to the English throne, he wrote a treatise on witchcraft that contains such gems as the claim that witches pay homage to Satan by kissing his bottom.[5] This remarkable king, so unlike any that England had seen before, died of a combination of a stroke and dysentery on 27 March 1625.

THE REIGN OF CHARLES I

When King Charles I peacefully inherited the throne after his father's death, at the age of 24, a panegyrist declared: 'Thou art that king and true-born *Caesar*, / Our greatest hap [fortune] and highest pleasure!'[6] Unfortunately, the domineering king proved to be about as divisive as Caesar, while failing to compensate for this fault with political or military greatness. Though he had spent most of his childhood in England, he had been taught by a Scottish tutor and had acquired his father's Scottish accent. His reign can be divided into four periods: a period of parliamentary rule (1625–9); a period of 'personal' or non-parliamentary rule, more sensationally named the Eleven Years' Tyranny (1629–40); a period of rising conflict between king and Parliament (1640–2); and a period of full-blown civil war culminating in the king's execution (1642–9).

At the beginning of his reign, the king married the petite French princess Henrietta Maria, a diplomatically advantageous match that turned old enemies into allies and challenged the dominance of Habsburg Spain in Europe. The hitch was that Henrietta practised Roman Catholicism, which was now, a century since the start of the Reformation, greatly unpopular in England. Grievances about the queen and other matters were frequently aired in Parliament during the first four years of the reign. Members of Parliament were particularly critical of the foreign policy blunders that characterized the war with Spain (1625–30), part of a wider European conflict called the Thirty Years' War (1618–48). They also denounced Lord Admiral Buckingham, an adviser and friend whom Charles had inherited from his father, as a poor strategist. Buckingham's enemies likened him to Sejanus, the overmighty minister to Emperor Tiberius in the first century. One of the many military debacles was the Cádiz Expedition of 1625, an Anglo-Dutch operation in which the English army imbibed too much Spanish wine on the job and had to be shipped home in disgrace.

MONEY TROUBLES

The House of Commons hit the king's pocketbook by repeatedly pushing back on his demands for revenue. The so-called Useless Parliament of May–August 1625 only agreed to grant the king a fraction of the money he requested, and in the 1626 Parliament, the Commons granted further tax revenue to the king but also impeached Buckingham of high crimes and misdemeanours. If Charles wanted to get his hands on the cash, he would have to allow the impeachment proceedings to run their course. Finding himself unable to tolerate this assault on the royal dignity, he chose to dissolve Parliament early and tried to get his money another way by resorting to a forced loan. There were some precedents for forced loans, such as Wolsey's Amicable Grant of 1525, but these should have served as a warning, not an encouragement. Despite its unpopularity, the forced loan was levied successfully, and five knights who refused to pay up were imprisoned *pour encourager les autres*. The forced loan satisfied Charles for a brief while, but the money soon ran out, so in January 1628 he found it necessary to summon a third Parliament.

Sir Edward Coke, who set great store by constitutional documents such as Magna Carta, suggested that the 1628–9 Parliament should draw up a Petition of Right to protest about the king's conduct. Most importantly, this petition requested that the king should only demand revenue by parliamentary consent, and that he should not order subjects to be imprisoned without giving a clear reason. Charles reluctantly authorized this petition because he was starved of funds, but he had no intention of keeping his word. This Parliament also drew up a remonstrance, or written protest, against Buckingham, which inadvertently encouraged a disaffected soldier named John Felton to assassinate the duke on 23 August 1628. After dissolving Parliament in March 1629, Charles resolved never to summon its members again, relying instead on such expedients as raising Ship Money, a form of non-parliamentary grant that was not customarily demanded in peacetime. Such high-handedness did nothing to ingratiate the king with the people.

There was also religious conflict. During Charles's personal rule, the disagreements between two rival groups of Protestant became increasingly acrimonious. The first were the Arminians, a 'High Church' party who rejected the Calvinist doctrine of predestination and supported the traditional Church hierarchy. They were led by William Laud, Archbishop of Canterbury from 1633, who kept an eagle eye on the smallest infractions of religious uniformity. The second were the puritans, ideological descendants of the Elizabethans of the same name, who continually struggled for further religious reform. Most so-called puritans either rejected the rule of bishops, or (more moderately) could live with bishops but refused to accept the doctrine that bishops ruled by divine right. Puritans feared that Arminianism was a high road to Roman Catholicism, noting with displeasure that the queen enjoyed significant freedom in protecting and advancing the careers of her fellow Catholics.

Charles was ultimately obliged to summon another Parliament in 1640, after an interval of eleven years, again because of impecuniosity: he needed cash to fight a rebellion by his Scottish subjects, also called the First Bishops' War. The rebellion was led by the Covenanters, who opposed Laud's interference with Scottish religion and wanted to abolish the office of bishop in Scotland. However, the assembly called into being became known as the Short Parliament because the king dissolved it after less than a month when he realized he was not going to get the result he wanted. Despite taking this summary action, Charles was painfully aware that it was impossible to defeat the Covenanters without parliamentary financing. To make matters worse, a Scottish army went on to occupy Newcastle after defeating a royal army at the Battle of Newburn in August 1640, and the soldiers refused to leave until they had been paid off.

THE LONG PARLIAMENT

With no other option, Charles sheepishly summoned another Parliament to meet in November 1640, the second in one year. By this point, it was clear that he had a very weak hand. The Scottish occupation in the north was a serious blow to the royal dignity because the king was expected above all to protect his people. If he could not secure the funds that only the English Parliament could provide, his entire regime was at risk of collapse. The November 1640 Parliament was named the Long Parliament, an apt name because it remained in existence for the following thirteen years, far longer than any Parliament had ever lasted before. Its members were fully conscious of the unprecedented power they held over the king. They began by impeaching the royalist Thomas Wentworth, Earl of Strafford, on allegations that he had urged Charles to employ an Irish army against English subjects. This allegation was probably spurious, and the impeachment trial fell through, but Parliament secured Strafford's execution by passing an Act of Attainder against him instead. William Laud was also unsuccessfully impeached and eventually (in 1645) convicted by act of attainder.

Members of Parliament pursued their political agenda by pass-ing several momentous acts in 1641. The Triennial Act stipulated that Parliament must be summoned at least once every three years. Another act abolished the Court of Star Chamber, a summary royal court that had been used to punish the king's enemies. Parliament also received, but did not immediately act upon, the so-called Root and Branch Petition from a delegation of zealous Londoners demanding the abolition of the office of bishop. Most importantly, the House of Commons drew up a great constitutional document called the Grand Remonstrance, prepared under the oversight of a committee of eight. In the traditional rhetoric of deference, the framers of the Remonstrance claimed that it was presented 'without the least intention to lay any blemish on your royal person, but only to represent how your royal authority and trust have been abused'.[7] In reality, it was a confident manifesto that enumerated hundreds of grievances against royal government over the past fifteen years and demanded a parliamentary veto on the king's choice of councillors.

Some parliamentarians were uneasy about the Remonstrance, while others reposed all their hopes in it. Oliver Cromwell, then merely one of the members for Cambridge, later claimed that if it had not passed, he 'would have sold all he had the next morning and have never seen England more'.[8] Ultimately, it passed the House of Commons by a very narrow margin and was presented to the king on 1 December 1641. If the king had cut his losses and resolved to live out the remainder of his reign subject to the political disabili-ties demanded by Parliament, he would probably have survived to bequeath the kingdom peacefully to his son, albeit a kingdom with diminished royal authority. But Charles was not the sort of man to stoop before his subjects.

Instead, he decided to appropriate Parliament's own weapon of impeachment. In early 1642, he presented the House of Lords with articles of impeachment against five leading anti-royalists in the Commons – John Hampden, Arthur Haselrig, Denzil Holles, John Pym and William Strode – on grounds of treason. When Parliament resisted his demands, since there was no precedent for an impeachment on the orders of the king, Charles led a band of armed supporters into the Commons to arrest the five members himself but found that they had already gone into hiding. As he succinctly put it, 'the birds are flown'.[9] The parliamentarians proceeded to draw up another list of demands, the Nineteen Propositions, which were delivered to Charles on 1 June 1642. In effect, the Propositions were 'terms for the King's unconditional surrender'.[10] They reiterated the requirement that councillors should only be appointed with parliamentary approval and urged the king to empower Parliament to reform the Church as its members saw fit. When the king peremptorily rejected the Propositions, it was clear that reconciliation was impossible. War was on the horizon.

THE ENGLISH CIVIL WAR

It is clear from the above that the English Civil War had manifold causes, including religious disputes, public hostility to irregular taxation and, perhaps most fundamentally, general opposition to a monarch who tended towards arbitrary rule. The parliamentarians were called Roundheads on account of cropping their hair shorter than the style popular at court, while the royalists were known as Cavaliers, derived from the Spanish noun *caballeros* ('gentlemen') and roughly meaning 'swashbucklers'. Most noblemen became Cavaliers, as did many who opposed the prospect of Church reform, while 'men with any kind of grievance – political, social, or economic – tended to find their way into the parliamentary ranks'.[11] The first battle of the English Civil Wars was fought at Edgehill in Warwickshire, near Banbury, on 23 October 1642. The king led the Cavaliers into battle himself, his regiments organized in diamond formation after the Swedish model, while the Roundheads were led by Robert Devereux, 3rd Earl of Essex. When the battle resulted in a stalemate, Charles withdrew to

A Cavalier

Oxford – whose citizens remained fiercely loyal to the king – to set up his wartime headquarters. The parliamentarians had the great advantage of possessing London, which was an important port as well as the centre of administration, and they also had an effective machinery for raising and collecting taxes. The royalists meanwhile, held virtually all the coalfields of the north.

The parliamentarians requested support from Scotland, while the royalists asked the same of Ireland, which was temporarily under the governance of the Irish Catholic Confederation in consequence of the 1641 Irish Rebellion. The Irish helped to finance the king but refused to provide soldiers, while Parliament agreed upon the Solemn League and Covenant with Scotland in September 1643. According to this agreement, the Scots promised to support the parliamentarians so long as they agreed to work towards the unification of the British Isles under a Presbyterian church. Scotland sent an army to fight on the parliamentarian side at the Battle of Marston Moor in North Yorkshire (2 July 1644), in which the royalists were defeated. One of the best performing officers at Marston Moor was Oliver Cromwell, who served under the Earl of Manchester. Cromwell came from a relatively humble, though financially secure, family in Huntingdonshire. Capitalizing on his new-found reputation, he successfully promoted the formation of a professional standing army that would supplement the ragged armies typically produced by local levies. The New Model Army, as it came to be called, was composed of over 20,000 soldiers, divided into eleven regiments of cavalry and twelve regiments of foot soldiers. It proved its worth at the Battle of Naseby in Northamptonshire on 14 June 1645, during which the parliamentarians effectively won the war, although the king did not surrender for another year.

As soon as the war was won, political divisions began to emerge between Parliament and the army, whose leaders provocatively set up their own quasi-parliamentary assembly, the Council of the Army. The army seized the captive king to use as a bargaining chip and impeached eleven members of Parliament. It also drew up a constitutional blueprint called the Heads of the Proposals (August 1647), intended to form the basis for an agreement with the king, but Charles rejected the plan. On the surface, Parliament and the army disagreed over such matters as soldiers' pay, but they were really engaged in a struggle over who was going to wield power in the new constitution. At the Putney debates held by the army in October, it was clear that everything was up in the air – should every Englishman have the vote? Was the king to be deposed?

There were also ideological disagreements between two types of 'puritan': most MPs were Presbyterians, while army leaders were generally Independents – the former wanted to establish a doctrinally unified Church ruled by elders, while the latter, more radically, wanted to grant freedom of worship to autonomous congregations of worshippers. Some army captains were Levellers, who sought to 'level' social distinctions by promoting popular sovereignty and extending the suffrage. One faction of Presbyterians, angered by the conduct of the army, decided it would be best to restore Charles I to the throne, thereby triggering a brief period of renewed conflict, the Second Civil War (February–August 1648). In a stunning reversal of alliances, the Scottish Covenanters supported Charles against the parliamentarians in return for vague promises of religious toleration. The Second Civil War ended when this new royalist coalition was defeated in battle at Maidstone in Kent (1 June) and at Preston in Lancashire (17–19 August).

KILLING A KING

Now the most pressing question for the Council of the Army was what to do about the stubborn Presbyterian majority in Parliament. On 6 December 1648, the army officers stationed Colonel Thomas Pride outside the Commons with a band of musketeers, who barred entry to the Presbyterians and only allowed Independents through, thus changing the composition of the legislature through sheer force. This coup, Pride's Purge, left only around fifty members in attendance, and so the assembly became known as the Rump Parliament. The members of the Rump set up a High Court to put the king on trial, led by John Bradshaw as Lord President. Though Charles refused to accept the authority of the court, he knew all too well that he was at its mercy: 'I am no Sceptic for to deny the Power that you have; I know that you have Power enough.'[12] After finding Charles guilty of tyranny and of levying war against his own subjects, this revolutionary court sentenced him to death, an unprecedented act. The two English kings deposed in the four-teenth century, Edward II and Richard II, had been surreptitiously murdered, not sentenced to death by a formal procedure. The king perceptively observed that if the new regime could treat a monarch like this, humbler subjects could expect to suffer even greater injustices in the future. He was led to execution outside the Banqueting House at Whitehall on 30 January 1649 and acted until the last with the dignity that befitted his royal state. When the axe came down, England found herself, for the first time in her history as a unified nation, without a reigning king or queen.

King Charles I

11

REVOLUTION AND RESTORATION (1649–1714)

For centuries government policy in England had been directed by the king and his council, while legislative authority had been exercised jointly by the three constituent elements of Parliament: king, Lords and Commons. Now the lowest member of that trinity was to supplant the others. After the king's surrender, the Commons passed a series of ordinances to further its radical religious agenda, prohibiting the celebration of Christmas and Easter in June 1647, and banning stage plays a few months later. On 4 January 1649, a month before the king's execution, the Rump Parliament declared that 'the people are, under God, the original of all just power', and that the House of Commons rightfully exercised this power on the people's behalf.[1] The House of Lords was abolished. In place of the privy council the revolutionaries substituted a Council of State, originally composed of forty-one members. In May, they declared England a Commonwealth and Free State – in other words, a republic.

TAMING IRELAND

Once the new government had established a workable constitution, it turned its attention to the reconquest of Confederate Ireland. To simplify, there were three socio-ethnic categories in Ireland: the Old English (Catholic and Protestant descendants of Anglo-Norman settlers), the New English (recent Protestant settlers) and the Gaelic Irish (the native majority), held in contempt by the Englishry. Among the Old English, in particular, there was significant support for Charles

Stuart's (son of Charles I) claim to the English throne. The Rump commissioned Cromwell, its greatest military commander, to sail to Ireland at the head of an army of 12,000 men. He arrived at Drogheda, a port town on the east coast, in September 1649. His men stormed the town and butchered around 3,000 soldiers, sparing around thirty to be shipped to the new English sugar colony of Barbados.

Though undoubtedly brutal, the Drogheda massacre was technically permissible according to the law of arms because the garrison had chosen not to surrender – a principle expounded, for instance, in Hugo Grotius's 1625 treatise *De jure belli ac pacis*. Nor was this a clear-cut story of one nation oppressing another, for there were Englishmen among Cromwell's victims in Ireland. The governor of Drogheda, Sir Arthur Aston, was an English-born Catholic. Still, Cromwell's expedition was admittedly lauded in chauvinistic terms. The poet Andrew Marvell declared: 'And now the *Irish* are ashamed / To see themselves in one year tamed.'[2] The innovative machinery of government that had been established by the Confederation was replaced with a restored colonial infrastructure governed by a Lord Deputy. Cromwell also defeated the Scots at the Battle of Dunbar on 3 September 1650, after they had rallied in favour of Charles Stuart.

THE FORTY MUSKETEERS

On returning from his military victories, Cromwell found himself at loggerheads with other members of the Rump. For example, whereas he wished to extend mercy to his royalist enemies as a way of building consensus, his fellow parliamentarians blocked and diluted his plans. With the support of the Council of the Army, Cromwell led forty musketeers to the House of Commons on 20 April 1653 and forcibly removed its members, declaring: 'You are no Parliament, I say you are no Parliament; I will put an end to your sitting.'[3] The banished MPs were replaced with 140 men of reliably radical religious views. This assembly was known as the Nominated Assembly or Barebone's Parliament, the latter a pejorative reference to one of the members for London, Praise-God Barebone, a zealous lay puritan of humble station who was mockingly taken to be a representative of the whole.

Despite some legislative achievements, Barebone's Parliament failed to settle a new form of national constitution. This responsibility therefore fell to the Council of the Army, which drew up England's first written constitution, the Instrument of Government, in 1653. The Instrument appointed Cromwell as Lord Protector of the Realm, giving him powers that had been exercised by the monarch under the old constitution, such as the right to summon Parliaments. It also replaced the large Council of State with a smaller body remarkably like the efficient Tudor privy council. The realm was now functioning rather like a monarchy, much to the chagrin of republicans. Two years later, the Protector established a military government throughout the realm, dividing England and Wales into ten districts governed by major-generals, responsible for mustering soldiers and enforcing moral discipline among civilians, for instance by closing pubs – a distinctly un-English brand of morality police. In the same year, England laid claim to Jamaica, which would later be developed into a successful sugar colony, fuelled by slave labour brought in from West Africa.

In 1657, Parliament offered Cromwell the kingly crown, presenting him with a supplication called the 'Humble Petition and Advice', but he refused the honour. A revised version of the petition called on Cromwell to establish a second house of Parliament, which would assume the constitutional role that had formerly been played by the House of Lords. Cromwell duly summoned an 'Other House' of around sixty low-born members in 1658, but he dissolved Parliament after only a few weeks and did not call another before his death from malaria on 3 September 1658. Though the Protectorate fell to his son, Richard Cromwell, it collapsed after a single year under this political lightweight. Richard resigned on 25 May, after which the Rump Parliament (which had been disbanded by Cromwell in 1653) was recalled. There were immediate disagreements between the army and the Rump, clearly a defining feature of revolutionary government, but General George Monck, a skilled diplomatist, managed to negotiate between the two sides and secured the restoration of the Long Parliament in December 1659. After that, a newly elected Parliament invited Charles II to take up his rightful crown, which he gladly accepted on 29 May 1660. One cultural development of the late 1650s should also be squeezed in here – Englishmen had the opportunity to taste tea for the first time, imported from China and served in coffeehouses in London and other cities.

THE RESTORATION OF CHARLES II

The restoration of the monarchy was met with a riot of popular acclamation, so much so that the king reportedly joked that 'it must have
been his own fault that he had been absent so long'. John Dryden
wrote an ode to the new king entitled 'Astraea Redux' (1660), or
'The return of the star goddess', which declared an end to factional
conflict and predicted an age of imperial expansion: 'Your much-
loved fleet shall with a wide Command / Besiege the petty Monarchs
of the Land.'[4] Charles II, the Merry Monarch, cut a very different
figure from the austere puritans who had run the country until very
recently. Tall and flamboyant, he lavished money on music and the
arts, and the royal bed was never without a mistress. Royal propagandists named him the Star King, but court wits gave him a different
nickname, Old Rowley, after a famously randy stallion in the king's
stables. Though the king had little patience for paperwork, he was
helped for a few years by Edward Hyde, Earl of Clarendon, a man
with great administrative ability who assumed the reins of government while the king enjoyed the perks of his position.

In the wake of the doctrinal laxity of the Commonwealth period,
Clarendon sought to clamp down on non-conformity and unorthodoxy with four laws known collectively as the Clarendon Code
(1661–5). The Corporation Act of 1661 declared it unlawful to
take up a municipal office, such as mayor or alderman, without
first receiving the sacrament according to Church of England rites.
The Conventicle Act of 1664 forbade religious meetings of more
than five persons that were not held in accordance with Anglican
rules, with the most severe punishment being seven years' transportation. Clarendon also plunged England into the Second Dutch
War in 1665 (the first had taken place under the Protectorate). This
war was provoked primarily by trading competition: although the
English had supported the Dutch in their struggle against Habsburg
Spain since the reign of Elizabeth, they now belatedly began to grasp
that they had been aiding the rise of a strong economic competitor.

WAR, FIRE AND PLAGUE

England suffered a national disgrace in 1667, the year John Milton's *Paradise Lost* was published, when a Dutch fleet managed to sail up the Thames to Chatham Docks, destroying or capturing several navy vessels. England's military failures sealed the fate of Clarendon, who was impeached and forced into exile, where he made the most of his unexpected leisure time by writing a celebrated history of the civil wars and interregnum period. Clarendon's administration was replaced by the so-called Cabal Ministry, an acrostic made up of the names of its ministers: Clifford, Arlington, Buckingham, Ashley and Lauderdale. That the Earl of Arlington and Lord Clifford were practising Catholics posed a grave concern to the Protestant political nation. In 1673, after Parliament passed the Test Act excluding Catholics from high office, the two men were forced to resign from the ministry. While the Second Dutch War was ongoing, there were also crises closer to home. An unprecedently severe outbreak of the plague in London from 1665 to 1666 killed tens of thousands of people. From 2–5 September 1666, the Great Fire of London, which originated with a careless mistake made in a bakery in Pudding Lane, destroyed most of the city, including 13,000 houses. This is why London, unlike other ancient English cities, retains little medieval architecture. Sir Christopher Wren was appointed to design new buildings to replace those lost in the inferno, most importantly the domed St Paul's Cathedral.

THE POPISH PLOT

The greatest political emergency of the reign, or so it was thought, was the Popish Plot of 1678, which came during the administration of Thomas Osborne, 1st Earl of Danby. This was a supposed Jesuit conspiracy to assassinate the king and force the succession of James, Duke of York, the king's Catholic brother. The 'discoverer' of the plot was Titus Oates, a tremendously ugly man with an oversized chin, who had been expelled from various institutions of religion and learning, including a Jesuit college. On finding himself an overnight celebrity, Oates enjoyed regaling his supporters with boastful tales about his intellectual powers. Sir George Clark has made an astute observation concerning the deceit: 'Once a false charge is made, uncritical people will always find circumstances which seem to point to its truth. They will do so the more readily if it is a charge against those whom they already hate and fear.'[5] Oates's story eventually fell apart, and he was convicted of perjury in 1685, but not until over thirty innocent people, including seven Jesuits, had been executed for treason in perhaps the greatest miscarriage of justice in English history. Another plot to assassinate the king, this one real, was the Rye House Plot (1683), orchestrated not by Catholics but by a small group of Whigs, three of whom were ultimately executed.

WHIGS AND TORIES

During Charles's reign, English politicians started to divide themselves into 'Whigs' and 'Tories', although these labels were originally pejorative and did not yet reflect a clear two-party political system. The Whigs were also called exclusionists because they wished to exclude the king's Catholic brother, James, from the succession; he was the heir apparent since Charles had no legitimate children, though there were many bastards. The Tories, on the other hand, supported the principles of the divine right of kings and indefeasible hereditary succession. The Tory doctrines were expounded in learned treatises and defended from every pulpit, for there was scarcely a local clergyman who was not also a good Tory. Led by Anthony Cooper, 1st Earl of Shaftesbury, the Whigs introduced an Exclusion Bill into the House of Commons in 1679, which would have excluded James from the throne, but the king, in a move reminiscent of his father, dissolved Parliament to scupper the plans.

Charles preferred to obtain secret funding from the king of France, and to take counsel from that old adversary of England, than to rely on his own disputatious subjects, a treacherous policy that would be continued by his successor. In spite of all this, Charles's reign was not devoid of achievements. One of the legal milestones of the period was the Habeas Corpus Act (1679), which strengthened individual protections against arbitrary imprisonment – a sign that despite the winsomeness of their new sovereign, Englishmen had not forgotten the excesses of monarchical government under Charles I.

When the king died of a stroke on 6 February 1685, the Tories had their way at first because the crown descended upon the rightful heir, King James. They could not have foreseen, however, that James would remain on the throne for just three years and ten months.

King Charles II

THE SHORT REIGN OF JAMES II

King James II, whose mother was Catholic, had converted to Catholicism as an adult. For his stubbornness and impetuosity, among other personal faults, he has been described as 'the worst and dullest of the Stuarts'. When he became king at the age of 51, he tried to reassure the realm that his religious convictions would not affect his public duties, vowing to preserve the status quo in church and state. However, Englishmen began to doubt his promise when they witnessed his policy of promoting fellow Catholics to office, contrary to the 1673 Test Act, which indeed he tried and failed to repeal. There were two rebellions in the very first year of his reign, the first led by the Earl of Argyll in Scotland and the second led by the Duke of Monmouth, Charles II's illegitimate son, in the West Country. Both rebellions were easily put down because Argyll's was bungled, and Monmouth, the 'Protestant Duke', failed to capture gentry support and was defeated by a royal army at the Battle of Sedgemoor. George Jeffreys, the irascible Chief Justice of the King's Bench, was sent westwards to try the English rebels, condemning over 300 men to death in local court sessions that became known as the Bloody Assizes. When it was suggested that a certain prisoner deserved mercy because he was on the parish (that is, in receipt of poor relief), Jeffreys reportedly replied, 'Do not trouble yourselves. I will ease the parish of the burden.'[6]

Kings of England had long been able to exercise a dispensing power, allowing them to grant exemptions from statute law, but there were questions about how extensively this power could be used. The normal kind of dispensation was a licence under the king's seal allowing an individual or group to evade some minor statutory rule. James made an untypically sweeping use of it in 1687 when he issued a Declaration of Indulgence wholly suspending the penal laws against Catholics and Protestant non-conformists. In a liberal age, James's policy of comprehensive toleration would have made him a hero, but in the seventeenth century, the relief extended to Catholics was offensive to many. It also alienated the king from the Tories, who would ordinarily have been his natural supporters. No less objectionable to English opinion was the king's scheme to disturb the balance of power in Ireland, dispossessing Protestant elites in the hopes of creating an Irish Catholic power base on which he might depend.

When James passed a second Declaration of Indulgence in 1688, seven bishops, including William Sancroft, Archbishop of Canterbury, petitioned him to withdraw it. The king responded by casting them all into the Tower of London, inadvertently transforming them into popular heroes. When the bishops were put on trial for seditious libel in June, they were defended by the best legal minds in the country and acquitted by the jury, occasioning a public explosion of mirth and celebration. In the same month, the king's wife, Mary of Modena, gave birth to a son (James Francis Edward Stuart). This came as a shock, because the two royals had been married for fifteen years without producing a surviving male heir. Protestants were alarmed because this new development seemed to promise a long-term Catholic dynasty. Some of the king's opponents spread a conspiracy theory that a male child had been smuggled into Mary's bed at the decisive moment, concealed inside a warming pan – a modern spin on the stories of changelings that loomed so large in the folklore of the time.

THE GLORIOUS REVOLUTION

An 'anti-popish' coalition of Whigs and Tories decided that the only solution to these challenges was to replace their rightful king with another. In July 1688, they invited William of Orange, the Calvinist Stadtholder of the United Provinces of the Netherlands, to enter England at the head of an army. William accepted this invitation, setting out for England with an awesome fleet of warships and a professional Dutch army, landing at Torbay in Devon on 5 November. Although James initially opened negotiations with the Stadtholder, he soon recognized that the game was up, fleeing the realm on 23 December after attempting to jam the wheels of government by casting the great seal into the Thames. A provisional government, composed of the peers of the realm, summoned a Convention to assemble in 1689 (technically not a Parliament since it had not been summoned by the king). The Convention declared that James had abdicated, and despite serious opposition from the Lords, ultimately agreed to offer the crown to William and his English wife Mary. Though James made one serious attempt to reclaim his throne with French support, arriving in Ireland in March 1689 and setting in motion a siege of Londonderry, the English citizens of the town successfully defended it against fearful odds, and James's army was conclusively defeated at the Battle of the Boyne (1 July 1690).

By future historians, William's coup would be called the Glorious Revolution, but contemporaries called it the 'happy revolution'. It was celebrated as the triumph of Protestantism over popery, liberty over bondage. Edmund Burke (1729–97), the Rockinghamite Whig who later became a conservative icon, would try to downplay the event as only 'a small and a temporary deviation from the strict order of a regular hereditary succession'.[7] The Whig apostle John Locke (1632–1704), on the other hand, believed that the Revolution confirmed his social contract theory of political power. This theory suggests that the relationship between rulers and ruled is governed by a voluntary unwritten agreement – subjects obey their rulers in return for justice and protection, and if rulers break the contract by acting tyrannically, then their subjects may legitimately rebel against them.

WILLIAM III AND MARY II

With the backing of the political establishment, the usurpers William and Mary were crowned at Westminster Abbey on 11 April 1689. As a daughter of James II, Mary brought legitimacy to the joint reign, while William brought extensive political experience, as well having a large dose of Stuart royal blood himself, being a grandson of Charles I. In theory, the rule of England, Scotland and Ireland was shared equally between the two monarchs, but in practice William was the more active. He had made it quite clear that he wanted to be king in his own right, not 'by apron-strings'. Mary deferred to William in everything, opining that women 'should not meddle in government'. William himself was reserved and cheerless, 'easier to love as an idea than as a man', embodying as he did the tradition of constitutional government.[8] On the plus side, he was a capable English speaker.

Despite broad popular approval of the coup of 1688, there remained significant support for James II among the Jacobites, who remained a force to be reckoned with for another half-century. Some professed adherents to the Jacobite cause were deadly serious, while for others it was a parlour game or a source of escapism. Almost immediately after William and Mary's accession, Parliament passed the Toleration Act (1689), which allowed non-conformists freedom of worship; this was relatively uncontroversial because the public no longer feared their activities, and indeed many non-conformists had joined hands with the Anglicans in opposition to James. Another act of the same year required all holders of religious or secular office to swear oaths of supremacy and allegiance, which resulted in the resignation of around

400 clergymen, the so-called non-jurors. This total included seven bishops, five of whom had, incredibly, been among those imprisoned by James for rejecting the Declaration of Indulgence.

The House of Commons also drew up a great document called the Declaration of Right, which was presented to the king in February 1689 and later passed as an act of Parliament. The Declaration stated that all taxation should be approved by Parliament; that there should be no standing army in peacetime without parliamentary consent; and that the privilege of liberty of speech in Parliament should be protected. It also abolished the king's dispensing power. The English monarchy had long been a constitutional, limited monarchy, and this new law further strengthened constitutional checks on the Crown, coming to be seen as a defining moment in the development of the English constitution. During the reign of William and Mary, Parliament began to scrutinize royal expenditure systematically for the first time, and Englishmen began to fully comprehend the doctrine of parliamentary sovereignty: the idea that the king in Parliament has 'an Unbounded Unlimited Reach' in the legislative sphere, as Daniel Defoe wrote in 1705 – or, according to a famous formulation, that Parliament could 'do anything but make a woman a man, and a man a woman'. Though the king once claimed that the newly empowered Parliament treated him 'like a dog', he was usually content to work closely with its members in the governance of the realm.[9]

THE NINE YEARS' WAR

William accepted the throne primarily because he wanted to use English money and manpower in his struggle against the Sun King, Louis XIV of France, who had been pursuing an aggressive policy of expansion, the *Réunions* policy, and who had personally humiliated William in 1682 by sacking the principality of Orange. On 7 May 1689, only a month after William and Mary's coronation, England declared war on France, joining an impressive anti-French coalition that included Spain and the Holy Roman Empire. The French won a significant naval victory against an Anglo-Dutch fleet off Beachy Head, Sussex, on 10 July 1690. However, the Allied fortunes turned in May 1692 when Admiral Edward Russell defeated a French invasion fleet at the six-day Battle of La Hogue, which confirmed

English naval supremacy. Lord Macaulay called it 'the first great victory that the English had gained over the French since the day of Agincourt'.[10] The Nine Years' War, as the larger conflict came to be known, also involved the deployment of English troops on the continent, where both sides mustered unprecedently large armies of up to 100,000 men. Hostilities continued until September 1697, when a peace treaty was signed at Rijswijk, near The Hague. William clashed with his ministers by suggesting the continued maintenance of a large standing army after the war had finished, which was widely regarded as un-English and a high road to tyranny.

Parliamentary elections were now held at least every three years in accordance with a new Triennial Act passed in 1694. Since government had become too complicated to be conducted solely by the king's privy council, this period saw the rise of government ministries, led by secretaries of state, who in turn delegated businesses to committees. During the reign of William and Mary, the Whig and Tory political parties became increasingly distinct, marking the distant origin of the modern system of two-party dominance in the United Kingdom. Though the parties remained fluid, with no formally defined structure or discipline, they had a degree of cohesion – Whig MPs met regularly at the Rose Tavern in Covent Garden. Contemporaries sometimes also referred to a 'country party', a loose affiliation of locally minded gentlemen in Parliament who defended the importance of personal liberty, a small state, low taxation and public decency.

It seemed probable that the king would throw his lot in with the Whigs rather than the Tories, who had historically promoted the hereditary right of James II. At first, he tried to build political consensus by appointing a mixed ministry of Whigs and Tories led by the Marquess of Carmarthen, but he began to drift away from this ideal in 1693, after a particularly turbulent parliamentary session, and he appointed more Whigs to key positions. Five of the leading Whigs (including Lord Somers and Charles Montagu, later Earl of Halifax) were nicknamed the Junto Lords, based on an erroneous version of the Spanish word *junta* (committee). William eventually became disillusioned with the Whig Junto, and he appointed another mixed ministry in 1699. The king may have been trying to find out whether viewpoint diversity or political unity was the secret to successful governance.

SCIENCE AND FINANCE

The reign of William and Mary was a high point in the Scientific Revolution (roughly 1626–1727). During this period a general acceptance of experimental science and empirical methods led to giant scientific and technological breakthroughs at a rate unseen since the Hellenistic Scientific Revolution of the fourth century BC. Prominent scientists included the astronomer Edmond Halley (1656–1742), who correctly predicted the 1758 return of the comet that bears his name, and the polymath Isaac Newton, who developed innovative theories concerning gravity and optics (1642–1727). New scientific discoveries led to a literary debate known as the Battle of the Books (beginning in 1690), as intellectuals argued about whether the modern learning was superior to the revered ancient classics. This period also witnessed the beginnings of a Financial Revolution, the development of a modern economy and the importation of advanced financial methods from the Netherlands, which was in part driven by policies introduced to help the government meet the costs of war. England's first 'stock market', situated in the various coffeehouses of Exchange Alley, was opened in the 1690s; a permanent National Debt was established in 1693; and the Bank of England was founded in 1694, which in 1708 won the right to be the only joint-stock bank in England. Mary died of smallpox on 28 December 1694, and on 8 March 1702, the king died of pulmonary fever, a month after suffering a serious fall when his horse tripped on a molehill. The regicidal mole responsible for the king's fall later became enshrined in Jacobite lore as 'the little gentleman in the velvet coat'.

THE REIGN OF QUEEN ANNE

Queen Anne, who reigned from 1702 to 1714, was a Stuart, daughter of King James II. Three days after her accession, she gave a speech to Parliament in which she made the most of her English birth: 'I know My own Heart to be entirely *English*,' she declared.[11] She was crowned in accordance with the Act of Settlement of 1701, hastily drafted when it became clear that William was going to die childless, and primarily intended to make sure that England would be ruled by Protestant monarchs until the end of time – which seems to have worked, because it is still in force today. This act also introduced some new limitations on the monarchy, stipulating, for example, that the nation should no longer go to war to defend foreign territories without parliamentary consent.

In Anne's reign it becomes possible to speak of a formally constituted Cabinet government. Every Sunday, the queen presided over a meeting of Cabinet ministers appointed by herself, in which official policy was formulated; in later reigns, the Cabinet would usually meet without the monarch. The overgrown privy council continued to assemble, but largely for the sake of formality, and it no longer made policy. At the same time, the political and organizational differences between Whigs and Tories became increasingly sharper, with each party vying for pre-eminence in Parliament. There were five parliamentary elections in total: 1702 (Tory landslide), 1705 (Tory victory), 1708 (Whig landslide), 1710 (Tory landslide) and 1713 (Tory landslide). This was an age of seriously partisan politics, as illustrated by a Whig-dominated Parliament's impeachment of the clergyman Henry Sacheverell in 1710 for preaching and publishing a sermon against religious toleration. Though Sacheverell's punishment was only a lenient three-year preaching ban, this case proves that freedom of speech – widely celebrated in eighteenth-century England – clearly had its limits.

THE WAR OF THE SPANISH SUCCESSION

Despite her Tory sympathies, the queen exercised moderation and restraint in her choice of ministers. On her accession, she appointed a mixed ministry of Whigs and Tories, led by the moderate Tories Lord Godolphin and the Duke of Marlborough ('the duumvirs'), who almost immediately involved England in the War of the Spanish Succession (1701–14). This war would last almost until the end of Anne's reign. As the name suggests, it was fought over the disputed succession to the Spanish throne after the death of Charles II of Spain in 1700. England, as a member of the Grand Alliance, supported the Habsburgs in opposition to the Bourbon king of Spain, Philip V. In 1702, John Churchill, Duke of Marlborough – Winston Churchill's ancestor – was appointed Commander-in-chief of the army. At Blindheim in Bavaria, Marlborough defeated a Franco-Bavarian army on 13 August 1704, the first major French defeat on land in sixty years, and he was rewarded with lands in Oxfordshire, where he built the spectacular Blenheim Palace to commemorate the victory. In the same year, Sir George Rooke captured Gibraltar in Spain, which remains to this day a British territory. The Allies also captured Barcelona in 1705. Marlborough helped to sustain popular support for the war by winning a great victory near the village of Ramillies in 1706, which cleared the way for Allied capture of much of the Spanish Netherlands. However, there were two serious defeats in the following year, at Almanza and Toulon, which somewhat dampened the nation's spirits. Incidentally, the war fuelled England's love of port wine, for the Methuen Treaty of 1703 reduced duties on wines from Portugal as a means of supporting an ally while hammering French wine exports.

THE BIRTH OF GREAT BRITAIN

Back at home, there was a government reshuffle in 1704, in which the queen retained Marlborough and Godolphin but replaced some leading Tory ministers with 'Harleyites', pro-war centrists who generally followed the line of Robert Harley (appointed Lord Treasurer). One of the burning questions of this time was the succession to the throne. According to the terms of the 1701 Act of

Settlement, the next in line for the English and Scottish crowns after Anne's death was the Electress Sophia of Hanover, a German descendant of James I. The Scottish Parliament defied this scheme in 1704 by passing the provocative Act of Security, claiming for itself an independent right to name a successor to the crown of Scotland. This dare could not go unchallenged if the English government wanted to ensure the success of the Hanoverian succession. And so, government lawyers drafted the most significant law of Anne's reign, the Act of Union, which formally united the realms of England and Scotland under the name of Great Britain, finalizing a process that had begun with the accession of James I a century earlier. The act was passed by both the English and Scottish Parliaments in 1707, a process sullied by the payment of bribes to Scottish members. It abolished the Scottish Parliament, so that from then on, Scotland would have to return members to the English Parliament, henceforth called the British Parliament. Scotland retained her own legal system and ecclesiastical framework. By and large, Scottish elites eventually got on board with the British project and would later play a full role in the development of the British Empire.

CLAMOUR FOR PEACE

When the Whig Party secured its only parliamentary majority of Anne's reign in 1708, the queen responded by appointing leading Whigs to high office. Gradually, the Whigs became a war party and the Tories a peace party, though Godolphin and Marlborough continued to support the war. Despite Britain's military successes, the War of the Spanish Succession was becoming increasingly unpopular. In 1712, Jonathan Swift urged an end to the fighting, claiming that nobody could 'be of opinion for continuing the war... unless he be a gainer by it'.[12] The later stages of the war strained the relationship between Anne, who was in a hurry to secure peace, and her chief ministers, who were not. After she sacked Godolphin in 1710 and Marlborough in 1711, Harley, now Earl of Oxford, emerged as the new leader of her government. In the winter of 1711–12, Anne packed the Whiggish House of Lords by creating twelve new peers in favour of peace – an unprecedented act soon decried as more tyrannical than anything done by Henry VIII.

The war was finally concluded by the Treaty of Utrecht (1713), which affirmed Philip's rule over Spain and the East Indies but forbade the union of the French and Spanish crowns. It also confirmed British possession of Gibraltar, Minorca, Newfoundland and Nova Scotia. The terms of this treaty suggested that perhaps Britain, not France, was now the hegemon of western Europe. However, Britain's readiness to come to terms with France without proper consultation with her allies gave rise to the unflattering nickname 'Perfidious Albion'. The queen, who was mocked in her own lifetime for being overweight, continually struggled with ill-health and died on 1 August 1714 at the age of 49. She left no heir, for despite seventeen pregnancies stemming from the efforts of her husband, Prince George of Denmark, she had only produced one child who survived into infancy, and he had died in 1700. In the afterglow of the War of the Spanish Succession, Britain's neighbours could not fail to notice that she had become one of the greatest nations in the world. It was about time for her to step into the centre of the world stage.

12

EARLY HANOVERIAN BRITAIN (1714–1760)

In 1883, the Cambridge historian Sir John Robert Seeley noted that the eighteenth century is commonly thought of 'as prosperous, but not as memorable ... everywhere alike we seem to remark a want of greatness, a distressing commonness and flatness in men and in affairs'. He also noted that the chief characteristic of the period was a rivalry between the expanding powers of England and France – 'a second Hundred Years' War' that would end with Napoleon's final defeat in 1815.[1] More perhaps than any other century, the eighteenth marks the beginning of the modern era: political life became rational and prosaic, while banking and mercantilism moved to the centre of public affairs. Architects and town planners came to prize rationality, refinement, order and symmetry; local elites and corporations competed to build the neatest town squares, the broadest paved avenues and the most well-ordered parks and gardens. The eighteenth century has been called the 'English century', an apt title if one holds a narrow view of what constitutes Englishness.[2] In terms of demographics, this century saw a population explosion, with unprecedented prosperity and advances in medicine and sanitation contributing to a rise in the English population from 5 million in 1701 to 8.7 million in 1801.

Sophia of Hanover predeceased Anne by a few months and so never had the chance to sit on the throne. The crown passed instead to her son George, who was 54. King George I was short, pot-bellied, lazy, spoke little English and was a man of questionable judgement. Notoriously, he had kept his adulterous ex-wife imprisoned for over two decades, doting instead on two mistresses, one overweight and the other tall and bony – cruelly referred to as the

Elephant and the Maypole. Nevertheless, George was a Protestant and therefore good enough for the establishment, who had his accession widely proclaimed after Anne's death. The king arrived in England in September, deliberately taking his time to prove that the Jacobites did not scare him. Despite some Jacobite manoeuvring among the elites in favour of the 'Old Pretender', James Francis Edward Stuart, there was a peaceful transfer of power. A Tory minister noted that 'there never was yet so quiet a transition from one government to another'.[3]

George had been Elector of Hanover for sixteen years. Prior to 1806, Germany and surrounding lands were governed by the Holy Roman Emperor, who was elected by territorial magnates, called electors (there were nine in this period). Hanover was a small electorate with Lutheran sympathies, comprising territory now part of the Netherlands and northern Germany. It was a pleasantly carefree place, 'with its cosy *gemütlich* little capital at Hanover, [and] its agreeable summer residence at Göhrde, where immense battues attested the precision of the electoral gun, and the orangeries the skill of the electoral gardeners'.[4] George had ruled over its happy people as a benign autocrat. He was thus ill-prepared for the turbulent world of English politics, with its many checks on the authority of the king.

THE WHIG SUPREMACY

Rather than skilfully seeking to balance power between the two political parties, as Anne had done, George sided almost exclusively with the Whigs, for he suspected the Tories of disloyalty and Jacobitism. In reality, only a few Tories were Jacobites, but two of their leaders, the Earl of Oxford and the Viscount Bolingbroke, had indeed been conducting secret negotiations with the Jacobite court in France. With the king's support, the Whigs set up an oligarchy that would last for over half a century, capturing much of the machinery of central and local government. They won a landslide victory in the general election of 1715 and cemented their power with the Septennial Act (1716), which raised the maximum length of a Parliament from three to seven years – a rather shameless bit of *realpolitik* since the Whigs had long been the champions of short Parliaments as a check on the royal prerogative. This was also an age infamous for parliamentary corruption, as the government perfected the mechanisms of securing majorities in the Commons by purchasing votes. The Whig ascendancy reflected not only the king's confidence but also political stability and consensus among the voting population: in an age where government policy meets broad approval, there is very little for the opposition to complain about.

THE FIFTEEN REBELLION

The new Whig ministry behaved vindictively towards its political enemies, launching parliamentary impeachments of Jacobitical Tories. Bolingbroke fled to France by surreptitiously leaving the theatre in the middle of a play. The Jacobites, who had missed their chance to rise up in opposition to the Hanoverian succession in 1714, belatedly called their adherents to arms. The Scottish Jacobite John Erskine, 6th Earl of Mar, signalled the start of the Fifteen Rebellion on 6 September 1715 by raising the Stuart standard at Braemar Castle near Aberdeen. However, the disorganized Jacobites lacked significant public support in England. For the following two months, they incited riots and mustered soldiers but never posed a serious threat to George's new regime. A Jacobite army of around 5,000 men surrendered at Preston on 13 November when its leaders realized they could not overcome the king's forces. The Old Pretender entered Dundee in January 1716 but hurried back to France after failing to win widespread support. In the moments they could spare, the Whigs also laboured to restore the health of public finances. As Chancellor of the Exchequer, Robert Walpole drew up a scheme to reduce the National Debt, which included the establishment of a 'sinking fund' of surplus revenue to pay off some of the Crown's debts each year. This policy would reduce the National Debt by around £6 million by 1742.

Though they could find common ground in opposition to the Jacobites, the Whigs were disunited in other areas of domestic and foreign policy. From 1717, disaffected Whigs who had been edged out of office by the king, including the recently dismissed Robert Walpole and the Viscount Townshend, established a shadow court at Leicester House under the auspices of Prince George, the king's son and heir, where they fraternized with the Tories and discussed measures for opposing the government's policy. But the tide turned in April 1720, when the Whigs settled their differences and the king repaired his relationship with the prince. Both Walpole and Townshend returned to office, though not yet the highest office. From now on, the most meaningful opposition to the government would come not from Leicester House and Parliament but from the pages of literary journals, most notably those graced by the pens of Jonathan Swift, Alexander Pope and other Tory wits.

THE SOUTH SEA BUBBLE

Eighteenth-century British businessmen continued to profit from the West Indian sugar colonies, fuelled by the Atlantic slave trade, though these did not play such a significant role in the home economy as is sometimes thought. This was an age of risk-taking and buccaneering. Some men, by making a few smart investments, acquired riches beyond their wildest imaginations, while others lost everything on madcap schemes. In 1720, many British investors faced financial catastrophe with the collapse of the South Sea Bubble. This was not wholly the result of foolish public speculation. In 1711, the South Sea Company had been founded to restructure part of the National Debt (which stood at about £50 million) by paying off public creditors and loaning to the government on more favourable terms. In return, the company enjoyed a monopoly of trade, including the slave trade, on the east and west coasts of South America. Since the company looked set to make great profits, many public creditors willingly traded government annuities for company stock, and total investment in the company reached nearly £20 million. Though the company never in fact managed to establish a thriving trade in South America, the company's share value continued to rise, in part because of 'bluff, hyperbole, lies and bribes' on the part of the company directors and other interested parties.[5] There was also a significant minority of noise traders: poorly informed individuals who trade on the basis of rumours or inaccurate information and thus contribute to the artificial raising of stock prices. The result was a colossal economic bubble that finally burst in September 1720.

Many investors were ruined in an instant; some took their own lives. Still, the crash did not cause an overall recession, and public confidence in the stock market quickly recovered.

The public apparently did not blame the government for the fiasco, for the next general election (1722) returned another sizeable Whig majority to the House of Commons. Some MPs and Cabinet members had taken bribes to look favourably on the company, for which the reprisals were immediate. The most prominent casualty was John Aislabie, who was removed as Chancellor of the Exchequer and replaced with the obese and ostentatious Robert Walpole – 'the very epitome of the selfish Whig oligarch' – in 1721. This was Walpole's reward for helping to restore economic stability and public confidence after the crash. The administration was now headed by Townshend and Walpole jointly – they were brothers-in-law, both born and bred in Norfolk. While Townshend was an aristocrat, Walpole was by birth a simple squire, but his was far the greater intelligence, and his pragmatic, common-sense policies generally won the day – 'peace, low taxes, unrestrained exports, and limited toleration for Dissenters'.[6] Walpole's motto was *Quieta non movere*, roughly translatable as 'Let sleeping dogs lie', which well encapsulates his preference for minimal government intervention.

The remainder of George I's reign was comparatively uneventful, except for the Atterbury Plot of 1721–2, in which Francis Atterbury, Bishop of Rochester, masterminded a desperate Jacobite attempt to remove the king. This plot fizzled out before it had even begun, although this did not prevent the Whigs from using the ensuing panic as an excuse to engross even more political power at the expense of their rivals. The king fell ill on 8 June 1727, initially attributing his ailment to over-consumption of oranges and strawberries, but his illness turned out to be more severe than that, and he died of a stroke at Osnabrück on 11 June.

GEORGE II AND ROBERT WALPOLE

Like his father, King George II was a native German speaker, born in Hanover on 10 November 1683, but he had managed to master the English tongue. Sir Robert Walpole, now a knight of the Garter, remained pre-eminent in state affairs, which gave a sense of continuity to British government despite the change of sovereign. Walpole had butted heads with George II when he was a prince, and thus fairly expected to lose his job when the old king died, but he was saved by his own talents and by his intimate friendship with George II's wife, Queen Caroline, who 'ruled her husband'.[7] Since it would have been foolish to discard a man of such ability, Walpole managed to consolidate his supremacy in government, heading a ministry that lasted until 1742.

Walpole is now considered to be England's first prime minister, and indeed his contemporaries referred to him as a prime minister. However, 'he did not have the power of a modern prime minister', since he served at the king's pleasure, did not appoint his own Cabinet, and never exercised absolute control over military affairs.[8] Strictly speaking, there was no formal office of prime minister until the reign of Queen Victoria; in Hanoverian Britain, the men whom historians call prime ministers were those politicians who presided over meetings of the Cabinet. Most but not all 'prime ministers' held the title of First Lord of the Treasury, a post that commanded the lion's share of official patronage. Walpole also made use of a small 'inner cabinet', which 'met frequently but informally to decide the broad outlines of policy'.[9] Policy was often presented to the whole Cabinet only after it had already been approved by the inner cabinet and the king.

Walpole suffered one of his worst political defeats in 1733. He drew up an Excise Scheme that sought to increase government revenue by levying an inland tax on tobacco and wine consumption. Similar duties were already payable on cocoa, tea and coffee. This scheme would have allowed him to reduce the land tax to one shilling in the pound, for he believed that landowners shouldered more than their fair share of taxation, but after strong opposition inside and outside of Parliament, Walpole was forced to withdraw it. Such was the unpopularity of the excise that the Whigs probably would have lost the subsequent general election of 1734, were it not for pocket boroughs and placemen. After 1734, Walpole enjoyed a parliamentary majority but clearly did not enjoy majority public support – that this was possible was a curious feature of the unreformed Parliament prior to 1832 (the year of the First Reform Act). Perhaps Walpole's feelings of paranoia in the face of a disapproving public helped to bring about the Licensing Act of 1737, which made it illegal to 'produce a play which did not carry the government's approval', one of the milestones in the history of English censorship.[10] It is suspected that Walpole had given covert support to a scandalous play attacking the royal family, *The Festival of the Golden Rump*, to create an artificial pretext for the new law. As for religious affairs, in the 1730s, the Oxford priest John Wesley emerged as the founder of Methodism, a religious movement that adhered to the doctrines of the Church of England but laid greater emphasis on preaching, Bible study and purity of life.

THE JENKINS' EAR WAR

George II's reign is more notable for foreign policy than for events closer to home. Always the pacifist, Walpole tried not to embroil Britain in continental conflicts. For example, he famously persuaded Queen Caroline that the British ought not to get involved in the War of the Polish Succession (1733–5): 'Madam, there are fifty thousand men slain this year in Europe, and not one Englishman.'[11] Nevertheless, the government could not ignore rising conflict between Britain and Spain, for which some of the fault lay on both sides. British merchants were regularly caught smuggling goods into Spanish ports in South America, while Spanish *guardacostas* (coastguards) obstructed legitimate British trade by vexatiously exercising their powers of searching ships. Parliament agreed to declare war on Spain in 1739, in part due to a persuasive speech from the young opposition MP William Pitt, later to distinguish himself as prime minister (William Pitt the Elder). This conflict was called the Jenkins' Ear War because of a symbolic story that the *guardacostas* had savagely cut off the ear of the Welsh captain Robert Jenkins in 1731.

Captain Edward Vernon won an early victory in Panama with only six ships, capturing an important fort at Puerto Bello, which occasioned the naming of Portobello Road in west London. One of the most memorable expeditions of the war was led by George Anson, who circumnavigated the globe between 1740 and 1744. His men captured the Spanish galleon *Nuestra Señora de Covadonga* in 1743, going all the way to Guangzhou in southern China to sell it before returning to England with chests full of treasure. Though

Anson was acclaimed as a hero who had remained strong in adversity, the voyage had little effect on the war effort, and 1,000 men perished in the undertaking. Walpole was never very enthusiastic about the Spanish war, and he was forced to resign in February 1742 after winning a general election in the previous year by a disappointingly narrow margin. This was not a tremendous blow because he was already of retirement age and was immediately raised to the peerage as Earl of Orford; in any case, he died just over three years later. The nursery rhyme 'Who killed Cock Robin?', about a robin killed by a sparrow, may have been written or rewritten in around 1742 as an allegory of Walpole's fall.

Despite his achievements, Walpole was constantly lambasted as corrupt during his lifetime, not only by hacks but also by the greatest writers of the age, including in John Gay's *Beggar's Opera* (1728) and Alexander Pope's 'Epistle to Bathurst' (1733). Walpole's opponents referred to his government as a 'Robinocracy', meaning that 'Robin' Walpole had set himself up as the wellspring of all patronage and political power. Some of these accusations carried weight. Walpole is known to have participated in illegal smuggling while in office, and it has been observed with justice that the 'legitimate proceeds of his public offices could not have provided Walpole with the huge sums needed to build his magnificent new palace at Houghton in Norfolk'.[12] That he was corrupt there can be no doubt, but he was also an effective statesman.

THE WAR OF THE AUSTRIAN SUCCESSION

The Spanish war that brought Walpole down was eventually absorbed into a larger-scale conflict, the War of the Austrian Succession (1740–8), in which Britain and Spain took opposing sides. Like the earlier Nine Years' War and the War of the Spanish Succession – and the later Seven Years' War – this conflict was in essence an attempt to resist French expansion. In March 1731, Britain had made an alliance with Austria in the Treaty of Vienna, promising to take the Habsburg side in the Austrian succession question. By agreeing to the Pragmatic Sanction of Charles VI (an imperial ordinance), Britain supported the eventual accession of Maria Theresa, Charles's daughter, as Archduchess of Austria, in opposition to the rival claim of Charles Albert, Elector of Bavaria. After Walpole's resignation in 1742, the fluent German speaker Lord Carteret (later Earl Granville) became chief minister for a brief period with the king's support, but he had no choice but to resign in November 1744. There had been serious parliamentary opposition to his foreign policy, which was only partially vindicated by the Battle of Dettingen (27 June 1743), where the combined forces of Britain, Austria and Hanover trounced the French. The king replaced Carteret with a 'Broad-Bottom' coalition ministry of Whigs and Tories, but this short-lived experiment in consensus was unsuccessful. Instead, a wholly Whig administration emerged under the premiership of Henry Pelham, with foreign policy directed by his brother, the Duke of Newcastle. The war was finally concluded in 1748 by the Treaty of Aix-la-Chapelle, confirming Maria Theresa's claim to Austria. Though it had been astronomically expensive, the war had 'worked like yeast in Britain's economy', boosting the efficiency and production levels of heavy industry.[13]

JACOBITES RESURGENT

War in Europe helped to revive the Jacobite cause that had lain dormant for a generation. The French provided troops to the incumbent Jacobite figurehead, Charles Edward Stuart, otherwise known as Bonnie Prince Charlie or the Young Pretender. In 1745, Charles adventured to seize the crown in the Forty-Five Rebellion. Having drawn an army from the Scottish Highlands, a land of chieftains, bards and heroes that had not yet been successfully incorporated into the British State, he defeated a royal army at the Battle of Prestonpans (21 September) before marching on England. He got as far as Derby, where a modern statue now commemorates his feat, but then decided to retreat because substantial English support had failed to materialize. He was ultimately routed at the Battle of Culloden near Inverness on 16 April 1746, the last serious battle on British soil, in which Scots fought on both sides. The British commander, the Duke of Cumberland, turned a blind eye to his officers' brutal treatment of wounded Jacobite soldiers after the battle, including burning them alive and clubbing them to death. Initially hailed as a hero, he was soon being described in the press as 'the Butcher'. In the wake of the battle, the British government sought to restrict traditional Highland customs, which could be seen as a kind of cultural resistance: in 1748, for example, it was made illegal to wear tartan. Incidentally, the fact that few English Tories joined in the rebellion made it increasingly hard to tar Toryism with the brush of Jacobitism.

Bonnie Prince Charlie

One of the last major domestic policies of the Pelhams' administration was the Jewish Naturalization Bill of 1753. The government sought to authorize Parliament to naturalize Jews on a case-by-case basis, a policy intended to draw wealthy Jews to Britain and 'to fill our island with industrious people'.[14] While this bill easily passed Parliament, it was vehemently opposed by the public, whose outrage forced lawmakers to repeal the act shortly after its passage. When Pelham died in 1754, he was succeeded as prime minister by his brother, Newcastle. Newcastle's ministry was hamstrung from the start by the fact that he was a peer, and thus unable to steer government policy through the House of Commons. He was eventually brought down by the Minorca fiasco of 1756, in which Admiral John Byng allowed the French navy to capture the lovely British territory rather than risking his men in battle.

THE SEVEN YEARS' WAR

This year also marked the outbreak of the Seven Years' War (1756–63) between Britain, Hanover and Prussia on the one side and France, Austria, Saxony, Russia and Sweden on the other. It was in essence a contest to decide who would dominate the world – the French or the British – so it was naturally fought on a global stage, especially in India and North America. The British East India Company, incorporated in 1600, had started out as a mere trading company but had gradually built up political as well as economic power in India, regularly clashing with its rival, the French East India Company. Robert Clive, a military captain employed by the Company and better known as Clive of India, won a major victory over the pro-French Nawab of Bengal, Siraj-ud-Daula, at the Battle of Plassey (Palashi) on 23 June 1757. The hapless Nawab had outraged British opinion by cramming a number of British citizens, possibly over a hundred, into a tiny cell nicknamed 'the black hole of Calcutta', where many of them perished. In his place, the East India Company installed the puppet ruler Mir Jafar, and claimed for itself the tax revenues of Bengal, then the most prosperous province in India. The victory at Plassey helped to lay the foundations upon which the British Raj would later be constructed, out of the pieces of the rapidly fragmenting Mughal Empire.

There were other military victories elsewhere, including in Germany, Portugal and France. Major General James Wolfe's bravura capture of Quebec from the French in 1759 paved the way for the British conquest of Canada, which was undoubtedly an attractive prize, no matter that Voltaire dismissed it as 'a few acres of snow'. So triumphant was the public mood that Horace Walpole boasted that 'one is forced to ask every morning what victory there is, for fear of missing one'.[15] Who could complain of the costs, totalling some £13.7 million per annum, when Britain was winning so many prizes, so much glory? It was no surprise that men who had studied almost nothing but Latin in school began to talk excitedly about a British answer to the Roman Empire. Sheltered from the turmoil of the battlefield and the hurly-burly of Parliament, George II spent his last days at Kensington Palace, where he died in 1760 after drinking a morning cup of hot chocolate. The British crown, which was becoming every day more prestigious in the eyes of the world, descended upon George III, grandson of George II, who had become Prince of Wales after his father's death in 1751.

13

LATER HANOVERIAN BRITAIN (1760–1838)

George III was the first English-born king in nearly five decades. 'Born and educated in this country,' he announced at his accession, 'I glory in the name of Britain.'[1] The personal authority of the monarch had been much eroded over the previous half-century, so much so that it was now generally agreed that policymaking should happen in the Cabinet, not in the palace. Though George asserted his traditional right to appoint government ministers, he had to choose men agreeable to Parliament if he wished to avoid muddle and conflict. That included his choice of prime ministers, who had to enjoy the confidence of Parliament if any business was to be dispatched with at least a modicum of efficiency. British government, in short, was increasingly Cabinet- and Parliament-centred, and less king-centred.

George's reign was a period of conservative revival after decades of Whig domination. The political landscape had become more complicated than a simple dichotomy between Whigs and Tories. The Whig Party had splintered into competing political factions that described themselves as Whig, led by men such as Lord Rockingham, George Grenville, and John Russell, 4th Duke of Bedford. Even the conservatives thought of themselves as a conservative Whig faction. There were eighteen successive ministries during George's long reign. On his accession, he inherited the Pitt–Newcastle ministry appointed by his grandfather, headed by Pitt the Elder and the Duke of Newcastle. Pitt and Newcastle resigned in 1761 and 1762, respectively, leaving the king's tutor and favourite, John Stuart, 3rd Earl of Bute, to enjoy a fleeting period of pre-eminence as prime minister (May 1762–April 1763).

Bute was a clever Scottish nobleman who had taught the king to entertain a high-minded view of his own majesty. His visionary character won the approval of great luminaries such as the author and critic Samuel Johnson and the printmaker William Hogarth, known for his satirical sketches of British life. He directed the peace negotiations with France that resulted in the 1763 Treaty of Paris. This treaty, which ended the Seven Years' War and formally apportioned large territories to Britain in North America, India and elsewhere, was nevertheless thought to be too lenient towards France, and Bute had to resign after a popular outcry. The radical MP John Wilkes wrote an article denouncing the peace and was expelled from the House of Commons for his pains, though the electors of Middlesex kept electing him again, which triggered a minor constitutional struggle when his election was repeatedly voided by the Commons.

TEA AND TAXES

After the Treaty of Paris, Britain had a strong claim, for the first time in her history, to being the most powerful nation in the world. But as Britain grew increasingly prosperous and mighty, and as the British Empire expanded, one colony in particular grew increasingly impatient with its subjection. In the years since the Virginia Company had founded the Colony of Virginia in 1606, and since the *Mayflower* had carried the first radical English puritans (or 'pilgrims') to Plymouth, Massachusetts, in 1620, thirteen colonies had grown up in North America: Connecticut, Delaware, Georgia, Massachusetts, Maryland, New Hampshire, New Jersey, New York, North Carolina, Pennsylvania, Rhode Island, South Carolina and Virginia. Eight of these colonies operated by virtue of royal charter, while the other five had different forms of constitution. All were subject to regulation by the British Parliament. The Stamp Act, passed in March 1765 during George Grenville's ministry, angered Americans by taxing them without their consent, and it had to be repealed in the following year under the supervision of the new prime minister, Lord Rockingham.

The ministry of Lord North (1770–82) agreed to suspend all British duties on imports into America except the tea duty, which was retained as a nominal statement of Britain's right to impose taxes on her American Colonies. The Tea Act of May 1773 then reduced duties on East India Company tea legally exported to America, ostensibly in an attempt to discourage smuggling. The following December, members of a political group called the Sons of Liberty responded by dressing up as native Americans and dumping the cargo of Company tea ships into Boston harbour, an incident that became known as the Boston Tea Party. The American colonists then openly rebelled against British rule, declaring independence on 4 July 1776. Supported by France, the Americans fought under the generalship of George Washington. The turning point of the war was the surrender of General Burgoyne at Saratoga on 17 October 1777, after which British fortunes steadily declined. At length the king's ministers were forced to the negotiating table. As Lord North concisely declared, 'Oh God, it is all over.'[2] The Americans secured confirmation of their independence in the Treaty of Versailles (3 September 1783). Pessimists thought that the British defeat marked the beginning of the end for the Empire, but they turned out to be wrong: it would continue to grow and thrive for another century at least.

THE GORDON RIOTS

During the American war, the British government faced additional problems at home, such as the Gordon Riots of 1780, in which a crazed anti-Catholic mob tyrannized London to protest about the implementation of a Catholic Relief Act that loosened traditional restrictions on practitioners of the Roman religion. It all began when Lord George Gordon organized a march to petition Parliament on 2 June. Since over 40,000 people were involved, it is not surprising that the march rapidly turned violent. The rioters went on a week-long rampage, attempting to storm the House of Commons, successfully storming Newgate Prison and destroying the private library of Lord Mansfield, Chief Justice of the King's Bench, in Bloomsbury. Hundreds of rioters were shot by soldiers, and twenty-five more were hanged after the event. Though Gordon himself was put on trial for treason, he was acquitted by the jury. The American war was lost, in part, because of the energies wasted on tackling these eruptions of internal instability. The constitution also came under strain at this time. Ministers and MPs were alarmed when the king began to magnify his own authority, having grown unsatisfied with his short reach in political affairs. However much it had been diluted, the imperious blood of the House of Stuart still coursed through the royal veins. The Commons passed a motion called Dunning's motion in April 1780, which boldly pronounced that 'the influence of the crown has increased, is increasing, and ought to be diminished'.[3]

The conservative Whig politician William Pitt the Younger, described by his opponents as a Tory, was appointed as prime minister in December 1783 after the collapse of a short-lived Whig coalition headed by Charles James Fox and Lord North, which the king had despised from day one. Pitt, who was only 24 years old on the day of his appointment, would hold this post until 1801. He was widely esteemed an honest man, yet he was loathed by radicals such as Samuel Taylor Coleridge and William Hazlitt on account of his austerity measures and the draconian laws passed against reformers and agitators in the 1790s, a period melodramatically described as Pitt's Reign of Terror. Pitt introduced Britain's first income tax, which was a startling innovation because direct taxation in England had traditionally been assessed on the basis of land and property ownership. He also oversaw the passage of an important colonial law, the India Act of 1784, which established a Board of Control for India with parliamentary oversight, though most Indian affairs remained nominally in the hands of the East India Company. Significantly, the Company retained control of colonial patronage rather than surrendering it into the hands of the Crown.

THE MADNESS OF KING GEORGE

In 1788, the king fell seriously ill. His ailment is often called the 'madness of King George', but the correct diagnosis is probably porphyria, a chemical disorder that can lead to mental confusion. George talked incessantly and incoherently, sometimes acting aggressively, and at one stage he declared his infatuation with Elizabeth Herbert, Countess of Pembroke (a grand lady in her late 50s). A mad-doctor called Francis Willis treated the king with a restraint chair and a straitjacket, as memorably dramatized in Alan Bennett's play and 1994 film *The Madness of King George*. It was announced on 17 February 1789 that George had recovered, but he relapsed in 1801, 1804 and 1810. The last of these relapses was permanent, and the Prince of Wales, later King George IV, was appointed as regent to take care of the king's active duties. The Regency period (1811–20) is remembered as a time of vice and pleasure among the ruling classes.

In some respects, the king's illness was not worrisome at all, but was in fact rather convenient, since it removed the embarrassing problem of a monarch who had been asking questions about his limited role in the constitution. A much more serious threat was posed by the French Revolution of 1789 – the violent overthrow of the French aristocracy and the execution of Louis XVI – which ultimately brought Britain into a war with the French Republic (starting with the War of the First Coalition, 1792–7). Britain was incited to act when France's Convention, or revolutionary Parliament, offered aid to any other countries that wished to overthrow their kings. The government, fearing popular support for a revolution in Britain, suspended the Habeas Corpus Act so that a group of radicals could be arbitrarily detained. Twelve were accused of treason on flimsy grounds, but they were saved by the common sense of a jury, whose members could not be convinced that demanding an English Convention was tantamount to calling for the death of George III – a case that proves the excellence of the jury system in restricting authoritarianism.

While trying to foment revolution in Britain, the French revolutionaries looked apprehensively upon the expansion of the British Empire. Excluded from power in India, they searched elsewhere for opportunities to counter British supremacy. Their eyes eventually fixed upon Egypt, whose native subjects had long been ruled by a supercilious caste of foreigners called the Mamluks, and which might therefore prove easy to conquer. As Napoleon Bonaparte declared in 1797, 'Truly, to destroy England, we must occupy Egypt.'[4] Napoleon, who fought sixty battles in his life and won fifty-three of them, has a claim to being the finest military strategist the world has ever seen. He successfully captured Egypt in 1798 and ruled it briefly as a colony, establishing the Institut d'Égypte in Cairo for the study of Egyptology. Ultimately, though, the French were forced to surrender Egypt after being defeated by Britain at the Battle of Alexandria. Napoleon overthrew the Directory, France's revolutionary government, in 1799, establishing himself as First Consul, in essence a military dictator, in 1800.

THE BIRTH OF THE UNITED KINGDOM

Back at home, one of the final achievements of Pitt the Younger's first ministry was to pass the 1800 Act of Union, which came into effect in January 1801. It united the kingdoms of Great Britain and Ireland, dissolving the Irish Parliament and decreeing that Ireland should thenceforth return MPs to Westminster. The Union Flag was duly updated to include the Irish red saltire. Pitt was forced to resign when the king heard about his plans to allow Catholic Irishmen to serve as MPs, but he returned to office in 1804. Napoleon was appointed as emperor of the French in the same year, and another war broke out between Britain and France in 1805. Napoleon attempted to invade Britain with Spanish support, but she was saved, not for the first time, both by her naval prowess and by mere geography, the English Channel forming a better frontier than even the most well-fortified borders on land. Napoleon was defeated by Admiral Horatio Nelson and the British Navy at the Battle of Trafalgar, fought off Cape Trafalgar in southern Spain on 21 October 1805. Nelson rallied his men by sending out a rousing maritime signal just prior to the battle: 'England expects that every man will do his duty.' He was fatally injured by a French musketeer and subsequently honoured, against his wishes, with an expensive state funeral.

After Pitt's death in 1806, Lord Grenville formed a short-lived all-star government named the Ministry of All the Talents, most notable for abolishing slavery in Britain in 1807 (slavery was not abolished in the colonies until 1833). Abolition was carried through at an enormous expense to the taxpayer because the government had to compensate slaveowners for their financial loss. In 1812, the prime minister Spencer Perceval was assassinated by a frustrated failed businessman, the only British prime minster to have suffered this fate. In 1814, Napoleon abdicated as emperor and was exiled to the Mediterranean island of Elba, a petty kingdom for him to rule and, with its white sands and clear waters, not an unpleasant place of retirement. He managed to escape from Elba in 1815, but the Duke of Wellington defeated him once and for all at the Battle of Waterloo in Belgium, fought about 8 miles from Brussels on 18 June, at the head of an army of British, Netherlanders and Germans. This defeat put an end to French dreams of becoming 'masters of the world'; Britain had won the second Hundred Years' War.[5] Napoleon was exiled to another agreeable island, this time St Helena in the South Atlantic, where he was kept under close guard until his death in 1821. At the Congress of Vienna (1814–15), chaired by the Austrian Prince Metternich, statesmen and diplomats pored over maps and old treaties, taking upon themselves the great task of restructuring the world in the wake of the Napoleonic wars. Britain was formally granted certain important colonies, including the Cape Colony in South Africa, Ceylon and Mauritius in the Indian Ocean, and Tobago and St Lucia in the West Indies.

THE INDUSTRIAL REVOLUTION

Far from the confines of drawing rooms and royal palaces, great technical advancements were being made in British industry and manufacturing. These would, in due course, lead the nation and then the world into the Industrial Revolution. The Preston-born businessman Richard Arkwright, working with the clockmaker John Kay, patented a successful roller spinning machine in 1769, which greatly increased the efficiency of textile production. Another Lancashire-born inventor, James Hargreaves, patented the spinning jenny, which allowed one worker to spin as much cotton as eight spinners working manually. In 1765, James Watt invented a steam engine that was far more efficient than earlier models. These pioneers paved the way for the mechanization of many other manual activities, a project that attracted significant investment in Britain because of a unique combination of cheap fuel and high wages. The Industrial Revolution had the incidental effect of bringing unprecedented prosperity and influence to the North and the Midlands, which became hotbeds of industry. The rise of factories for mass production provoked riots by the Luddites, a covert group who opposed the mechanization of labour and set out to destroy the new labour-saving machines. They are said to have been named after a disaffected Leicester apprentice called Ned Ludlow or Ned Ludd.

Industrial development was not the only driver of social discontent. Another source of unhappiness was the unpopular Corn Law, passed in 1815 to impose protectionist tariffs on corn and thus making it almost impossible to import foreign produce. This law benefitted English producers but not consumers, whose quality of life deteriorated because they had to spend a higher proportion of their income on food. The Corn Law was traditionally seen as a self-serving decree designed to benefit landowners at the expense of the common man, 'one of the most naked pieces of class legislation in English history'.[6] This does not tell the whole story, for the legislators had other concerns in mind, such as the need to incentivize British farmers so that the country would not become overly reliant on foreign produce.

THE PETERLOO MASSACRE

Such arguments, of course, rang hollow in the ears of hungry men. In March 1817, 5,000 Manchester weavers dubbed 'the blanketeers' marched towards London. They were carrying blankets on their shoulders with the intention of sleeping in the capital until their petition for radical reform had been granted, but were quickly dispersed. On 16 August 1819, there was another huge political rally in Manchester, organized to call for annual Parliaments, universal suffrage and 'liberty' in general. There have been various estimates of the size of the rally, but it is generally agreed that there were around 40,000 participants, half from Manchester and half from elsewhere. Two British cavalry regiments were charged with keeping order, the 15th Hussars and the Cheshire Yeomanry, who charged into the crowd and caused a stampede. There was violence on both sides, and some of the protesters were armed, but undoubtedly the soldiers bore most of the blame, for over 600 civilians were injured and eighteen killed. The events of 16 August became known as the Manchester Massacre or the Peterloo Massacre, the latter a reference to the location (St Peter's Field) combined with an ironic allusion to the Battle of Waterloo.

The government's instinctive response was to blame the protesters, and Parliament passed the Seditious Meetings Act in 1817, which strengthened existing restrictions on political meetings and reaffirmed the rule that assemblies of more than fifty persons were illegal unless authorized in advance. However, the public sympathized with the plight of the Manchester protesters, and so the massacre helped to amplify the calls for political and social reform that characterized the late eighteenth and early nineteenth centuries. King George III's physical and mental health was very poor in the last decade of his life. In his final years he was blind and detached from reality, taking pleasure only in playing the harpsichord. He passed away at Windsor Castle on 29 January 1820, leaving the throne to his son.

THE REIGN OF GEORGE IV

King George IV, who ascended the throne at the age of 57, has been described as 'amiable but egotistical and capricious'.[7] After his accession, he immediately involved the realm in a dishonourable domestic crisis. His relationship with his German wife, Caroline of Brunswick-Wolfenbüttel, had been appalling from the start; he had reportedly needed a glass of brandy to get through the first meeting with his beloved. The two became utterly estranged in 1796, from which date the queen lived the high life in the Mediterranean, surrounding herself with handsome admirers such as the sporty Bartolomeo Bergami. On George's insistence, the Milan Commission was set up in 1818 to gather evidence of the queen's activities abroad. When he became king, he tried to secure a divorce by introducing a bill in Parliament that accused Caroline of 'licentious, disgraceful, and adulterous intercourse'.[8] She probably was an adulteress, but since George was an adulterer himself, he could hardly take the moral high ground. Caroline enjoyed overwhelming public support, and once the bill had passed the House of Lords, the Cabinet decided to drop it rather than risk an embarrassing defeat in the Commons. Caroline accepted a pension of £50,000 per annum on the condition that she quit the United Kingdom permanently, but she died soon after, either of intestinal problems or, as it is said, of heartbreak.

THE TORY ASCENDANCY

The Tory Party enjoyed a parliamentary majority for the whole of George IV's reign. The Tories still thought of themselves as a Whig faction, but had gained sufficient cohesion that it is possible to describe them as a party in the modern sense. The most important prime minister of the reign was Robert Jenkinson, Earl of Liverpool, normally referred to as Lord Liverpool, who served from 1812 to 1827. Son of an MP and baptized at Westminster, Liverpool had been destined for a political career. He was expert at building political consensus, but some argued that he was an unthinking conservative: it was joked that if he had been present on the day of Creation, he would have cried, 'O God, let us preserve the chaos!' Benjamin Disraeli later called him 'the Arch-Mediocrity'.[9] Nevertheless, he had some seemingly sensible views, including the idea that governments frequently do more harm than good when intervening in financial affairs, an insight drawn from the laissez-faire economic principles of the Scottish philosopher Adam Smith. Four decades earlier, Smith had published his seminal *Inquiry into the Nature and Causes of the Wealth of Nations* (1776), which argued that private consumers serving their own interests benefit society more than if they were to consciously seek the 'public good': each individual is 'led by an invisible hand to promote an end which was no part of his intention ... By pursuing his own interest he frequently promotes that of the society ...'.[10] Liverpool's foreign secretary was the political genius George Canning, who later served as prime minister for a few months in 1827.

The social and economic unrest that had characterized the reign of George III continued under his son. At the very outset of the reign, a group of radical activists led by Arthur Thistlewood planned to assassinate the entire Cabinet while they were having dinner at the house of the Earl of Harrowby, Lord President of the Council, and then to proclaim a new British republic. Rather like the Babington Plot of Elizabeth's reign, this conspiracy was infiltrated by a government spy who helped to gather evidence on the culprits. The conspirators were arrested in a loft in Cato Street, near Edgware Road, on 23 February 1820. Five of them were executed, while the rest were transported to New South Wales, which had been claimed for Britain in 1770 by James Cook, captain of the HMS *Endeavour*, and was used as a penal colony. When the conspirators' heads were severed after hanging, the inept hangman dropped one of them, provoking a voice to call out from the crowd, 'Butterfingers!'[11]

Five years later, Britain was racked by a financial crisis caused in part, like the South Sea Bubble of 1720, by incautious mass speculation. In 1824 and 1825, over 600 companies were floated on the stock market, with a total capitalization of over £300 million. Many of these companies were significantly overvalued and financed with paper money. The banknotes of this time were simply pieces of paper promising that a bank would pay out a stated sum in gold whenever the holder of the note demanded it.

Smaller banks were free to issue as many notes as they pleased, so it was possible for a bank to issue more 'money' than it really held, in expectation of future profits. When the investment bubble burst in the troubled winter of 1825, over seventy banks failed. The government believed that this crisis was caused by the feebleness of the county banks, so it saw an act through Parliament in 1826 that allowed smaller banks outside London to operate on a joint-stock basis.

CATHOLIC EMANCIPATION

The great question of the age was the relief, or 'emancipation', of Roman Catholics, who had been formally excluded from public office since the seventeenth century, along with a range of other civil disabilities. The Whigs, still languishing in parliamentary opposition, were united in their belief that Catholics should not suffer discrimination, while the Tories were divided on the matter. There was a degree of public support for the idea because it was hoped that emancipation would placate Ireland. In 1828, during the Tory administration of the Duke of Wellington, the Test and Corporation Acts were repealed, allowing Roman Catholics to occupy high and municipal office without special permission. Wellington did not support Catholic emancipation in principle, but he believed it would prevent civil war in Ireland, and he was politician enough to recognize that the tide of opinion was against him. He thought it was wiser 'to consent to a bad Bill than to run a serious risk of civil disturbance'.[12] In the following year, the Roman Catholic Relief Act was passed to allow Catholics to sit as MPs, to vote in elections and to own land, so long as they swore a new oath of civil allegiance to the king. This oath replaced the Oaths of Supremacy and Allegiance, first introduced in 1534 and 1606 respectively, and it was comparatively inoffensive to Catholics. Though the king strongly opposed the Relief Act, his ministers insisted upon it. On 4 March 1829, he wrote to Wellington: 'I have decided to yield my opinion to that which is considered by the Cabinet to be for the immediate interests of the country... God knows what pain it causes me to write these words.'[13]

'Reform' was a word on everyone's lips in the early nineteenth century. The clamour for change was typified by the figure of Jeremy Bentham, an idealistic man of a million schemes who designed an all-seeing prison named the Panopticon and constantly pestered government ministers to make sweeping changes to the structure of government, society and the law. The increasing liberalization of public opinion is reflected in the criminal law reform of the period, spearheaded by Wellington's Home Secretary, Robert Peel, a Lancashire-born Tory whom we shall have more to say about in the following chapter as an influential prime minister. Under the traditional system, a person could be hanged for picking a pocket and other trivial crimes, but the Criminal Statutes Repeal Act (1827) abolished most capital offences. These reforms coincided with the introduction of England's first professional police force in Greater London, the Metropolitan Police (nicknamed 'Bobbies' after the diminutive form of Robert Peel's first name). Eventually, modern police forces would be rolled out across the entire nation. George IV died on 26 June 1830, at the age of 67, having spent the last months of his life indulging in all the food and drink that would be in short supply on the other side: it is recorded that for breakfast one morning he ate a pie containing two pigeons and three beefsteaks, and washed it down with Moselle wine, champagne, port and brandy. Since he had no surviving issue, the crown passed to William, the third son of George III.

WILLIAM IV AND THE FIRST REFORM ACT

William IV, the Sailor King, inherited the throne at the ripe age of 64, an honour he would have missed out on had George lived for seven more years. William had served in the Royal Navy since his early teens and had lived a far from saintly life, fathering ten children with an actress called Dorothy Phillips. If nothing else, William was fiercely patriotic, illustrated by the fact that when he inherited the crown, he replaced the French and German royal chefs with British staff. The most important event of William's reign was the passage of the First Reform Act (4 June 1832), during the Whig premiership of Charles Grey, 2nd Earl Grey, while the country was in the midst of a terrible cholera epidemic. Calls for parliamentary reform had been a feature of political life for many years. The unreformed House of Commons was made up of 558 MPs, whose seats were distributed in a way that no longer reflected the relative importance of constituencies: for example, decayed port towns continued to send members to Parliament, whereas Birmingham, now an important industrial centre, sent none.

Criticism was directed principally towards the so-called rotten boroughs or pocket boroughs: urban constituencies with electorates so small that the result was either decided by aristocratic influence or could otherwise be easily manipulated. Some constituencies resembled the satirical Dunny-on-the-Wold in *Blackadder*, whose electorate consisted of only one voter, along with three cows, a hen and a 'dachshund named Colin'. The First Reform Act was designed to rationalize the distribution and representation of constituencies. It was supported both by Whigs and by Ultra Tories (the right wing of the Tory Party), the latter believing that Catholic emancipation would never have been passed by a more representative Parliament. Other politicians fiercely opposed reform: the king only assented to the legislation reluctantly, while the Tory Duke of Wellington obstinately protested that Britain already 'possessed a legislature which answered all the good purposes of legislation, and this to a greater degree than any legislature had ever answered in any country whatever'.[14]

Nevertheless, the sceptics and the defenders of England's 'ancient constitution' lost this battle. The Reform Act did away with sixty borough constituencies altogether, while forty-seven more had their representation reduced. Birmingham, Manchester and Leeds gained MPs, and the number of county MPs rose by nearly 60 per cent. There was no attempt to allow poorer men to vote: the qualification for voting in county elections was still ownership of freehold land worth 40 shillings, as it had been for centuries, although Parliament now allowed richer landowners to vote even if they held no freehold. Overall, the size of the electorate rose from around 3.2 per cent to around 4.7 per cent of the population, so Britain was still a long way from universal suffrage. The old Palace of Westminster was burned to the ground in 1834 by a bungled incineration of Exchequer tally sticks, once used to keep track of royal finances, in furnaces beneath the House of Lords. This opened the way for an iconic redesign of the houses of Parliament in the Gothic Revival Style by Sir Charles Barry and A.W.N. Pugin, including a new eastern clock tower colloquially referred to as Big Ben (the nickname originally applied only to the bell).

SOCIAL REFORM AND EMPIRE

The Whigs also passed social legislation, including the 1833 Factory Act, which made it unlawful for children under 13 to work more than eight hours a day, and for children over 13 to work more than twelve hours. The 1834 Poor Law was more morally dubious, for it decreed that no poor relief should be provided to paupers unless they consented to be relocated to workhouses, where they would be forced to engage in dull and exhausting labour. In the religious sphere, William's reign saw the beginning of the Oxford Movement, led by John Keble, Edward Bouverie Pusey and John Henry Newman, the last of whom later converted to Catholicism and became a Cardinal. These men sought to restore High Church principles, including respect for ceremony and clerical authority, to an increasingly liberal Church of England. King William died in 1837, after the onset of several illnesses including acute asthma.

The British Empire had expanded greatly during his reign, with the acquisition of the Cape of Good Hope, the Gambia and the Gold Coast in Africa; Singapore, Malacca and part of Burma in Southeast Asia; and Western and South Australia. It must be understood that the British Empire was not unique, but rather the most successful example of a common type. The nineteenth century was by all accounts the age of empire: almost the whole world was carved up between the British, Spanish, Portuguese, French, Dutch, German, Italian, American, Russian and Ottoman empires. There was no overall strategy to Britain's acquisition of territories, which all came into British hands in different ways, sometimes almost by accident; in 1883, a Liberal historian would declare that Britain had 'conquered and peopled half the world in a fit of absence of mind'.[15] And yet, Britain's imperial possessions were to contribute immeasurably to her power and influence in the century to follow.

14

VICTORIA AND EDWARD (1838–1910)

Queen Victoria, granddaughter of George III and last of the House of Hanover, was crowned in the summer of 1838 at the age of 18. Physically, she could not have been more different from her well-built predecessor and uncle, William, for she never attained a height of above 4ft 11in. Her childhood had been solitary. As a teenager, she had been subject to the cultlike influence of her stepmother, the Duchess of Kent, and Sir John Conroy, comptroller of the duchess's household and possibly also her lover. This pair set up the so-called Kensington system to exercise exclusive influence over the princess and prevent her from finding supporters elsewhere. Fortunately, Victoria was a woman with her own mind and impatient to free herself from their control. As soon as she was queen, she banished Conroy from the court and excluded the Duchess from power. In 1840, she married her first cousin, the German Prince Albert of Saxe-Coburg and Gotha, and willingly submitted to his powerful influence. She held decidedly unprogressive views on women's affairs, arguing that a woman should be 'a helpmate for a man' (a phrase from Genesis 2:18), and that woman would 'become the most hateful, heartless, and disgusting of human beings were she allowed to unsex herself'.[1] Inconsolable when Albert died in 1861, she spent the next four decades of her life in mourning.

Lord Melbourne was prime minister at the time of Victoria's accession, and he remained in office until 1841. His character is so hard to pin down that 'his three twentieth-century biographers might have been writing about different people'.[2] He certainly attained a reputation for indolence; it is said that his preferred response to any scheme of reform was 'Can't you let it alone? It will do very well if you only let it alone.'[3] During Melbourne's administration, Britain fought the First Opium War with China (1839–42), in which the main bone of contention was China's clampdown on illegal British transportation of opium into China, normally done with the connivance of rogue local officials. Opium smoking had been practised in China for over a millennium, but it had been ineffectively outlawed in 1729. After winning a victory against the Daoguang Emperor (the sixth of ten Qing Dynasty emperors), the United Kingdom assumed control of Hong Kong, which would not be returned to China until 1997. Later, in 1899, Britain would also acquire the north-eastern port of Weihaiwei, in an attempt to counterbalance Russian, German and Japanese forays into China. Britain was China's biggest trading partner by the end of the nineteenth century.

ROBERT PEEL

The queen trusted Melbourne and was sorry when he was succeeded by the Liberal Tory Robert Peel in 1841. Peel has been described, paradoxically, both as the 'founder of modern conservatism' and as 'the architect of Victorian Liberalism and Free Trade'.[4] He split his party over the issue of Corn Law repeal. The protectionist Corn Laws, which subjected foreign corn imports to high tariffs, had been unpopular ever since the passage of the first Act in 1815, for it was thought that they drove food prices up for the sole benefit of British landowners. The Manchester-based Anti-Corn Law League was a vocal opponent, organizing campaigns and parties to spread its free-trade message. The Radical MPs Richard Cobden and John Bright promoted free trade in addresses to Parliament, arguing that it would help to draw mankind together in bonds of peace, 'thrusting aside the antagonism of race, creed, and language'.[5] Despite concerted opposition from the right wing of his own party, Peel managed to secure the repeal of the Corn Laws in 1846 with support from a coalition of interest made up of Liberal Tories (117 MPs), Whigs and Radicals. However, Peel was thereafter forced to resign, and his policy success broke the Tory Party, which would not manage to regroup and recover power for nearly three decades.

CHARTISM

Both Peel and his successor as prime minister, the Whig Lord John Russell, had to confront a series of challenges and terrible crises. One was the Irish potato famine (1845–50), caused by the pathogen *Phytophthora infestans*, which led to one-eighth of the population of Ireland dying of starvation (1 million souls). The potato famine increased the rate of Irish emigration to England, which began to happen on a massive scale. The British government was excoriated in Ireland for its lacklustre response. This period also saw the rise of a radical working-class movement called Chartism. Life was tough for the urban working class, who worked excruciatingly long hours and, as often as not, lived in squalid one-room homes. The Chartists drew up the People's Charter of 1838, which called for universal manhood suffrage and payment for MPs. They founded the National Charter Association in Manchester in the summer of 1840, and a national 'monster' petition presented to Parliament in 1842 gathered over 3 million signatures. The Chartists also disseminated their ideas through poetry and newspaper columns, the most well-known paper being the *Northern Star*. One bit of Chartist doggerel about the potato famine condemned Irish landlords who 'spend in luxury the peasant's gain / Whilst they who till their native soil / Are dying fast from hunger's pain'.[6] Parliament dismissed the Chartists' demands, whereupon the agitators responded by organizing industrial strikes.

The movement came to a head in 1848, the 'year of revolution', in which republicans and revolutionaries seized power or forced reforms in France, Germany, Austria, Italy and elsewhere (and in which Marx and Engels's *Communist Manifesto* was first published). The Chartists organized a mass demonstration at Kennington Common in Lambeth on 10 April 1848. In the event, the demonstrators dispersed quietly when instructed to do so by police. The Chartists seemed to have failed, and yet with the passage of time their demands would ultimately be satisfied: the property qualification for MPs was abolished in 1858, and universal manhood suffrage was introduced by the Representation of the People Act in 1918. Only after 1918 was Britain truly a democracy – a country governed by the people. It is sometimes forgotten, in the context of world history, just how new democratic government is.

If Chartism illustrated the fault lines of British society, the Great Exhibition of 1851 demonstrated Britain's confidence. This exhibition, co-organized by Prince Albert and held at the Crystal Palace in Hyde Park for six months, was designed to showcase products, wonders and curiosities from around the world, including glass fountains, telescopes, fabrics, statues, precious stones, industrial machinery and even a reconstructed royal court in medieval style. In February 1852, Russell's government was replaced with the short-lived 'Who? Who?' Conservative ministry, so-called because of the relative obscurity of its members. Lord Derby was prime minister, while Benjamin Disraeli served as Chancellor of the Exchequer. William Gladstone, at this time a Peelite Tory, undermined confidence in the government by picking holes in Disraeli's creative budget, thus kindling an enmity between the two men that would last for the best part of three decades. Upon the collapse of his government, Derby was replaced by the Scottish aristocrat Lord Aberdeen at the head of a coalition of Whigs and Liberal Tories, under whose watch Britain entered the Crimean War (1853–6).

THEIRS NOT TO REASON WHY

The Crimean War, in which Britain, France and Turkey fought side by side against Russia, was essentially an attempt to restrict Russian southward expansion during the slow break-up of the Ottoman Empire, which threatened to disturb the balance of power in the East. The trigger event was the Ottoman sultan's rejection of the 1853 Vienna Note, a plan to ensure peace drawn up by the Great Powers (Great Britain, Austria, France and Prussia). The sultan's refusal was influenced by the advice of the headstrong British ambassador at Constantinople, Sir Stratford Canning. In October 1853, British and French troops arrived at the Dardanelles Strait (also called the Gallipoli Strait) – a narrow waterway of crucial strategic significance connecting Europe with Asia – with the purpose of protecting Constantinople from Russian invasion. War was then officially declared in March 1854. Most of the fighting took place in the Crimean Peninsula, a landmass to the south of the Ukraine surrounded by the Black Sea that had been annexed by Russia in 1783. At the high point of the conflict, over half of British national expenditure went towards the war effort. In October 1854, about 600 cavalrymen from the Light Cavalry Brigade were needlessly sent into harm's way at the Battle of Balaclava near Sebastopol, thanks to poor communication of orders from the generals. About 200 of them died. This blunder was almost immediately commemorated in the poem 'The Charge of the Light Brigade' by the poet laureate, Alfred, Lord Tennyson:

> "Charge," was the captain's cry;
> Theirs not to reason why,
> Theirs not to make reply,
> Theirs but to do and die,
> Into the valley of Death
> Rode the six hundred.[7]

The Allies captured Sebastopol in September 1855, effectively winning the war. When a peace treaty was drawn up on 30 March 1856, Russia was the clear loser, but the high British expenditure and casualty rates (around 22,000 British soldiers dead) were widely criticized by the public at home. Florence Nightingale, a self-trained nurse from a privileged family, rose to fame in her efforts to improve conditions for wounded and sick soldiers in the Crimea, though her importance has been described as 'somewhat overinflated'.[8] The Jamaican-born Mary Seacole, daughter of a Scottish soldier and a mixed-race mother, also provided a degree of medical support and comfort to the British troops by setting up an institution called the British Hotel to provide amenities for army officers. She later wrote a successful autobiography about her experiences entitled *The Wonderful Adventures of Mrs Seacole in Many Lands* (1857).

THE INDIAN MUTINY

Lord Aberdeen, blamed for mismanaging the war effort, was replaced by the Whig (later Liberal) Lord Palmerston in 1855, an aggressive proponent of British interests on the world stage who had previously served as Home Secretary. Two years later, the public was shocked to hear of the Indian Mutiny of 1857, alternatively named the Indian Rebellion. Bengali soldiers in the employment of the East India Company rebelled against British rule at Meerut, near Delhi, triggered by rumours that new Enfield rifles were lubricated with pig fat (offensive to Muslims) and cow fat (offensive to Hindus), or that the British fed Hindus grain mixed with ground-up beef bones.

The military mutiny escalated into wholesale revolution, and the soldiers captured Delhi on 11 May. There were outrages on both sides, and British public opinion hardened against the Indian people: Charles Dickens – remembered as a lovable liberal – wrote in a private letter that if he were Commander-in-chief in India, he would seek to 'exterminate the Race upon whom the stain of the late cruelties rested'.[9] Parliament responded to this crisis by passing the Government of India Act (1858), transferring the rule of India from the East India Company to the Crown. This marked the beginning of almost a century of direct rule in India: the British Raj. Eighteen years later, Victoria was granted the title Empress of India.

This was a time of reform and revolution on all fronts. In 1859, Charles Darwin published *On the Origin of Species* with the London publisher John Murray, which introduced the theories of biological variation and natural selection into mainstream society. Meanwhile, British geologists such as Charles Lyell demonstrated the true age of the earth, which had traditionally been thought to be about 6,000 years old.

Charles Darwin

GLADSTONE AND DISRAELI

In the political realm, a notable constitutional milestone came with the Second Reform Act of 1867, passed during the third administration of Lord Derby, which doubled the British electorate. The years following the Second Reform Act saw the ascendancy of two great political leaders, the first being William Gladstone, leader of the Liberal Party. Having begun as a loose grouping of Whigs and Radicals, the Liberal Party had gradually developed into a well-defined organization, now replacing the Whig Party as the Conservatives' main rival. The Liberal Party was characterized by its championship of liberty in all its manifestations. Gladstone served as prime minister four times (1868–74, 1880–5, 1886 and 1892–4). Having begun his political career as a Tory, he had been transformed into a progressive Liberal. He was a preachy politician, a workaholic who believed that Parliament could be an engine not just of political but also of moral change. His interventionism in domestic affairs was tempered by a belief in thrift and self-help and by his constant desire to reduce government spending.

The thorn in Gladstone's side was Benjamin Disraeli, leader of the Conservative Party, who had made quite a reputation as a popular novelist before his two terms as prime minister in 1868 and from 1874 to 1880. Baptised as an Anglican, he was Britain's first and only Jewish-born prime minister. More languid and practical than Gladstone, he became the queen's pet. In a typical attack on Gladstonian liberalism, he argued that government should be based not upon 'abstract principles' but upon 'the influence of tradition and upon the strength that results from experience'.[10] His politics were defined by a strong attachment to England's ancient constitution, which he thought was the source of her welfare and liberties, although he was quite willing to make cautious, practically conceived reforms. His greatest defect was an unwillingness or inability to acquire a command of detail.

When Gladstone was first appointed as prime minister in 1868, his two priorities were to secure retrenchment (that is, to cut government expenditure) and to disestablish the Anglican Church of Ireland; the latter policy was achieved surprisingly easily with an act of Parliament passed in 1869. There were many other reforms, including the opening of Oxford and Cambridge to men of all

Christian denominations and the introduction of a Civil Service examination in 1870 to ensure that appointments to government departments were made according to merit. This was sometimes called the 'Chinese' principle because China had had a meritocratically appointed civil service for centuries. The 1870 Education Act established school boards to maintain the quality of education throughout England, and secret voting in general elections was established with the Ballot Act of 1872. The swift pace of change evidently did not please everyone, for Gladstone was voted out of office in a Tory landslide in 1874.

Disraeli, who had only served for ten months in his first stint as prime minister, was now reappointed to the premiership, and his second administration lasted until 1880. He led the government from the Commons until 1877, when he was created Earl of Beaconsfield and thus whisked away to the Lords. His administration was dominated by foreign policy, which he found far more interesting than the kind of domestic reforms favoured by Gladstone. With the support of most Tory MPs, Disraeli intervened in the Russo-Turkish War of 1877–8 by sending the British Navy to the Dardanelles, an act of strength that successfully forced Russia to the negotiating table. The Congress of Berlin convened in 1878, chaired by the great German Chancellor Otto von Bismarck. Here Britain played a major role in negotiating the Treaty of Berlin (July 1878), which prohibited further Russian naval expansion and allowed Britain to lease Cyprus in return for offering military assistance to the Ottoman Empire. In 1879, the Zulu War broke out in South Africa, which started unpropitiously with a British defeat at Isandlwana at the hands of King Cetshwayo, though the British army was eventually triumphant. The most famous victory was at Rorke's Drift, where around 100 British troops fought off 4,000 Zulu warriors. Despite his diplomatic successes, Disraeli was defeated in the general election of 1880, mainly because of discontent caused by a faltering economy.

During his election campaign, Gladstone had set out his party's principles and opposition to 'Beaconsfieldism' in a celebrated series of speeches at Midlothian (Edinburghshire), where he was subsequently elected as one of the county's two MPs. These speeches were heard by tens of thousands of people. In his third Midlothian speech, he took a jab at Disraeli's interventionist foreign policy by warning that 'the consequences of an unwise meddling with foreign affairs... will find their way to your pockets in the shape of increased taxation'.[11] To her displeasure, the queen found that she had no choice but to reappoint Gladstone as prime minister in April 1880, an office that he combined with the Chancellorship of the Exchequer for the first two years. One of the achievements of Gladstone's second administration was the 1881 Irish Land Act, passed in response to agitation from the Land League, which sought to strengthen the rights of Irish tenants against their landlords. Parliament also passed the Third Reform Act in 1884, which increased the size of the British electorate to around a quarter of the adult population.

Gladstone resigned in 1885 after a government bill was defeated in the Commons, but by 1886 he was back in office, and he made the historic decision of committing the Liberal Party to the policy of Irish Home Rule, that is, to seek the reestablishment of a separate Parliament in Ireland, which had long been the rallying cry of Charles Stewart Parnell and other Irish Nationalist MPs. Like Robert Peel's Corn Law repeal four decades earlier, Gladstone's policy split his own party, and turned many lifelong Liberal voters into Conservatives. His First Home Rule Bill was defeated in the Commons in 1886, after which Lord Salisbury was appointed as prime minister at the head of a coalition of Conservatives and Liberal Unionists (that is, those Liberals who opposed Irish Home Rule). During his final period of tenure as prime minister (1892–4), Gladstone managed to get a Home Rule bill passed in the Commons, but it was dashed in the Lords, where over 400 peers voted against. The Grand Old Man, as Gladstone had become known to his contemporaries, was once again forced to resign.

THE BOER WAR

After the fall of a brief interim Liberal ministry headed by the Earl of Rosebery, Lord Salisbury was reappointed prime minister in 1895. The final years of Salisbury's third premiership were dominated by the Boer War (1899–1902). The Boers were a race of farmers of Dutch descent who governed two republics located to the north of the British Cape Colony: the Transvaal Republic and the Orange Free State. There was ongoing conflict between the British and the Boers, partly fuelled by the number of Britons – contemptuously called 'outlanders' – who had arrived in the Transvaal to mine diamonds. War finally broke out in 1899, and Britain successfully annexed both Boer republics. The conflict, which was formally concluded by the Peace of Vereeniging in May 1902, cost the British treasury over £200 million, and both colonies were in any case regranted self-government a few years later. During the war, Britain housed displaced women and children in 'concentration camps' to be fed and sheltered, a fact later seized upon by the Nazi official Hermann Göring to argue that the British could take no moral high ground on the subject. The new Liberal leader, Sir Henry Campbell-Bannerman, condemned the camps as 'methods of barbarism', which they no doubt were, though it must be remembered that internment camps were an ordinary part of warfare in the nineteenth and twentieth centuries.[12] The War Office sent altruistic British women into the camps to check their conditions, including the suffragist Millicent Fawcett, but many camps remained unsanitary, and a shocking 20,000 inmates died. Salisbury resigned as prime minister on 11 July 1902.

Outside the realm of politics, Victoria's reign is known for the development of the railways, funded not by the state but by private investment. This led to some inefficiency, as rival companies sometimes built different lines to the same place. The Portsmouth-born civil engineer Isambard Kingdom Brunel was appointed to oversee the construction of the Great Western Railway connecting London with Bristol in 1833, when he was only 26. The late Victorian period was also a time of imperial expansion, in part spurred on by Germany's rival territorial ambitions. Major European powers staked competing claims to lands in Africa in a period of rivalry that became known as the Scramble for Africa. Later British imperialism had a prominent moral dimension. When the Scottish missionary David Livingstone explored sub-Saharan Africa, the unknown continent, he hoped to disseminate 'Christianity, Commerce and Civilization'. Some other notable imperialists were General Gordon, who served in China after the Second Opium War (1856–60) and was killed by Mahdists (a radical Muslim sect), in Sudan in 1885;

Cecil Rhodes, who made a fortune in the diamond fields of South Africa and became prime minister of the Cape in 1890; and Colonel Robert Baden-Powell, founder of the Boy Scouts, who withstood the Boers at the Siege of Mafeking (1899–1900). Late Victorian public-school boys were brought up to acquire the abilities, values, knowledge and character necessary to assume positions of responsibility across the globe – this was the great age of field sports, the classics, adventure stories and a stiff upper lip. Queen Victoria, who had reigned for longer than most people could remember, passed away on 22 January 1901.

Queen Victoria

THE REIGN OF EDWARD VII

King Edward VII, son of Victoria and Albert, was the first monarch of the House of Saxe-Coburg–Gotha (known from 1917 as the House of Windsor). In his early years, he had been something of a playboy, fond of gambling, smoking, yachting, hunting and womanizing. Now in his late 50s, he was popular with the public at large, and somewhat more active in political affairs than his mother had been, especially in the realm of foreign policy. Very soon after his accession, the published philosopher and Conservative politician Arthur James Balfour was appointed prime minister. Balfour's ministry, which lasted for two and a half years, was not a great success. Foreign policy, headed by the Marquess of Lansdowne, was dominated by fears of Russian and German expansion. It worked to Britain's benefit that Japan decided to go to war with Russia in 1904 and – to everyone's surprise – won. Britain and Japan had been in an anti-Russian alliance since 1902, which was to last until 1923.

As for domestic policy, Balfour's ministry has been described as 'stumbling from one disaster to another'.[13] He and Joseph Chamberlain divided Conservative opinion by expressing views on free trade that were contrary to the prevailing orthodoxy, as they believed that tariffs ought to be introduced both to protect imperial trade and to retaliate against protectionist trading partners. One real achievement was the Education Act of 1902, which brought all schools under the jurisdiction of Local Educational Authorities, and thus helped to standardize the quality of education, but even this act did nothing to increase the government's popularity at the time.

THE LIBERAL ASCENDANCY

The Tory Party, which had governed England for eighteen of the past twenty years, now found that its run of success was over. At a general election in 1906, the Liberal Party won an incredible 400 seats out of a total of 670, inaugurating nearly two decades of Liberal domination of Westminster. The government also counted many Labour MPs among its allies. H.H. Asquith, who became prime minister in 1908, is best remembered for having founded the welfare state. The government introduced a state pension and a system of National Insurance, the brainchild of the Chancellor of the Exchequer, David Lloyd George. The welfare state was built on the foundation of a thriving economy: Britain still produced more than a quarter of global manufacturing exports. It was also overdue, since 30 per cent of the nation lived in poverty. Still, well-intentioned reforms sometimes had unintended negative consequences. For example, in response to a 1908 law limiting miners' work shifts to eight hours, employers began to divide each day into three eight-hour shifts, which meant that miners were forced to work at unreasonable times – this was the cause of the Durham Coal Strike of 1910. Some socialists supported the labour reforms, while others thought they were a cynical attempt to buy off working-class opponents. The Liberal government also oversaw a massive expansion of the civil service, despite the opposition of small-state advocates such as the constitutional lawyer A.V. Dicey.

Many of these changes were also anathema to the House of Lords, of whose members about 60 per cent identified as Conservative. The Lords triggered a constitutional crisis in 1909 by voting down Lloyd George's People's Budget, breaching a century-old unwritten convention that the Lords should not veto money bills. By threatening to pack the House of Lords through the mass creation of Liberal peers – a strategy lifted from Queen Anne's playbook – Asquith successfully coerced the Lords into agreeing to the Parliament Act of 1911. This act ordained that the Lords could not veto or amend money bills, and that they could only veto other Commons bills for a maximum of two years. Asquith's opponents in the Commons called him a traitor, in contravention of the rules of unparliamentary language.

King Edward died in the midst of the People's Budget crisis, in 1910, after catching a serious cold. He was succeeded by his middle-aged son, George. The country that George V came to rule was very different from that which had been inherited by his grandmother, Victoria. Indeed, H.G. Wells foretold in his 1901 book *Anticipations* – which also predicted inventions such as air conditioning – that the twentieth century would be a time of 'social confusion' because of rapid technological changes.[14] While the leisured classes were still living it large, their inexorable decline had begun. Labourers and servants, meanwhile, found that their traditional occupations were swiftly disappearing with the popularization of labour-saving machines. Other great changes were afoot in the religious sphere. English thought and culture were becoming increasingly secular, as the established Church lost much of its influence on the hearts and minds of the nation. Just over forty years later, the poet Philip Larkin would wonder what would happen to the nation's churches when they 'fall completely out of use'.[15] At the close of the relatively stable Edwardian period, there were also only four years to go until the outbreak of the Great War, when hell would be unleashed upon the world.

15

THE EARLY TWENTIETH
CENTURY (1910–1953)

King George V reigned for the duration of the First World War and died three years before the outbreak of the Second. He was not cut from the same cloth as his predecessor, for in place of mistresses and bad habits he substituted seriousness, soberness and frugality. He was also unimpeachably English, once declaring that no true Englishman would refuse an offer of roast beef on a Sunday. His seriousness and patriotism help to explain why the monarchy continued to flourish in Britain during the quarter-century of his reign, while elsewhere 'the world witnessed the disappearance of five Emperors, eight Kings and eighteen minor dynasties'.[1] This was, however, an age of social and cultural fragmentation. British society ceased to be understood as an organic whole and began to look instead like a patchwork of rival interest groups, with farmers pitted against landowners; artisans against employers; conservatives against liberals; and men against women – an unfortunate trend that has its parallels in the present day. The popular historian George Dangerfield wrote that this was the age of the 'strange death' of liberalism, the end of what had been the dominant philosophy in British politics for half a century. Britain's last ever Liberal prime minister hung up the keys to Downing Street in 1922, and the Labour Party was poised to replace the Liberals as the Conservatives' chief opponent.

The early years of George V's reign witnessed a concerted effort to secure women the vote in general elections. The National Union of Women's Suffrage Societies (NUWSS), founded in 1897 by Millicent Fawcett, organized 'respectable' campaigns that involved debates and petitions to Parliament, while the Women's Social and Political Union (WSPU), founded in 1903 by Emmeline and Christabel Pankhurst, rsorted to violence, vandalism and militancy. The former group are often called 'suffragists', and the latter, 'suffragettes'. One well-known suffragette was the Oxford-educated Emily Wilding Davison, who died after throwing herself under the king's horse at the Epsom Derby in June 1913 (one year after the sinking of the RMS *Titanic*). Not all suffragettes were heroines. Mary Richardson, who vandalized a nude female painting by Diego Velázquez in the National Gallery to further the cause, later became a card-carrying fascist. Some crossed the line into promoting hatred of men, and their peace-loving allies suspected that such attitudes hindered the cause. Suffragettes imprisoned for offences often went on hunger strike, which Parliament tried to solve with the so-called Cat and Mouse Act (1913). This act allowed starving prisoners to be temporarily released and then recaptured once they had eaten a good meal. After much campaigning, women over 30 finally gained the vote in 1918, and the minimum age was lowered to 21 in 1928.

THE FIRST WORLD WAR

The First World War was fought between the Central Powers (chiefly Germany, Austria–Hungary and Turkey) and the Allies (chiefly Great Britain, France, Italy, Japan, Russia and the United States). Prior to the outbreak of war, tension had been building between the great powers of Europe due to their rival territorial ambitions. For example, Russia was determined to frustrate German plans to seize control of the two Turkish Straits (the Dardanelles and the Bosphorus). Historians disagree over whether Germany deliberately sought a war or whether hostilities broke out almost by accident. One of the most unconventional arguments is that the war had no 'profound causes' but was caused unwittingly by military preparations and railway timetables.[2] Early twentieth-century Germany was strikingly militaristic, and there is some evidence that she had been planning a naval war against Britain since at least as early as 1901. The British army, meanwhile, had been reorganized in preparation for large-scale conflict by Richard Burton Haldane at the War Office.

A crisis in the Balkans was the spark that finally set the tinder-box alight. Austria annexed Bosnia–Herzegovina in 1908, and six years later, a Bosnian nationalist called Gavrilo Princip, funded by the government of Serbia, responded by assassinating the Austrian Archduke Franz Ferdinand with a bullet through the throat. This triggered a chain of events leading to the outbreak of world war: Austria–Hungary declared war on Serbia (which was under Russian protection) on 28 July 1914, and Germany declared war on Russia, France and Belgium between 1 and 4 August. When Germany invaded Belgium on 4 August, Britain, who had signed the Treaty of London in 1839 to guarantee Belgian neutral-ity, declared war on Germany. The country was immediately placed on a war footing. Parliamentary elections were suspended. Some believed that the war would be 'over by Christmas', though this phrase was nowhere near as ubiquitous at the time as popular tradition suggests; the new War Secretary, Lord Kitchener, accurately pre-dicted that the war would last four years. Germany too had hoped for a swift victory: the objective of her 'Schlieffen Plan' was a rapid conquest of France before the Allies had had time to mobilize, but this plan failed because the Allies checked Germany's advance at the First Battle of the Marne (6–12 September 1914). The remainder of the fighting on France's eastern border, the so-called Western Front, assumed the form of louse-ridden trench warfare and painful stalemate.

New weapons and strategies robbed the hostilities of any chivalry that might have characterized past warfare: this was a war of barbed wire, poison gas, tanks (a new invention) and heavy artillery. One fearful innovation was the German Zeppelin, a hydrogen airship used to drop bombs on strategic infrastructure, often killing civilians in the process. This was also a truly global war. Over 1 million Indians fought for the Allies, while the first president of China, Yuan Shikai, agreed to send 140,000 illiterate peasants to France to work as indentured labourers on the Allied side. Almost immediately after the outbreak of war, Britain blockaded Germany, cutting off her supplies of contraband such as rubber and textiles, and constraining German exports. In the Gallipoli Campaign of 1915–16, the Allies, supported by Australian and New Zealand forces, attempted to force the Dardanelles Strait and occupy Constantinople, but Kemal Atatürk, later president of Turkey, managed to fight them off. After this defeat, Asquith succumbed to pressure to incorporate Conservatives into his Cabinet in the spring of 1916.

LIONS LED BY DONKEYS?

Britain imposed a policy of general conscription in May 1916, the first time this had ever been attempted, which saw 6 million able-bodied men between the ages of 18 and 51 join the army. A particularly horrific battle in the same year was the Somme (1 July–13 November 1916), orchestrated by General Sir Douglas Haig, which has become a byword for pointless slaughter. Over 100,000 Allied troops were mown down in return for very modest strategic gains, which led to a grim joke that Haig proved himself an excellent Scottish general by getting so many English soldiers killed. The Remembrance Day poppy is an allusion to the poppy-strewn fields surrounding the River Somme in Picardy.

Asquith, who lost his own son at the Somme, resigned on 6 December and was replaced by another Liberal whose star was in the ascendant, David Lloyd George. Affectionately nicknamed 'the Welsh Wizard', Lloyd George headed an efficient War Cabinet of five men. In December 1916, France won a pyrrhic victory at the Battle of Verdun, which had a restorative effect on French morale but required such expenditure of men and materials that it crippled the army. By the end of 1916 it was obvious to everyone that the Central Powers had the upper hand, but the Allies eventually clawed victory from the jaws of defeat, in part thanks to the intervention of the United States. The US President Woodrow Wilson, who had initially been reluctant to join the war, was persuaded to change his mind by Germany's expanding use of submarine warfare, which posed a threat to American shipping. The US Congress declared war on Germany on 6 April 1917.

A few months later, Haig (now promoted to Field Marshal) planned a British offensive in Flanders supported by Canada, the Third Battle of Ypres, also called the Battle of Passchendaele (July–November 1917). As at the Somme, Haig won a limited victory at a tremendous cost of life. The British government introduced rationing in 1918, a successful policy that ensured an equitable distribution of food. Food shortages caused much greater trouble in Germany, where desperate citizens began taking to the streets to demand peace. Unfortunately, there were fundamental divisions between the Reichstag (German parliament) and the military leadership as to what such a peace should look like. Russia, racked by the Bolshevik Revolution, exited the war with the Treaty of Brest-Litovsk in March 1918. Germany eventually concluded an armistice with the other Allied powers on 11 November 1918, after the Allies smashed through the Hindenburg Line in October. By the time the armistice was signed, around 750,000 British lives had been lost.

A peace conference called in Paris was dominated by representatives from the so-called Big Four: Great Britain, France, Italy and the United States. The Treaty of Versailles was signed on 28 June 1919, based largely on Woodrow Wilson's Fourteen Points. The War Guilt Clause (Article 231) stated that 'Germany accepts the responsibility... for causing all the loss and damage to which the Allied and Associated Governments and their nationals have been subjected'. This admission of guilt made it possible for the Allies to demand from Germany billions of pounds in reparations, which aroused German resentment; some of the victors were of the opinion that the Allies should 'squeeze the orange until the pips squeak'.[3] Although Lloyd George signed the treaty, he had reservations about the wisdom of reparations. Likewise, the economist John Maynard Keynes argued that the reparations were a betrayal of the terms of the November armistice.

THE INTERWAR YEARS

A general election was called almost immediately after the end of the war. Lloyd George retained the premiership at the head of a Conservative-majority coalition, while the Labour Party increased its number of seats from thirty-nine to fifty-nine. In a by-election held the following year (1919), the constituency of Plymouth Sutton elected Britain's first ever female MP, a wealthy American named Nancy, Viscountess Astor, who used her position in the Conservative Party and the House of Commons to press for temperance and improvements to education. Meanwhile, there were ongoing troubles in Ireland. Parliament had approved the Home Rule Act in 1914, paving the way for Irish self-government, but Irish politicians were impatient that its provisions had still not been enacted. In 1919, the Sinn Fein party set up an Irish Parliament, the Dáil, and a network of republican courts without the permission of the British government. More extreme tactics were brought into play by the Irish Republican Army (IRA), founded in January 1919, which stockpiled arms and began a guerrilla war against the British administration.

The British government decided to fight fire with fire by introducing two units of special constables to Northern Ireland, the Black and Tans and the Auxiliary Division, the latter of which has been described as 'an autonomous terror squad'.[4] Lloyd George secured the passage of the Government of Ireland Act in 1920, which sought to establish two Irish Parliaments, a southern assembly at Dublin and a northern assembly at Belfast. The Ulster Unionists reluctantly accepted this settlement, but Sinn Fein denied the authority of the southern Parliament. In a treaty signed on 6 December 1921, the British government conceded to the Irish demands, and effectively authorized a partition between Northern Ireland and an independent Free State of Ireland (formally established in December 1922 and named the Republic of Ireland after 1937). Far from solving the Irish problem, this treaty set the stage for the Irish Civil War of 1922–3, fought between the Irregulars, who rejected the treaty, and the Army of the Irish State, who accepted it.

THE RISE OF LABOUR

Coalition government came to an end in 1922, when Lloyd George was succeeded as prime minister by the Canadian-born businessman Andrew Bonar Law, leader of the Conservative Party, who served for just over six months before resigning due to infirmity. He was replaced by another Conservative, Stanley Baldwin, in May 1923. Baldwin was a man of integrity, even to the point of priggishness, and one could see that he was motivated by fiercely held moral and political ideals. Though he knew how to project authority, he was nervous and awkward under the surface; he detested parties, constantly fidgeting with his pipe and unsure what to do with his hands. Baldwin immediately called an unnecessary general election to consolidate his position, but to his horror, the Conservative Party lost ninety seats and thus also lost their parliamentary majority.

After a government bill failed to pass the Commons in January 1924, Baldwin resigned the premiership and gave way for Britain's first ever Labour government, under the leadership of James Ramsay MacDonald. It is necessary to backtrack slightly to explain Labour's rise to power. The Third Parliamentary Reform Act of 1884 had allowed, for the first time, a significant number of working-class men to vote. The socialist Independent Labour Party (ILP), led by the Scottish trade unionist and former miner Keir Hardie, was founded in 1893. Hardie, who wore an iconic deerstalker hat, oversaw the creation of an alliance between the socialists and the trade unionists, who had frequently found themselves locking horns (the trade unions traditionally supported the Liberal Party). The new alliance was cemented by the creation of the Labour Representation Committee (LRC) in 1900, led both by trade unionists and socialists.

The LRC became even more popular among trade unionists after the Taff Vale judgment of 1901, in which the House of Lords affirmed that employers could sue unions for damages; between 1901 and 1902, membership of the LRC more than doubled to 861,000. In 1906, the LRC was renamed the Labour Party. The party's newfound importance is reflected in the fact that Labour ministers served in the wartime coalition government. However, between 1906 and 1918, the number of Labour MPs hovered at around thirty-five to sixty. The real breakthrough came in the general election of 1922, held five years after the Bolshevik Revolution in Russia, in which Labour fielded 414 candidates and won 142 seats, beating the Liberal Party for the first time but still lagging far behind the Conservatives. Most of Labour's electoral gains were in formerly Liberal working-class constituencies. In 1924, Labour won 191 seats, enabling the party to form a short-lived minority government. Many of the new Labour MPs were from mining and other labouring backgrounds.

The Labour prime minister Ramsay MacDonald, with his lilting voice and handlebar moustache, was the illegitimate son of a maidservant, born in the small Scottish fishing town of Lossiemouth. He began his political career in 1888 as a campaign organizer for a minor Liberal politician, and he joined the ILP in 1894 and later became secretary of the LRC. He was on very good terms with King George, though he could be a windbag; Winston Churchill quipped that he had 'the gift for compressing the largest number of words into the smallest amount of thought'. MacDonald could not implement a full socialist policy because of his reliance on Liberal support, so he focussed on improving working and living conditions for the poor. His principles became somewhat compromised by the perks of high office and the realities of governance, perennially the 'occupational hazard of Labour leaders'.[5]

COMMUNISM AND FASCISM

When MacDonald lost a vote of no confidence in 1924, a general election was called for 29 October. Four days before the election, a sensational letter was published in the press that had allegedly been written by the Russian Grigory Zinoviev, chairman of the Comintern's executive committee. This letter encouraged British communists to infiltrate the Labour Party as a means of advancing the Communist Revolution. It may have been forged with the connivance of British officials at the very top, to scare voters into voting Conservative. Whether or not this letter had an appreciable effect on the election result, Labour lost forty seats, and the Conservatives were propelled back into power. Baldwin was reappointed as prime minister, and this time he served until 1929, with Winston Churchill as his Chancellor of the Exchequer. Foreign Secretary Austen Chamberlain helped to arrange the Locarno Pact of 1925 between Germany, France and Britain, which reaffirmed the Treaty of Versailles and opened the way for Germany's admission to the League of Nations, founded in the hopes of preventing a future war. Another of the ministry's priorities was to restore trust between industrialists and their employers. As a result it exercised a political moderation that led to accusations of 'semi-socialism', though Labour saw things differently, charging the prime minister with being in thrall to 'organized capital'.[6] Baldwin managed to put down Britain's first and only general strike after only nine days in 1926, which bolstered his political reputation.

Labour returned to power in 1929 after winning 287 seats in the general election of 30 May, which gave it a majority over the Conservatives in Parliament but not an overall majority. The firebrand Oswald Mosley, who had joined the Labour Party in 1924, was appointed as Chancellor of the Duchy of Lancaster, a moderately important non-Cabinet role. This was to prove the high point of his career in the Labour Party, for he soon left to institute the short-lived New Party, and after the failure of this venture, he founded the British Union of Fascists in 1932. However, the militaristic and mob tendencies of fascism scared off genteel support, and so Mosley's fascist movement ultimately foundered after reaching a high point of 20,000 members. Fascism would resurface in Britain after the end of the Second World War, with regular clashes between fascists and anti-fascists on the streets of London. One of the defining moments of the 1929–31 Labour administration, and indeed one of the defining moments of British naval history, was the Five-Power Naval Conference of January 1930, in which Britain agreed to the principle of parity between the British and US Navies, ending Britain's long stretch of naval pre-eminence.

UNEMPLOYMENT

One of Ramsay MacDonald's greatest challenges was widespread unemployment, which had reached a level of 2 million as early as 1921 and was now further exacerbated by the global repercussions of the 1929 Wall Street Crash, reaching a peak of 3 million by 1933. After the Cabinet repeatedly failed to agree on an appropriate response to unemployment, the prime minister had the king dismiss its members and set up a National Government consisting of four Labour ministers, four Conservative ministers and two Liberals. Baldwin was appointed Lord President of the Council, essentially MacDonald's second-in-command. At the general election of October 1931, this National Government won 554 seats, most of them held by Conservative MPs, and Ramsay MacDonald was expelled from the Labour Party. England was thus in the odd position of having an apostate 'Labour' prime minister and a mostly Conservative government and Commons. In 1932, about fifty years since Gladstone had called protectionism an 'exploded doctrine', the government introduced a protective tariff on manufactures in an attempt to arrest economic decline.[7] Two years later, an Unemployment Act was passed to regularize the system of unemployment relief. Though his mental and physical health declined during these years, MacDonald tried to retain a grip on Cabinet business and attended conferences concerning reparations and disarmament, which failed to arrest the drift towards war. Adolf Hitler was appointed Chancellor of Germany in January 1933, and he announced in March 1935 that his government would disregard the Versailles restrictions on German rearmament.

THE ABYSSINIAN CRISIS

Labour performed poorly in the general election of 1935, polling at only fifty-two seats, and Baldwin, now aged 67, was once again appointed as prime minister. The most notable event of Baldwin's third ministry was the Abyssinian crisis. On 3 October 1935, Italy – under the leadership of the fascist prime minister Benito Mussolini – invaded Abyssinia (Ethiopia) in the hopes of establishing an Italian empire. This was in clear violation of Italy's obligations as a member of the League of Nations. Britain considered sanctioning the export of oil to Italy in retaliation, but it soon transpired that this would be impracticable. Instead, the British foreign secretary Sir Samuel Hoare and the French prime minister Pierre Laval hammered out the secret Hoare–Laval Pact (1935), which would have allowed Italy to keep hold of Abyssinia, but the plan had to be dropped after it was leaked and publicly denounced for its lack of principle. The Italian army captured the Abyssinian capital,

Addis Ababa, in the spring of 1936, and Emperor Haile Selassie fled into exile. Not only did these events provoke criticism of the British government at home, but they also utterly undermined the credibility of the League of Nations. King George V died in the midst of this crisis, on 20 January 1936, at the age of 70, after making enquiries about the state of the Empire.

THE ABDICATION OF EDWARD VIII

George V was succeeded by his eldest son, King Edward VIII, who travelled by aeroplane from Sandringham to London to be proclaimed king, an unprecedented mode of transport for a sitting monarch. John Betjeman, later poet laureate, captured the mood of public astonishment at Britain's new king, who seemed to herald the beginning of a fresh and modern era:

> Old men who never cheated, never doubted,
> Communicated monthly, sit and stare
> At the new suburb stretched beyond the run-way
> Where a young man lands hatless from the air.[8]

But the reign of this hatless king would end before the year was out. Despite the usual flood of panegyric that followed his accession, there was concern over the king's love affair with the American divorcee Wallis Simpson, whom he had first met in 1931, and who was still married to her second husband. Though Edward and Wallis had an apparently pleasant romantic life, some courtiers and politicians believed the king was infatuated. The situation was complicated further by the fact that both king and mistress apparently had a soft spot for Nazism and fascism.

Matters came to a head in the autumn of 1936, when it transpired that Wallis Simpson was planning to divorce her husband. In November, the king told the prime minister, Stanley Baldwin, that he intended to wed Wallis; Baldwin replied that if he did, he would have to abdicate, given Wallis's divorcee status. The king found few men on his side because he had proved himself temperamentally ill-suited to the official business of kingship.

On hearing of the prime minister's resolve, Wallis tried to persuade Edward to give up the idea of marriage, but his mind was set, and he renounced the throne on 11 December 1936. In a farewell broadcast to the nation, he bluntly declared: 'I now quit altogether public affairs.'[9] Styled Duke of Windsor after his abdication, he married his sweetheart at the Château de Candé in Touraine, a fairytale Renaissance castle. The newlyweds visited Nazi Germany, where Edward saluted the Führer and surveyed the improvements the German government had been making to the working conditions of labourers – a great propaganda win for the Nazi party.

THE REIGN OF GEORGE VI

The new king of Great Britain and Northern Ireland, George VI, was crowned on 12 May 1937, with his predecessor listening in to the ceremony on the radio. George's family life was more agreeable to the public than Edward's. Married to a scandal-free noblewoman, he doted on his two daughters, and his unimpeachable character helped to maintain the popularity of the monarchy: as the Labour politician Herbert Morrison declared in 1954, 'no monarchy in the world is more secure or more respected by the people than ours'.[10] Though his vices were few, George was afflicted by a speech impediment that made the public-speaking duties of a monarch painful for him. Sixteen days after the king's accession, Neville Chamberlain replaced Stanley Baldwin as prime minister, having previously served as Chancellor of the Exchequer for six years. Born in Birmingham, Chamberlain had lived an eventful life, including a youthful venture to grow sisal, a plant used for making rope, in the Bahamas.

Chamberlain is best remembered as the prime minister who 'appeased' fascist Italy and Nazi Germany. When Germany flagrantly breached the Treaty of Versailles by remilitarizing the Rhineland in March 1936 and invading Austria in the same month, Britain rewarded her bad behaviour by agreeing to roll back many of the limitations imposed by the treaty. Britain also lifted sanctions that had been imposed against Italy during the Abyssinian crisis. At the Munich Conference of 29–30 September 1938, Britain and France agreed to concede to Germany the Sudetenland, a slice of German-speaking Bohemia and Moravia that had been given to the newly formed Czechoslovakia after the First World War. Chamberlain returned to Britain in high spirits and delivered an infamously misguided speech in front of the media on the runway of Heston Aerodrome. He presaged the arrival of European peace, naively trusting Hitler's assurances to that effect. Contrary to popular memory, he did not say, 'I have in my hand a piece of paper', but rather, 'This morning I had another talk with the German Chancellor, Herr Hitler, and here is the paper which bears his name upon it as well as mine.'[11]

Three journalists later published a pseudonymous pamphlet entitled *Guilty Men* (1940), which argued that appeasement was a foolish policy responsible for encouraging German aggression. This remains the most influential view, although historians have argued for decades about the precise nature of appeasement and about the wisdom of the policy. Revisionist historians such as A.J.P. Taylor attempted to rehabilitate Chamberlain's reputation by arguing that he could not have foreseen Hitler's territorial ambitions. Ian Kershaw has argued that British and French politicians suffered from a naivety that sprang from their gentlemanly background: 'Their upbringing, experience and political schooling left them utterly unprepared to encounter a gangster on the international stage.'[12] In any case, appeasement did nothing to arrest the march towards world war. Hitler almost immediately broke the promises he had made at the Munich Conference by pushing further into Czechoslovakia, occupying Prague and establishing Bohemia and Moravia as German protectorates. Chamberlain finally abandoned his pacifism, committing Britain to war if Germany should continue her course of aggression.

THE SECOND WORLD WAR

The combatants in the Second World War included Germany, Italy and Japan (the Axis Powers) and Great Britain, France, the United States, the Soviet Union and China (the Allies). The Republic of Ireland remained neutral, as did Sweden, Switzerland, Portugal, Spain and Turkey. Germany's initial strategy, sometimes termed *Blitzkrieg*, or 'lightning warfare', was to capture as many enemy targets as possible before the Allies had an opportunity to prepare effective defences. On 1 September 1939, Hitler invaded Poland without formally declaring war, and a couple of weeks later, the Soviets also invaded from the east, the plan being that both aggressors would carve up the country between them. On 3 September, Britain declared war on Germany. Rationing was reintroduced in Britain in the following January. In the spring of 1940, Germany occupied Copenhagen and Oslo and captured all the main ports of Norway. Winston Churchill, First Lord of the Admiralty, explained the details of the German achievements in a rambling speech to the House of Commons on 11 April, in which, according to those present, he seemed totally exhausted.

Britain's prospects were already beginning to seem bleak. On 9 May 1940, Chamberlain resigned to make way for a war coalition consisting of Conservative, Labour and Liberal MPs. He was replaced as prime minister on 10 May by Churchill, a man who had a mixed record of political success and was far from universally popular among the upper echelons of the Conservative Party. Having begun his career as a Conservative MP, he had joined the Liberal Party in 1904 after falling out with his own party over the issue of free trade (which he supported). He had served in Asquith's Liberal Cabinet from 1908, as Home Secretary from 1910 and as First Lord of the Admiralty from 1911, in which capacity he had overseen the catastrophic Gallipoli Campaign of 1915–6. In 1924, he had been welcomed back into the Conservative Party and appointed as Chancellor of the Exchequer. He was 65 when he finally attained the premiership.

Immediately after his appointment, Churchill had to deal with an emergency that could have lost Britain the war: the stranding of hundreds of thousands of British and French soldiers at Dunkirk (Dunkerque), a charming port town on the northern tip of France. On 10 May 1940, Britain had sent the British Expeditionary Force to France. After being defeated at the Battle of Sedan, the British and French armies were forced to retreat to a poorly defensible position, and Churchill thought that Britain was on the brink of 'the greatest military disaster in our long history'. Fortunately, on 25 May, the British commander Lord Gort saved the day by sending the 5th and 50th Divisions to block the advance of the German army and buy time for an Allied retreat to Dunkirk. On

27 May, the Allies began a naval evacuation of troops named Operation Dynamo. Over the next six days, around 250,000 British soldiers were brought back to Britain, many in small vessels. Then, between 3–4 June, around 53,000 French soldiers were similarly evacuated. Churchill delivered his most celebrated speech in the House of Commons, lauding the close-run rescue mission and expressing his confidence that the British people 'shall prove ourselves once again able to defend our island home, to ride out the storm of war, and to outlive the menace of tyranny'.[13] Later that month, Paris was captured, and Germany and France signed an armistice that effectively indicated France's surrender.

Churchill now had to decide whether to come to terms with Germany, whose war machine seemed unbeatable, or to fight to the death, and after some wavering he settled on the latter course. On 10 July 1940 began the three-month-long Battle of Britain,

Sir Winston Churchill

a series of air campaigns fought between the RAF and the German Luftwaffe. Germany launched an ambitious attack on British targets on 18 August, but her pilots were successfully engaged by RAF fighters, who destroyed or captured over seventy German aircraft. On 7 September, Germany changed her strategy from bombing strategic military targets to bombing civilians in London, which of course became known as the Blitz. Though the RAF successfully countered German day raids, its pilots were less successful in defending against nocturnal attacks. The Battle of Britain officially ended on 31 October, but German air raids continued after this date; for instance, there was a significant raid just after Christmas 1940.

THE USSR AND THE USA ENTER THE WAR

Immediately prior to the outbreak of war, Germany and the Soviet Union had signed a non-aggression pact, but this was purely a matter of strategic convenience; Hitler had himself identified Russia as Germany's greatest threat in *Mein Kampf* (1925–7), and the Nazis thought that Bolshevism was a Jewish conspiracy. On 22 June 1941, Germany unilaterally broke the non-aggression pact by invading the Soviet Union, tempted by the rich natural resources of Russia. The Nazi invasion, Operation Barbarossa, was a three-pronged attack aiming to capture Leningrad, Kiev and Moscow. The conflict between these two titans was by far the deadliest part of the entire war. While Kiev swiftly fell into German hands, Moscow and Leningrad proved to be more difficult targets. In September, the Nazis besieged Leningrad, cutting off the city's supply lines and allowing a million of its citizens to starve to death. German tanks got within 12 miles of Moscow in November but were driven back just as victory was within sight.

Another giant, the USA, entered the war in 1941. On 7 December, Japan made a surprise attack on Pearl Harbor, a United States naval base on Oahu Island, Hawaii. Hundreds of aircraft and several battleships were destroyed, including the USS *Arizona* and *Oklahoma*. The Japanese intended to keep the Americans occupied and immobilized while they attempted to make conquests in Southeast Asia, but their action had the effect of provoking the US Congress, which had heretofore favoured neutrality, to declare war against Japan the very next day. On 9 December, China declared war on Japan, Germany and Italy, and on 11 December, Germany declared war on the USA. The Japanese made astonishing progress in picking off British possessions in Southeast Asia, capturing Singapore in February 1942 and Burma (where George Orwell had once served as a policeman) in May. A major turning point came in late October, when a British army serving under Field Marshal Montgomery defeated its German and Italian opponents at the Second Battle of El-Alamein in Egypt, triumphing over the great German general Erwin Rommel. The Allies thereby checked Germany's territorial ambitions in North Africa and ensured continued access to the vital resources of the Middle East. And then, in the bitter Russian winter of 1942–3, the German 6th Army – barely sustained on rations of horse soup – was wiped out by the Red Army near Stalingrad (Volgograd).

The sensible thing at this point would have been for Germany to surrender, but Hitler ploughed on, and some Germans indulged in the fantasy that a top-secret death ray would soon give their country the decisive advantage. Britain reacted by prioritizing air campaigns, bombing towns and cities to wear down German morale. These campaigns were led by Air Marshal Arthur 'Bomber' Harris, who believed (in the words of Norman Stone) that 'if smashing cities did not win the war outright, it was because they were not being smashed hard enough'.[14] In fact, the bombing campaigns, which reduced urban centres and charming medieval towns to ruins, were arguably counterproductive because they intensified the Germans' hatred of their adversaries and commitment to go on fighting. In Operation Chastise, carried out on the night of 16 May 1943, an RAF squadron commanded by Guy Gibson wrecked two German dams with bouncing bombs designed by the engineer Barnes Wallis, flooding the Ruhr valley and crippling German industrial production for months. The story of an engineer contributing so imaginatively to the war effort has long captured the public imagination, having its parallels in the classical story of Archimedes helping to defend Syracuse against the Romans.

The end of the war was near at hand. Allied troops, in a combined British, American and Canadian operation, landed in Normandy on 6 June 1944 and liberated France from Nazi occupation. Their success was due in part to the efforts of British codebreakers working at Bletchley Park in Milton Keynes as part of a secret project called Ultra. These codebreakers, the most famous being Alan Turing, helped the Allies to crack German ciphers and stay one step ahead of their enemies. As a Cambridge don in the 1930s, Turing had invented the programmable computer, but his brilliant life ended tragically. After the war, in 1952, he was convicted for homosexual activity and chose to undergo oestrogen treatment rather than going to prison, before committing suicide two years later. Soviet troops surrounded Berlin on 16 April 1945, and two weeks later, Hitler swallowed a cyanide capsule and shot himself in the head. An Allied victory was declared on VE Day (Victory in Europe Day), 8 May 1945. President Truman ordered the US air force to detonate atomic bombs over Hiroshima and Nagasaki on 6 and 9 August, forcing Japan's surrender. The total death toll in Europe and Russia had been over 40 million (355,000 British lives were lost, including 60,000 civilians).

POST-WAR BRITAIN

Winston Churchill was voted out of office on 5 July 1945 in a surprise Labour landslide. He was replaced by the Oxford-educated Labour leader Clement Attlee, Britain's second Labour prime minister. Known as Clem to his close associates, Attlee had previously served in the wartime coalition. He was a family man of gentle demeanour, modest and unassertive, though he could be surprisingly decisive when occasion required. One of Attlee's achievements as prime minister was the expansion of the welfare state, of which some of the groundwork had been laid by Churchill's administration. Sir William Beveridge's 1942 report *Social Insurance and Allied Services* had promised the implementation of 'cradle to grave' welfare measures. The National Insurance Act of 1946 expanded the provisions of the similarly titled Act of 1911: now National Insurance covered the entire population, offering unemployment, sickness and retirement benefits in return for monthly contributions. The National Health Service (NHS), designed to run on socialist principles, was set up in 1946 by the health minister Aneurin Bevan. Some of the founding principles of the NHS had been framed by the Conservative health minister

Sir Henry Willink a few years earlier. In the economic sphere, the Attlee administration operated a policy of cautious nationalization of industries and institutions, including the Bank of England in 1946 and coal mines in 1947. The United Kingdom began to receive financial assistance from the United States as part of the Marshall Plan of 1948, an attempt to rebuild the economies of western Europe. In the same year, the Labour government conducted a purge of communists in its ranks and within the civil service, believing them to be a threat to civil order.

The Labour government also continued the inevitable process of dismantling the British Empire. At its height, the Empire had encompassed about a quarter of the world's land surface but was now 'turning into millions of acres of bankrupt real estate, partly ungovernable and partly not worth governing'.[15] If the nineteenth century had been the age of empire, the later twentieth century was to be the age of the small, self-governing nation state. The United States, not Britain, was to be the world hegemon in the post-war order, and Britain could maintain her own strategic interests on a shoestring by retaining sovereignty over little islands dotted around the globe – the British Overseas Territories. In 1947, about six months before the assassination of Mahatma Gandhi, the UK Parliament passed the Indian Independence Act, which renounced India as a colonial possession and set up a partition between majority Hindu India and majority Muslim Pakistan, which, it was hoped, would bring peace to the subcontinent.

The United Kingdom also withdrew from Palestine (mandated to Britain since 1920) in 1948, opening the way for the establishment of a Jewish state there. Many former colonies joined the Commonwealth, a loose voluntary association of nations and territories. As for the United Kingdom, its population was still overwhelmingly white British: it has been estimated that there were only 103,000 ethnic minority residents in England and Wales in 1951, out of a total population of around 43.8 million (i.e., 0.2 per cent of the population). The ethnic minority population gradually increased with growing immigration from the Commonwealth. For example, 500 Jamaican immigrants arrived in England on the HMT *Empire Windrush* in the summer of 1948. Britain was slowly being transformed from 'white world-imperial power to multi-racial middle-ranking European state'.[16]

In the general election of 23 February 1950, Labour was returned to office but with a reduced overall majority of only five seats. The party performed relatively poorly in part because of their perceived mismanagement of affairs, but also for technical reasons such as constituency boundary revisions. In another general election held on 25 October 1951, the Conservatives won an overall majority of seventeen seats and returned to power, with Winston Churchill again appointed as prime minister. A few months later, on 6 February 1952, King George VI passed away. Though his daughter's reign was not to be dominated by the evils of world war, there were to be other challenges.

THE LATER TWENTIETH CENTURY TO THE PRESENT DAY

When Queen Elizabeth II was crowned at Westminster Abbey on 2 June 1953, the service was captured on video camera for the first time in history, with the BBC's footage narrated by Richard Dimbleby. About a third of the population were by now regular TV viewers. Elizabeth was 27 and had been married for five years to Philip Mountbatten, Duke of Edinburgh, a Navy lieutenant who had formerly been Prince of Greece and Denmark. Though Churchill remained in Downing Street for the first few years of Elizabeth's reign, his best days were past; he was deaf, irritable and unpredictable. At his last Cabinet meeting on 5 April 1955, he agreed to resign but expressed private reservations about the competence of his successor, Anthony Eden. Taller but less robust than Churchill, Eden had served two terms as Foreign Secretary before his appointment as premier. He was rather prickly and prone to anger. Not only did he have the unenviable job of following in the footsteps of 'the greatest Englishman of history', but there were also worries about his health.[1] He decided to call a general election for May 1955 to bring legitimacy to his administration, though he could technically have waited until October 1956, under the terms of the 1911 Parliament Act. Eden and his rival, Clement Attlee, campaigned tirelessly throughout the country, and the result was a Conservative victory: 345 seats against Labour's 277 and the Liberal Party's 6.

THE SUEZ CRISIS

The most notable event of Eden's administration was the Suez crisis (July–November 1955). The Suez Canal in Egypt is a 120-mile waterway connecting the Mediterranean with the Red Sea, which has long served as a major shipping lane. It was built with French money between 1859 and 1869 by the Suez Canal Company, in which the British government bought shares during Disraeli's second administration. The Constantinople Convention of 1888 stipulated that ships of any country had the right to navigate the canal in peace and war. Britain had long stationed troops in the area to protect its interests, but in 1954, her representatives signed the Suez Canal Base Agreement, naively promising to evacuate troops from the region. Two months after the evacuation was completed, the President of Egypt, Gamal Abdel Nasser, declared the nationalization of the canal, contrary to reassurances he had made to the British government. Nasser gave this takeover an air of legality by promising to compensate shareholders, but the canal company's offices and infrastructure were immediately seized by the Egyptians. The nationalization of the canal was retaliation for Britain's recent decision to renege on its promise to fund construction of the Aswan Dam. It posed an immediate threat to British and global financial interests, since most Western oil supplies were transported through the canal.

Britain prepared to take military action if necessary, and Eden set up a Cabinet body called the Egypt Committee to plan how to retake the canal and, it was hoped, to oust Nasser. At first, the government tried to solve the problem through diplomacy, and the United States strongly warned against a military response, but there was a sense of urgency because Britain could not risk losing fuel supplies before the approach of winter. In October, Eden approved a secret French–Israeli scheme to take back the canal. The plan, subsequently discussed in meetings of the Cabinet, was for Israel to invade Egypt as an excuse for Britain and France to enter the region as supposed peacemakers. The British stressed that they were not *encouraging* an Israeli invasion of Egypt; they were only deciding what to do if such an invasion should transpire – a fine distinction that helped them to avoid a degree of responsibility.

Israel did indeed invade Egypt on 30 October, whereupon British and French forces arrived to 'stabilize' the region. However, the conspiracy had been too obvious. It was impossible for Britain to keep its plans secret, partly because the CIA detected an increase in cipher communications between Paris and Tel Aviv. The Canadian Foreign Minister, Lester Pearson, suggested defusing the situation with the creation of a United Nations Emergency Force (UNEF) to keep peace in Suez, a plan for which he won the Nobel Peace Prize. Though a slim majority of the British public supported Eden's actions, the political opposition took a toll on the prime minister's health, and he unwillingly resigned on 9 January 1957. At his last Cabinet meeting, he tearfully berated ministers: 'You are all deserting me, deserting me.'[2]

YOU'VE NEVER HAD IT SO GOOD

Harold Macmillan succeeded Eden as leader of the Conservative Party and prime minister. Macmillan was a man of good parts who struggled with nerves before major public speaking occasions. The political cartoonist Victor Weisz, pen name 'Vicky', created a long-running cartoon strip satirizing the prime minister as an incompetent superhero called Supermac, but ironically this only increased the public's affection for Macmillan. He initially managed to reduce inflation and bolster the party's reputation, and in the general election of October 1959, the Conservatives won an increased majority, after having campaigned on the slogan: 'Life's better with the Conservatives. Don't let Labour ruin it.' This is commonly misremembered as 'You've never had it so good', based on something Macmillan had said in 1957: 'Let's be frank about it, most of our people have never had it so good.'[3]

Despite the optimism of sloganeers, the economy took a minor downturn after the election, and so ministers felt the need to increase the volume of British exports. In 1961, Macmillan decided to apply for British membership of the European Economic Community (EEC), the precursor of the European Union. On 14 January 1963, the president of France, General de Gaulle, used his veto to block Britain's application – a blow to Macmillan that is remembered as 'de Gaulle's "non"'. The French believed that the United Kingdom was 'the Trojan Horse of Washington'.[4] De Gaulle said 'non' to Britain again in 1967 when she reapplied for membership, and she did not manage to join the EEC until 1 January 1973 (a couple of years after de Gaulle's death). As for Britain's relationship with the rest of the world, Macmillan's government oversaw further decolonization, with The Gambia, Nigeria, Sierra Leone and Uganda gaining independence between 1960 and 1965.

THE PROFUMO AFFAIR

Macmillan made an unprecedently aggressive Cabinet reshuffle on 13 July 1962, sacking seven ministers in an attempt to restore the Conservative Party's popularity and his own grip on the government. This reshuffle was nicknamed the Night of the Long Knives, an allusion to the 1934 Nazi purge. However, it had little effect, for the credibility of Macmillan's government took a hit in 1963 from which it never recovered, due to the so-called Profumo affair. The married, middle-aged Secretary of State for War, John Profumo, had been having an affair with a 19-year-old model and dancer, Christine Keeler. This girl had apparently been procured by an osteopath called Stephen Ward, who was thought to be part of a 'sordid underworld network' of elite sex trafficking. Keeler was also in a relationship with a Russian attaché called Eugene Ivanov, which raised the possibility of Soviet espionage, especially given Profumo's sensitive role and responsibility in government. Profumo lied to members of Parliament on 22 March, claiming that though he was 'on friendly terms' with the girl, 'there was no impropriety whatsoever'. He also threatened to 'issue writs for libel and slander if scandalous allegations are made or repeated outside the House' (accusations made within the Commons were protected by the parliamentary privilege of liberty of speech).[5] Soon after, however, clear evidence emerged to prove Profumo a liar, and he was forced to resign when found guilty of contempt of Parliament.

Amidst rumours of an official cover-up, this scandal marked the beginning of the end for Macmillan. Immediate resignation was out of the question as the world waited to see whether human civilization would be consumed in a nuclear apocalypse during the Cuban Missile Crisis of October 1962, but the crisis was averted when Nikita Khrushchev agreed to move Soviet nuclear warheads out of Cuba. Macmillan resigned as prime minister on 6 June 1963 (a few months before the BBC broadcast the first episode of *Doctor Who*). Sir Alec Douglas-Home, who renounced his peerage to qualify for the Conservative leadership, replaced Macmillan as prime minister. He served for only twelve months before his party was defeated in the general election of 1964, ending a thirteen-year stretch of Conservative government. He was forced to resign as party leader by his irate colleagues; Reginald Maudling, later Home Secretary, said that the way the prime minister was treated proved that 'the old rules of public life applied, namely that there is no gratitude in politics, and you should never kick a man until he is down'.[6] Although barely remembered, Douglas-Home sometimes comes up in quizzes as the only British prime minister to have played first-class cricket.

LABOUR AND IMMIGRATION

In the 1964 election, Labour won a slim overall majority of four seats. The Yorkshire-born Harold Wilson was appointed as Britain's third Labour prime minister. Although he had read Philosophy, Politics and Economics (PPE) at Oxford and owned a house in London, Wilson was still something of a social outsider, which added to his charm: in his first audience with the queen, he wore a suit jacket instead of a morning coat in contravention of Palace etiquette. Blunders such as this, however, did not stop him from becoming one of Her Majesty's favourite prime ministers. The new government passed various socialist measures, including the introduction of a capital gains tax and a corporation tax, and the reintroduction of rent controls by repeal of the 1957 Rent Act. While praiseworthy in intent, such measures led ultimately to a loss of trust in British sterling and the selling off of currency, which was thought to be overvalued, causing great financial hardship.

Wilson called another general election for March 1966, in which the party increased its overall majority to ninety-seven. In the following year, the Chancellor of the Exchequer, James Callaghan, attempted to ease continuing financial pressures by devaluing the pound in relation to other currencies by 14 per cent, which was supposed to promote British exports. Although Wilson stressed that this did not mean that the 'pound in your pocket' had lost value internally, the devaluation hit consumers by raising the cost of imports and therefore leading to price rises. People struggling with the cost of living might have been cheered up somewhat by England's victory in the World Cup Final against Germany on 30 July 1966. Commonwealth immigration to Britain continued at pace during the Wilson administration. Parliament passed the first Race Relations Act in 1965 to prohibit racial discrimination in public and to criminalize incitement to racial hatred. Still, the government accepted that there was 'justifiable concern' across the political spectrum about the large number of immigrants arriving in Britain fraudulently and sought to tighten controls.[7] Wilson also had his work cut out with the prime minister of the self-governing colony of Southern Rhodesia (modern Zimbabwe), the oddly charismatic Ian Smith, who approved a unilateral declaration of independence in 1965.

RIVERS OF BLOOD

Rising levels of immigration led to public discontent, which was channelled by figures such as Enoch Powell, a Birmingham-born, classically educated Tory politician who had served in the Second World War. Contrary to popular belief, Powell was not a fascist, but rather a 'parliamentarian and libertarian who repudiated economic corporatism'.[8] In the late 1950s, he had been active in denouncing the murder of African prisoners in Kenya by British guards, unlike some of his fellow Conservatives. But it is the Birmingham speech of 20 April 1968 – delivered in the same year the Beatles released the White Album – that everyone remembers. He argued that some British people had been 'made strangers in their own country', with their 'neighbourhoods changed beyond recognition, their plans and prospects for the future defeated'. He also quoted the Roman poet Virgil to prophesy future racial strife in Britain: 'Like the Roman, I seem to see "the River Tiber foaming with much blood".'[9]

This speech may have been a 'revolt against the accepted complacency of Establishment London, or simply a reflection of a fatal maverick streak'.[10] The leader of the opposition, Edward Heath, responded by kicking Powell out of the Shadow Cabinet.

On 5 May, the prime minister responded to Powell in a public speech, also delivered at Birmingham, decrying 'racialism' but also affirming the government's commitment to strengthening immigration restrictions. This riposte was described by the *Guardian* as a 'sermon on the brotherhood of man'.[11] The economic highlight of the 1960s was the discovery of oil in the North Sea in 1969, which would allow Britain to become a self-sufficient energy producer by 1980. In May 1970, Wilson formally advised the queen to dissolve Parliament and called a general election for 18 June. He campaigned heavily on the theme of 'responsibility', but the fact that he had to stress this word indicates that voters may have doubted how far the government had acted responsibly.

TED HEATH

Although many opinion polls wrongly predicted another Labour victory, voters returned a Conservative majority to Parliament in 1970, on a seventy-seven-seat swing. Edward Heath, who had been waiting for his chance for five years, became prime minister. Born into a very humble family, Heath had won a grammar school scholarship followed by a place at Oxford, and his talents commended him to all. On his accession to the premiership, Ted Heath appointed Margaret Thatcher as Secretary of State for Education – the only woman in the Cabinet. Amazingly, Heath captained the British sailing team to victory in the 1971 Admiral's Cup, an unprecedented achievement for a sitting prime minister, and one that helped to enhance his public image. In the same year, Heath's government passed the Industrial Relations Act to improve relations between businesses and trade unions, an unpopular and pretty well useless law. On 15 February 1971, the UK's currency was decimalized, and the old pre-decimal system whereby £1 was worth 20 shillings and 1 shilling was worth 12 pence, which had been in place for a millennium, was consigned to the history books. The most significant event of Heath's premiership was Britain's entry into the EEC in January 1973, mentioned earlier, with support from some Labour MPs and opposition from others, including Tony Benn. Entry into the EEC was also opposed by Enoch Powell.

THE TROUBLES AND INFLATION

In Northern Ireland, Heath was forced to deal with the early stages of the Troubles, a long period of sectarian unrest (roughly 1968 to 1998). He found himself up against the IRA, who used terrorist tactics to press for greater political representation of Catholics at Stormont, the Northern Irish Parliament. The British government assumed direct rule of Northern Ireland in 1972, sending about 20,000 soldiers to keep the peace. Another grave problem was spiralling inflation, which had not been such a major problem in England since the Tudor age. Britain and the USA both faced serious inflationary pressures, caused in part by their governments' attempts to ease unemployment by printing more money, and possibly exacerbated by President Richard Nixon's decision to take his country off the gold standard in 1971.

Heath's government believed that rising wages were the main driver of inflation. The US economist Milton Friedman had recently published a pamphlet entitled *Inflation: Causes and Consequences*, which set out the monetary theory of inflation: in short, that general inflation (as opposed to localized price rises) can only be caused by a money supply that expands more quickly than overall productivity. But since this theory was not yet widely credited, Heath's decision to focus on cost-push inflation was understandable. At first, he resolved to avoid introducing statutory limits on wages or prices, seeking to solve the problem by negotiating with trade unions. But the government eventually changed gears and introduced prices and incomes regulation with the 1973 Counter-Inflation Act – part of a package of policies vapidly termed the 'dash for growth'. Although the government arguably helped to increase national prosperity, it did not manage to check inflation, which had reached a rate of over 20 per cent by 1975. Naturally, the trade unions strongly opposed wage controls, and in early 1974, the National Union of Mineworkers announced its intention to strike.

After failing to broker a deal, Heath called a general election for 28 February 1974, which returned a hung Parliament. Harold Wilson was propelled back into office, this time at the head of a minority government. At a general election held in October, hot on the heels of the previous one, Labour increased its share of parliamentary seats to win an overall majority of three seats. The backdrop of the election was continuing terrorist violence from Irish Catholic radicals, as IRA bombs exploded with sickening regularity in pubs, car parks and government buildings across the UK. Parliament passed the Prevention of Terrorism Act in 1974, which introduced severe new penalties and granted the police sweeping powers in relation to terrorist activities.

MARGARET THATCHER

Margaret Thatcher was elected leader of the Conservative Party in 1975, having stood as the 'standard-bearer of free market economics', in opposition to the socialist agenda pursued to some extent by both parties since the Second World War.[12] Thatcher had been educated at Oxford (Chemistry) and had worked as both a chemist and a lawyer. On 16 March 1976, Wilson surprised his colleagues by resigning as prime minister in favour of his Foreign Secretary, James Callaghan, a man with extensive experience in government. Wilson claimed that he was resigning on account of his age (he was 60) but he may actually have been blackmailed into doing so after MI5 got its hands on incriminating papers from his desk – a claim made in Peter Wright's 1987 book *Spycatcher: The Candid Autobiography of a Senior Intelligence Officer*. The end of Callaghan's government was precipitated by the so-called Winter of Discontent, a series of strikes in 1978–9 by workers in the public and private sectors. Trains stopped running, uncollected rubbish piled up in the streets and the lights were going out. The public voted, quite naturally, for change.

The Conservatives won a landslide victory in the general election of 3 May 1979, with an overall majority of forty-three seats, thanks in part to a skilful public relations campaign organized by the London firm Saatchi & Saatchi. Thatcher therefore became the UK's first female prime minister. Some sectors of the economy were thriving in the 1970s and '80s, such as the British computer industry, which had not yet lost out to American competition. The Cambridge firm Sinclair Research put out several personal computers in the 1980s, including the Sinclair ZX80. But other industries were failing, as is inevitable in an age of transition. The new Chancellor of the Exchequer, Geoffrey Howe, thought it was better to tackle inflation than to maintain an artificially high level of employment. By January 1982, the unemployment rate was 2.67 million, having risen nearly 50 per cent in four years. Unemployment led to unrest, and unrest led to countrywide riots.

A distraction from the unemployment crisis came with the military government of Argentina's decision to invade the Falkland Islands, known to the Spanish-speaking world as Las Malvinas, on 2 April 1982. These islands, situated off Argentina's east coast and teeming with penguins, had been in British possession since 1832. Thatcher sent a 'task force' of a hundred ships to the South Atlantic and controversially ordered the sinking of the Argentine cruiser *General Belgrano* by submarine-launched torpedoes on 2 May, even though it was sailing away and was outside an exclusion zone drawn up by the British. On 21 May, a team of Royal Marines and SAS forces recaptured the islands as part of Operation Sutton, overcoming a much larger Argentine force. The 'Falklands Factor' contributed to Thatcher's phenomenal success in the election of June 1983, alongside the fact that the government had brought inflation down. Although the party's overall share of the vote was 1 per cent lower than it had been in 1979, it gained over a hundred more seats this time – a quirk of the first-past-the-post system.

PRIVATIZATION AND THE POLL TAX

As a free marketeer, Thatcher believed that the government should not be expected to prop up failing industries. Ironically, it was thanks to Labour's nationalization of coal in 1947 that the government held the fate of the coal industry entirely in its own hands. Ian MacGregor, Thatcher's chairman of the National Coal Board, began to order the closure of unprofitable mines but came up against determined opposition from Arthur Scargill, president of the National Union of Mineworkers. The predictable result was a miners' strike, which lasted from March 1984 to March 1985, when the miners ultimately agreed to go back to work even though they had won no concessions from the government. In the first year of the strike, an IRA bomb nearly annihilated the entire Cabinet at the Brighton Grand Hotel, where the Conservative Party was holding its annual conference – a modern-day Gunpowder Plot. While overseeing the closure of mines, Thatcher also orchestrated the privatization of government assets, including British Airways, Cable and Wireless, Jaguar, Rolls-Royce and part of British Rail. The underlying theory was that state-owned companies are often unprofitable and uncompetitive, but one Labour Lord criticized the policy as 'selling off the family silver to pay for the groceries'.[13] Thatcher also deregulated the London Stock Exchange in 1986, which soon enabled the City of London to become the financial capital of Europe. At this time, 10 per cent of the British population held 49 per cent of the marketable wealth – perhaps only a sign of the Pareto principle at work, but for some it demonstrated the unfairness of modern global capitalism.

The Iron Lady's uncompromising economic policies were hated by many, but she proved that she commanded the support of a majority of the electorate in June 1987 when she won her third consecutive election, the first time a party leader had achieved this since 1826. The Conservatives won 42.2 per cent of the vote, compared to Labour's 30.8 per cent, on a 75.5 per cent turnout. Only four months after the Conservative victory came Black Monday, 19 October, when the value of British stocks and shares fell by £50 billion, part of a global financial slump caused by a poorly performing American economy. Thatcher made one of the greatest missteps of her premiership in 1988 by introducing the poll tax (predecessor of the current council tax). This was a flat-rate local tax levied on all residents of a local community, not just householders, as had been the case under the old system of local rates taxation. The tax was even opposed by her own Chancellor of the Exchequer, Nigel Lawson. Many low-income households simply refused to pay, and there were tax riots in London. Thatcher was also becoming out of step with her own party, which was increasingly Europhile. She resigned as leader of the Conservatives on 22 November 1990, just over a year after the fall of the Berlin Wall, and about the same time that the English computer scientist Tim Berners-Lee invented the World Wide Web, an information retrieval service making use of computer networking technology invented by US engineers.

JOHN MAJOR

John Major, who took over as prime minister, differed from Thatcher in his leadership style: 'Government was no longer by confrontation but rather by discussion.'[14] He cultivated an approachable manner and was instantly recognizable from his fashionably oversized glasses. One of his first acts in office was to send troops to liberate Kuwait from Iraqi occupation as part of the international Operation Desert Storm (January–February 1991). Saddam Hussein, president of Iraq since 1979, had invaded the small, oil-rich kingdom five months earlier. Western intervention in this conflict, the Gulf War, resulted in Iraq's withdrawal from Kuwait. At a general election on 9 April 1992, Major pulled off another Conservative victory, leading the party to an overall majority of twenty-one. In 1993, despite opposition from some Conservatives, the British Parliament ratified the Maastricht Treaty (1992), which renamed the EEC as the European Union (EU) and set out a plan for greater European cooperation not just in the economic sphere but also in foreign policy, law and security. Major was quite happy to agree to terms that Thatcher would have refused to contemplate and so, by a process of gradualism, British law and government were becoming increasingly integrated into a European whole.

What of Labour? Since it was now nearly two decades since they had won an election, the party clearly needed to regroup and, to use an ugly term, rebrand. In July 1994, the centrist Tony Blair was elected as Labour leader. He launched a memorable slogan encapsulating his political aims: 'New Labour, New Britain'. New Labour 'went all out in its drive to prove its adherence to the capitalist system', despite opposition from Tony Benn, Jeremy Corbyn, Ken Livingstone and other leftists in the party.[15] Meanwhile, the Conservative Party suffered from unfavourable media attention, with some of its MPs accused of corruption, immorality and 'sleaze'. Its run of success was over.

NEW LABOUR

In advance of the general election of 1 May 1997 – held, incidentally, a couple of months prior to the publication of J.K. Rowling's first Harry Potter novel – the Conservatives campaigned on the slogan 'Britain is Booming, Don't Let Labour Blow It'. But this warning was not enough to prevent a Labour landslide. The party won a remarkable 418 seats, and Blair was appointed as Britain's fifth Labour prime minister. About a quarter of this crop of Labour MPs were educators by profession, including fifty-four schoolteachers and fifty-seven lecturers, while only twenty-nine were lawyers. Over a hundred were women, a group described in the tabloids as Blair's Babes, and five women were appointed to the Cabinet, another record. At least ten members of the Cabinet had been educated at public schools, while five had graduated from Oxford or Cambridge. A few months after the Labour victory, Princess Diana (who had divorced from Prince Charles in 1996) died in a car accident in Paris along with her friend Dodi Fayed, son of the billionaire owner of Harrods. The circumstances of her death have naturally led to conspiracy theories, with some suggesting that she was assassinated on the orders of MI5.

Labour engaged in a process of constitutional reform, for instance by establishing devolved representative assemblies in Scotland and Wales, and by cutting down the number of hereditary peers in the House of Lords. Blair also introduced Britain's first national minimum wage in 1998. In Ireland, the Good Friday Agreement, signed in Belfast in April 1998, established a system of government in Northern Ireland that was palatable to both Catholics and Protestants, a vital step towards establishing peace after decades of sectarian strife. Before polling day, Blair had claimed that his top three priorities for government were 'education, education and education'.[16] He went on to institute a wide range of education reforms in concert with his blind Secretary of State for Education, David Blunkett, which included limiting class sizes in schools, introducing a numeracy hour in primary schools, and encouraging international students to study at British universities. In preparation for the year 2000, Blair's government authorized the construction of the Millennium Dome in Greenwich in south London (now the O2 Arena), designed by the architect Richard Rogers. Widespread fears of a 'millennium bug' that would cause computers to malfunction across the globe turned out to be unfounded. In June 2001, Blair was re-elected as prime minister. His next two terms were dominated by Britain's involvement in controversial US-dominated wars in Afghanistan and Iraq.

Afghans were no strangers to international warfare, having fought three wars with Britain and one with the Soviet Union since 1839. During the Soviet–Afghan War of 1979–89, the Afghan resistance had been financed and armed by the United States. After the conclusion of this war, a political organization called the Taliban rose to power, seeking to unify the government of Afghanistan and strengthen the hold of Islamic law. The Taliban captured Kabul, Afghanistan's temperate capital, in 1996 and declared an Islamic Emirate. The Taliban leader Mullah Mohammed Omar tolerated the activities of the terrorist organization al-Qaeda within Afghan borders. Al-Qaeda was led by Osama bin Laden, a wealthy Saudi national. Bin Laden issued a *fatwa* against the United States in 1996, apparently hoping this would be the first step towards a new Islamic world order.

On 11 September 2001, nineteen al-Qaeda militants hijacked four American passenger jets. Two were piloted straight into the twin towers of the World Trade Center in New York City, while a third crashed into the Pentagon in Arlington, Virginia. The fourth, intended for the Capitol Building in Washington, DC, crashed prematurely. Three thousand civilians were killed. The militants were of several nationalities, and none were Afghans, although some had trained in Afghanistan. The US President George W. Bush demanded that the Taliban hand over the other al-Qaeda militants or face reprisals, but Mullah Omar argued that 'turning over Osama would only be a disgrace for us'.[17] The USA made its first airstrike on Taliban sites in Afghanistan on 7 October 2001, the first stage of the grandiosely named 'Operation Enduring Freedom'. The United Kingdom supported America with troops, of whom about 500 were killed prior to the conclusion of the war in 2021, when the Taliban rose to power once more.

The Iraq War

Blair also involved the United Kingdom in war with Iraq, where the USA staged a coup to topple the administration of Saddam Hussein. This conflict, which lasted from 2003 to 2009, was less easily defensible than the war in Afghanistan. The pretext furnished by the White House in conjunction with the US intelligence agencies was that Iraq held weapons of mass destruction, which turned out to be untrue. Exactly why US official opinion coalesced around the war remains unclear, though some critics blamed special interest groups such as arms companies, the oil industry and the 'Israel lobby'.[18] This war resulted in the loss of 179 British soldiers. Back at home, Blair won his third election on 5 May 2005. Although he had a reduced majority, he was the first Labour prime minister to serve three terms. Something about the changeable nature of British politics can be detected in the fact that Blair and Thatcher, as different from each other as chalk and cheese, are the only prime ministers for the past two centuries to have been elected for three consecutive terms. Two months after the election, on 7 July 2005, four radicalized British Muslims from West Yorkshire launched suicide bomb attacks on a bus and three underground trains in London, killing fifty-two people as well as themselves. Blair's third term was his most accomplished in terms of policy achievements, including reforms to the NHS, secondary education, the welfare state and nuclear energy. However, in part due to the unpopularity of the continuing Iraq war, Blair felt compelled to resign the premiership on 28 June 2007. Financial inequality had grown during his three terms in office, with the share of wealth held by the richest strata of British citizens continuing to rise.

THE FINANCIAL CRISIS

Blair was succeeded as Labour leader and prime minister by his Chancellor of the Exchequer, Gordon Brown, a Scotsman with a PhD in History. Brown's administration coincided with the 2007–8 global financial crisis, triggered by the bursting of a housing bubble in the USA that had grown up on cheap credit. The UK Treasury decided in February 2008 to nationalize Northern Rock, one of the country's largest mortgage lenders, and took other action to protect the economy. Britain is still struggling with the after effects of the financial crash. In May 2009 came the parliamentary expenses scandal, in which the *Daily Telegraph* revealed that MPs from all major parties had been wasting taxpayers' money by abusing the parliamentary expenses system. This scandal damaged the reputations of both the Conservatives and Labour. Though Brown was a man of superior intellect, and pretty authentic as politicians go, he could never match Blair's simulated charisma. Just days before the general election of 6 May 2010, his handlers staged an awkward filmed conversation with an elderly Labour voter from Rochdale called Gillian Duffy. Moments after the cameras were switched off, the prime minister was caught on a hot mic describing her as a 'bigoted woman', a comment which seemed to reflect his disrespect for ordinary voters. Change was in the air.

THE CONSERVATIVE RESURGENCE

The May 2010 election resulted in a hung Parliament, and the Conservatives formed a government with the (nominally centrist) Liberal Democrats – the first coalition government since 1945. The Conservative leader David Cameron became prime minister, with the Lib Dem leader Nick Clegg serving as deputy prime minister. Both men had gone to public schools and were Oxbridge-educated. The new Chancellor of the Exchequer, George Osborne, spearheaded an austerity plan that reduced many welfare payments and cut public-sector employment. The government also introduced a new payment called Universal Credit to simplify (and arguably pare back) the welfare system and introduced Work Capability Tests for benefits claimants. In 2011, Clegg supported the Conservative plan to raise maximum undergraduate university fees to £9,000 a year, breaking one of his party's election pledges and undermining the Liberal Democrats' credibility. In the summer of the same year there were riots in London and other cities, ostensibly in response to the killing of Mark Duggan by Metropolitan Police officers.

The United Kingdom played host to the Olympics in 2012, the third time it has ever done so. Some drew unfavourable comparisons between the 27 July opening ceremony and the more spectacular Beijing Olympics opening ceremony of 2008. In August 2012, Australian national Julian Assange, who had released top-secret US documents on the website WikiLeaks, was granted asylum in the Ecuadorean embassy in London, where he would remain for the next seven years. In other news, there were repeated calls from the ascendant Scottish National Party (SNP) for a reconfiguration of the British constitution. After a victory in the 2011 Scottish parliamentary elections, SNP leader Alex Salmond had declared that his government had the 'moral authority' to hold a referendum on Scottish independence.[19] Such a referendum was eventually held on 18 September 2014, when over 55 per cent of voters in Scotland opted to remain part of the United Kingdom. Then, in the British general election of 7 May 2015, the Conservatives won a small overall majority, largely thanks to a collapse in support for the Lib Dems. Cameron returned to Downing Street as the head of a Conservative-only government. Ed Miliband resigned as Labour leader and was succeeded by the far-left favourite Jeremy Corbyn, who had served in Parliament for over three decades. Corbyn would go on to enjoy incredible support from some sections of society, especially the young, but he would ultimately fail to translate this into an election victory.

BREXIT

The Conservative leadership had long heard calls from the Eurosceptic wing of their own party to reconsider the role of the United Kingdom in Europe. Early in 2015, Cameron agreed to schedule an 'in or out' referendum on the UK's membership of the European Union. He opposed the idea of withdrawal and hoped he could pull off a success similar to the Scottish independence referendum. On 9 October 2015, the Vote Leave campaign was launched under the leadership of the political strategist Dominic Cummings. Cummings ran the campaign with the awareness, in the words of one of his allies, that 'people in market towns in the Midlands hate London, hate the elites, think more money should go to the NHS, hate bankers and are not very keen on foreigners'.[20] On 19 February 2016, the European Council in Brussels attempted to placate British Eurosceptics by agreeing on an 'emergency brake' for immigration, meaning that the government would temporarily be able to limit European migrants' benefits in the first four years after their arrival in the UK. Two days later, Boris Johnson, then Mayor of London, decided that he would support the Leave campaign. The referendum was held on Thursday, 23 June after ferocious and often nasty campaigning on both sides. On a turnout of 72.2 per cent (about five points higher than the typical general election), 51.9 per cent voted to leave the EU.

As Cameron watched the results coming in all night, it gradually
dawned on him that his side had lost. He announced the next day
that he would resign, declaring that the British people had made a
'very clear decision'. Home Secretary Theresa May went on to win
the Conservative leadership election, after Boris's leadership campaign was undermined by the defection of key allies such as Michael
Gove. In March 2017, May triggered Article 50 of the Lisbon Treaty,
the formal first step in leaving the EU. She called a general election,
hoping that popular support for Brexit would boost her party's
Commons majority of only seventeen seats. But the Conservatives
lost their slim majority, precisely the opposite of what was intended,
and had to rely thenceforth on a 'confidence and supply' deal with
Northern Ireland's Democratic Unionist Party (DUP).

The Cabinet formulated an exit plan in May 2018 at Chequers, a
country house in Buckinghamshire used as a prime ministerial residence. This plan would have committed the UK to a 'soft' Brexit,
meaning that she would still follow some EU rules and that there
would be freedom of movement between the UK and the EU. It
soon became clear, however, that there was serious opposition to
this plan within the Conservative Party. May's Brexit blueprint was
rejected twice in the Commons, on 15 January and 12 March 2019,
after which some commentators helpfully pointed out that Albert
Einstein's supposed definition of insanity was doing the same thing
twice and expecting a different result. May resigned on 7 June and
was succeeded by the more colourful and popular Boris Johnson on
24 July, who had been waiting in the wings for the top job. At a general election on 12 December, general frustration over delays to Brexit
helped the Conservatives to win a large overall majority. The UK then
formally left the European Union on 31 January 2020. The long-term
effects of this momentous decision remain to be seen, though in the
short term it seems to have harmed British economic interests.

COVID-19

Two days prior to Brexit Day, on 29 January 2020, the UK had its
first confirmed cases of the novel coronavirus Covid-19, which was
discovered in two guests at the Staycity Hotel in York. Initially, the
World Health Organization advised against mask-wearing and flight

restrictions, but on 11 March it declared a pandemic. The UK went into lockdown on 23 March, with citizens forbidden to leave their homes except to buy essentials and to exercise once every day. This was given legal force by the Coronavirus Act, passed on 25 March, and the prime minister himself caught the virus two days later. The lockdown was partially lifted on 13 May, whereupon a three-tier system was introduced so that different regions of the UK could be placed into separate categories of risk, with different restrictions – Medium (indoor gatherings of no more than six people), High (no indoor gatherings) and Very High (no outdoor gatherings).

Britain was placed under lockdown once again from 5 November to 2 December, after which the nation reverted to the tier system. A new, higher tier was introduced on 19 December, named Tier 4, which no doubt sounded better than 'Very, Very High'. On 30 December, the government granted emergency approval for a vaccine developed by the University of Oxford and AstraZeneca, which promised a route out of the pandemic. A third lockdown was imposed on 6 January 2021, which was relaxed in stages between March and May. On 19 July, most restrictions were lifted, although some were reimposed in December. The government then began to transition to a more relaxed approach termed 'Living with Covid', with virtually all remaining restrictions removed in early 2022. From February, Covid patients no longer had to isolate themselves upon testing positive. It is estimated at the time of writing (December 2022) that just under 200,000 people have died of Covid in the UK, about 0.3 per cent of the population, though the methodology for collecting these statistics has been called into question. To put that in perspective, about 20,000 people die of influenza in England and Wales each year.

Boris Johnson, who had led the government throughout the pandemic, found his premiership increasingly dogged by scandals, and he announced his resignation as party leader on 7 July 2022. Liz Truss, formerly Foreign Secretary, was appointed as prime minister on 6 September after winning the leadership contest, though she was forced to resign forty-four days later after losing the confidence of the party, making her the shortest-serving prime minister in British history. Her Majesty Queen Elizabeth II, the longest-reigning British (and English) monarch, passed away at Balmoral Castle, reportedly her favourite residence, on 8 September, just two days after inviting Truss to form a government. She was 96 years old.

What comes next? England's influence remains inescapable. The educated speak English the world over; English law and finance are everywhere renowned; and many countries have clones of the British parliamentary system. England's universities, never mind their undoubted failings, have earned their reputation for excellence. Even the most trivial and fatuous academic work produced in England finds admirers and imitators across the globe. True, there are other areas in which England is performing poorly. The UK's faltering economy is propped up by an endless supply of hopeful immigrants. Perhaps England's finest days are already past, or perhaps she has not yet made her greatest contribution to world history. Who can say? The future is the province of pundits and prophets, not historians. Time will tell. It will fall to future historians to record the rest.

ENDNOTES

CHAPTER 1

1   L.S. Stavrianos, *A Global History: From Prehistory to the Present*, fifth edn. (Englewood Cliffs, NJ: Prentice Hall, 1991), p. 32.
2   E. Cary, trans., *Dio's Roman History*, vol. 8 (London: William Heinemann, 1925), p. 85.
3   S. Ireland, *Roman Britain: A Sourcebook*, third edn. (Abingdon: Routledge, 2008), p. 160.

CHAPTER 2

1   C. Wickham, *The Inheritance of Rome: Illuminating the Dark Ages, 400–1000* (New York: Viking, 2009), p. 25.
2   N.J. Higham and M.J. Ryan, *The Anglo-Saxon World* (New Haven: Yale University Press, 2013), p. 188.
3   J. Whitaker, ed., *The Life of Saint Neot: The Oldest of All the Brothers to King Alfred* (London: John Joseph Stockdale, 1809), p. 236.
4   E. John, 'The Age of Edgar', in J. Campbell, E. John and P. Wormald, eds., *The Anglo-Saxons* (Ithaca: Cornell University Press, 1982), p. 168.
5   J.A. Giles, *Roger of Wendover's Flowers of History*, vol. 1 (London: Henry G. Bohn, 1849), pp. 314–315.
6   T. Forester, ed., *The Chronicle of Henry of Huntingdon* (London: Henry G. Bohn, 1853), p. 199.
7   C. Williamson, trans., *The Complete Old English Poems* (Philadelphia: University of Philadelphia Press, 2017), p. 455.
8   W. Besant, 'The Future of the Anglo-Saxon Race', *The North American Review* 163, no. 477 (1896), pp. 129–143; R.J. White, *A Short History of England* (Cambridge: Cambridge University Press, 1967), pp. 37–38.

CHAPTER 3

1   S. Morillo, ed., *The Battle of Hastings: Sources and Interpretations*
     (Woodbridge: The Boydell Press, 1996), p. 46.
2   J.A. Giles, ed., *The Anglo-Saxon Chronicle*, new edn. (London: G. Bell and
     Sons, 1914), p. 139.
3   S.E. Finer, *The History of Government*, vol. 2 (Oxford: Oxford University
     Press, 1997), p. 899.
4   W.C. Hollister, *The Making of England to 1399*, eighth edn. (Boston:
     Houghton Mifflin, 2001), p. 155.
5   R. Bartlett, *England Under the Norman and Angevin Kings, 1075–1225*
     (Oxford: Clarendon Press, 2000), p. 38.
6   Hollister, *The Making of England*, p. 163.
7   Hollister, *The Making of England*, p. 162.
8   D. Carpenter, *The Struggle for Mastery: Britain 1066–1284* (London:
     Penguin, 2004), p. 164.
9   Carpenter, *Struggle for Mastery*, p. 172.

CHAPTER 4

1   Gerald of Wales, *Giraldi Cambrensis Opera*, ed. J.S. Brewer, vol. 1 (London:
     Longman, 1861), p. 52; Carpenter, *Struggle for Mastery*, p. 205.
2   J. McGovern, 'The Origin of the Phrase "Will no one rid me of this turbulent
     priest?"', *Notes & Queries* 68, no. 3 (2021), p. 266.
3   W. Scott, *Ivanhoe* (London: Marcus Ward & Co., 1878), p. 379.
4   Carpenter, *Struggle for Mastery*, pp. 247–255.
5   J. Gillingham, *Richard the Lionheart* (New York: Times Books, 1978),
     p. 219.
6   Carpenter, *Struggle for Mastery*, pp. 272–273.
7   C.R. Cheney, 'King John and the Papal Interdict', *Bulletin of the John
     Rylands Library* 31, no. 2 (1948), p. 295.
8   W. Holden, trans., *Magna Carta* (London: W. Holden, 1887), pp. 21–22.
     Chapter 39 is numbered 29 in the 1225 version.
9   J. Baker, *The Reinvention of Magna Carta 1216–1616* (Cambridge:
     Cambridge University Press, 2017), p. 1.

CHAPTER 5

1   Carpenter, *Struggle for Mastery*, p. 312.
2   Carpenter, *Struggle for Mastery*, p. 338.
3   C.L. Kingsford, ed., *The Song of Lewes* (Oxford: Clarendon Press, 1890),
     line 24.
4   Carpenter, *Struggle for Mastery*, p. 380.
5   M.T. Clanchy, *England and its Rulers, 1066–1307*, third edn. (Malden, MA:
     Blackwell, 2006), p. 294.

6   M. Powicke, *The Thirteenth Century, 1216–1307* (Oxford: Clarendon Press, 1953), p. 421.

7   A. Musson, 'Second "English Justinian" or Pragmatic Opportunist? A Re-Examination of the Legal Legislation of Edward III's Reign', in J.S. Bothwell, ed., *The Age of Edward III* (Woodbridge: York Medieval Press, 2001), p. 69.

8   G. Lapsley, 'John De Warenne and the Quo Waranto Proceedings in 1279', *The Cambridge Historical Journal* 2, no. 2 (1927), p. 111.

9   S. Payling, 'The House of Commons, 1307–1529', in C. Jones, ed., *A Short History of Parliament* (Woodbridge: The Boydell Press, 2009), p. 79.

10 W. Stubbs, *Chronicles of the Reigns of Edward I and Edward II*, vol. 2 (London: Her Majesty's Stationery Office, 1883), p. xlix.

11 B. Wilkinson, 'The Coronation Oath of Edward II and the Statute of York', *Speculum* 19, no. 4 (1944), p. 447.

12 M. Prestwich, *Plantagenet England, 1225–1360* (Oxford: Clarendon Press, 2005), p. 189.

13 T.F. Tout, *The Place of the Reign of Edward II in English History* (Manchester: Manchester University Press, 1914), p. 74.

14 Prestwich, *Plantagenet England*, p. 197.

15 15 Edward II, 'Revocatio novarum Ordinationum', printed in *Statutes of the Realm*, vol. 1 (London: Dawsons of Pall Mall, 1810), p. 189.

16 C. Marlowe, *The troublesome raigne and lamentable death of Edward the second* (London: R. Robinson, 1594), signature no. L4v [scene 24]. Marlowe's version has only one assassin, named Lightborn.

17 N.A. Cervo, 'Marlowe's Edward II', *The Explicator* 58, no. 3 (2000), p. 123.

CHAPTER 6

1   B. Wilkinson, *The Constitutional History of England, 1216–1399: With Select Documents*, vol. 2 (London: Longmans, 1958), p. 174.

2   W.M. Ormrod, *Edward III* (New Haven: Yale University Press, 2011), p. 90.

3   Ormrod, *Edward III*, p. 149.

4   Ormrod, *Edward III*, p. 239.

5   C. Babington, ed., *Polychronicon Ranulphi Higden monachi Cestrensis*, vol. 2 (London: Longman, 1865), p. 167.

6   D. Green, *The Hundred Years War: A People's History* (New Haven: Yale University Press, 2014), p. 29.

7   R. Horrox, *The Black Death* (Manchester: Manchester University Press, 1994), p. 84.

8   Ormrod, *Edward III*, p. 474.

9   G.L. Harriss, *Shaping the Nation: England 1360–1461* (Oxford: Clarendon Press, 2005), p. 437.

10 R.B. Dobson, *The Peasants' Revolt of 1381*, second edn. (London: Macmillan, 1983), p. 347.

11 Dobson, *The Peasants' Revolt*, p. 167.

12 B. Wilkinson, *The Later Middle Ages in England, 1216–1485* (London: Longmans, 1969), p. 169; G.H. Martin, ed., *Knighton's Chronicle 1337–1396* (Oxford: Clarendon Press, 1995), p. 484.

13 Aristotle, *Politics*, trans. E. Baker and rev. R.F. Stalley (Oxford: Oxford University Press, 1995), p. 121 [III. 14]; Lord Acton, 'Beginning of the Modern State', in *Lectures on Modern History*, ed. J.N. Figgis and R.V. Laurence (London: Macmillan, 1921), p. 51.

CHAPTER 7

1   C. Given-Wilson, *Henry IV* (New Haven: Yale University Press, 2016), p. 1.

2   *Henry V*, act 3, scene 1.

3   F. Taylor, 'The Chronicle of John Strecche for the Reign of Henry V (1414–1422)', *Bulletin of the John Rylands Library* 16, no. 1 (1932), p. 147.

4   Harriss, *Shaping the Nation*, p. 574.

5   M.R. James, ed., *Henry the Sixth: A Reprint of John Blacman's Memoir* (Cambridge: Cambridge University Press, 1919), p. 30.

6   B. Wolffe, *Henry VI*, new edn. (New Haven: Yale University Press, 2001), p. xix; Finer, *History of Government*, vol. 2, p. 907.

7   A.L. Kaufman, *The Jack Cade Rebellion of 1450: A Sourcebook* (Lanham, MD: Lexington Books, 2019), pp. 114–115.

8   C. Richmond, 'Beaufort, Edmund, first duke of Somerset (c. 1406–1455)', *Oxford Dictionary of National Biography*.

9   C. Richmond, 'The Nobility and the Wars of the Roses: The Parliamentary Session of January 1461', *Parliamentary History* 18, no. 3 (1999), p. 262; Harriss, *Shaping the Nation*, p. 642.

10 C. Ross, *Edward IV* (Berkeley: University of California Press, 1974), p. 44.

CHAPTER 8

1   S.B. Chrimes, *Henry VII*, new edn. (New Haven: Yale University Press, 1999), p. 68.

2   S. Cunningham, *Henry VII* (London: Routledge, 2007), p. 110.

3   G.R. Elton, *England under the Tudors*, second edn. (London: Methuen, 1974), p. 72.

4   Elton, *England under the Tudors*, p. 77.

5   J.O. Halliwell, ed., *Letters of the Kings of England*, vol. 1 (London: Henry Colburn, 1846), p. 302.

6   G.W. Bernard, *The King's Reformation: Henry VIII and the Remaking of the English Church* (New Haven: Yale University Press, 2005), p. 21.

7   J. Gairdner, ed., *Letters and Papers of Henry VIII*, vol. 11 (London: Her Majesty's Stationery Office, 1888), p. 510.

8   M.L. Bush, *The Pilgrims' Complaint: A Study of Popular Thought in the Early Tudor North* (Farnham: Ashgate, 2009), p. 251.

9   M.H. Dodds and R. Dodds, *The Pilgrimage of Grace 1536–1537 and the Exeter Conspiracy 1538*, vol. 2 (Cambridge: Cambridge University Press, 1915), p. 36.

10 31 Henry VIII, *c.* 14.

CHAPTER 9

1   B. Cummings, ed., *The Book of Common Prayer: The Texts of 1549, 1559, And 1662* (Oxford: Oxford University Press, 2013), p. 19.

2   M. Stoyle, '"Kill all the gentlemen"? (Mis)representing the Western Rebels of 1549', *Historical Research* 92, no. 255 (2019), pp. 50–72; Edward VI, *A message sent by the Kynges majestie to certain of his people, assembled in Deuonshire* (1549), signature no. B5r.

3   J. Guy, *Tudor England* (Oxford: Oxford University Press, 1988), p. 208.

4   M.J. Armstrong, *History and Antiquities of the County of Norfolk*, vol. 10 (Norwich: M. Booth, 1781), p. 35.

5   Elton, *England under the Tudors*, p. 208.

6   G.W. Sprott, ed., *The Second Prayer-Book of King Edward the Sixth, 1552* (Edinburgh: William Blackwood and Sons, 1905), p. 159.

7   J. McGovern, 'A Herald's Account of Mary I's Oration at the Guildhall (1 February 1554)', *Notes & Queries* 66, no. 3 (2019), p. 388.

8   J.N. King, ed., *Foxe's Book of Martyrs: Select Narratives* (Oxford: Oxford University Press, 2009), p. 154.

9   L. Strachey, *Elizabeth and Essex: A Tragic History* (New York: Harcourt, Brace and Company, 1928), p. 16. Beatrice of Savoy, King Henry III of England's mother-in-law, was Elizabeth's ancestor.

10 L.S. Marcus, J. Mueller and M.B. Rose, eds., *Elizabeth I: Collected Works* (Chicago: University of Chicago Press, 2000), p. 182.

11 F. Bacon, *The Works of Francis Bacon*, vol. 3 (London: Baynes and Son, 1824), p. 73.

12 T. Norton, *To the Queenes Maiesties poore deceiued subiectes of the northe contreye, drawne into rebellion by the Earles of Northumberland and Westmerland* (London: Henry Bynneman for Lucas Harrison, 1569), signature no. B2r.

13 R. Lockyer, *Tudor and Stuart Britain: 1485–1714*, third edn. (Abingdon: Routledge, 2005), p. 213.

14 P.E. McCullough, *Sermons at Court: Politics and Religion in Elizabethan and Jacobean Preaching* (Cambridge: Cambridge University Press, 1998), p. 85.

15 J. Marriott, *This Realm of England: Monarchy, Aristocracy, Democracy* (London: Blackie & Son, 1938), p. 185; P. Lake, *Anglicans and Puritans? Presbyterianism and English Conformist Thought from Whitgift to Hooker* (London: Unwin Hyman, 1988), p. 7.

16 G. Mattingly, *The Armada* (Boston, MA: Houghton Mifflin, 1959), p. 265.

17 William Shakespeare, *Richard II*, A.B. Dawson and P. Yachnin, ed., (Oxford: Oxford University Press, 2011), p. 4.

18 A. Gajda, *The Earl of Essex and Late Elizabethan Political Culture* (Oxford: Oxford University Press, 2012), p. 29.

19   Y. Winters, 'The 16th Century Lyric in England: A Critical and Historical
     Reinterpretation: Part I', *Poetry* 53, no. 5 (1939), p. 258.
20   Sir W. Raleigh, *The Works of Sir Walter Raleigh*, vol. 1 (London: R. Dodsley,
     1751), p. 273.
21   J.R. Tanner, ed., *Constitutional Documents of the Reign of James I*
     (Cambridge: Cambridge University Press, 1930), p. 4.

CHAPTER 10

1   W. Barlow, *The summe and substance of the conference* (London: Valentine
     Simmes for Matthew Law, 1605), pp. 79–80, 82.
2   J.R. Tanner, ed., *Constitutional Documents of the Reign of James I*,
     pp. 90–91.
3   P. McCullough, ed., *Lancelot Andrewes: Selected Sermons and Lectures*
     (Oxford: Oxford University Press, 2005), p. 147. The Biblical reference is to
     Exodus 12.
4   L. Levy Peck, *Court Patronage and Corruption in Early Stuart England*
     (London: Routledge, 1993), p. 24.
5   James VI and I, *Daemonologie in forme of a dialogue, divided into three
     bookes* (Edinburgh: Robert Waldegrave, 1597), p. 37.
6   P.M., *King Charles his birthright. By P.M. Gentleman* (Edinburgh: John
     Wreittoun, 1633), signature no. A3v.
7   J.P. Kenyon, *The Stuart Constitution, 1603–1688: Documents and
     Commentary*, second edn. (Cambridge: Cambridge University Press, 1986),
     p. 208.
8   G. Davies, *The Early Stuarts, 1603–1660*, second edn. (Oxford: Clarendon
     Press, 1959), p. 121.
9   Davies, *Early Stuarts*, p. 123.
10   M.A. Kishlansky, *A Monarchy Transformed: Britain 1603–1714* (London:
     Penguin, 1997), p. 150.
11   Davies, *Early Stuarts*, p. 128.
12   F. Hargrave, ed., *A Complete Collection of State-Trials and Proceedings for
     High Treason*, vol. 1 (London: T. Wright for C. Bathurst &c., 1776), p. 992.

CHAPTER 11

1   *Journal of the House of Commons*, vol. 6 (London: His Majesty's Stationery
     Office, 1902), p. 111.
2   A. Marvell, 'An Horatian Ode upon Cromwell's Return from Ireland', in *The
     Poems of Andrew Marvell* (London: Heinemann, 1969), p. 120.
3   Kishlansky, *A Monarchy Transformed*, p. 187.
4   Davies, *Early Stuarts*, p. 259; J. Dryden, 'Astraea Redux', in *Poems* (Oxford:
     Clarendon Press, 1958), p. 24.
5   G. Clark, *The Later Stuarts, 1660–1714*, second edn. (Oxford: Clarendon
     Press, 1955), p. 93.

6   T.B. Macaulay, *The History of England*, ed. H. Trevor-Roper (London: Penguin, 1986), pp. 480, 123.
7   J. Hoppit, *A Land of Liberty? England 1689–1727* (Oxford: Clarendon Press, 2002), p. 25; E. Burke, *Reflections on the Revolution in France*, second edn. (London: J. Dodsley, 1790), p. 23.
8   Hoppit, *Land of Liberty*, pp. 20, 151, 135.
9   A.V. Dicey, *Lectures Introductory to the Study of the Law of the Constitution* (London: Macmillan & Co., 1885), p. 39; Hoppit, *Land of Liberty*, pp. 27, 144.
10 Macaulay, *History of England*, p. 475.
11 *Journal of the House of Lords*, vol. 17 (London: Her Majesty's Stationery Office, 1803), p. 68.
12 J. Swift, *The conduct of the allies, and of the late ministry, in beginning and carrying on the present war* (London: John Morphew, 1711), signature no. A2r.

CHAPTER 12

1   J.R. Seeley, *The Expansion of England; Two Courses of Lectures*, second edn. (London: Macmillan, 1914), pp. 20–21, 28.
2   White, *Short History of England*, p. 179.
3   Hoppit, *Land of Liberty*, p. 384.
4   B. Williams, *The Whig Supremacy 1714–1760*, second edn. (Oxford: Clarendon Press, 1962), p. 14.
5   Hoppit, *Land of Liberty*, p. 335.
6   Hoppit, *Land of Liberty*, pp. 410, 412.
7   J.H. Plumb, *The First Four Georges* (New York: Macmillan, 1957), p. 64.
8   H.T. Dickinson, *Walpole and the Whig Supremacy* (London: English Universities Press, 1973), pp. 66, 70.
9   Dickinson, Walpole and the Whig Supremacy, p. 71.
10 P. Langford, *A Polite and Commercial People: England 1727–1783* (Oxford: Clarendon Press, 1989), p. 49.
11 Dickinson, *Walpole and the Whig Supremacy*, p. 134.
12 Dickinson, *Walpole and the Whig Supremacy*, p. 73.
13 Plumb, *The First Four Georges*, p. 91.
14 Langford, *Polite and Commercial People*, pp. 223–224.
15 S. Schama, *A History of Britain*, vol. 2 (London: BBC, 2001), p. 452; G. Agar-Ellis, ed., *Letters of Horace Walpole*, vol. 3 (London: Richard Bentley, 1833), p. 352.

CHAPTER 13

1   J. Cannon, 'George III (1738–1820)', *Oxford Dictionary of National Biography*.
2   Langford, *Polite and Commercial People*, p. 554.
3   Langford, *Polite and Commercial People*, p. 548.

4   A. Roberts, *Napoleon and Wellington: The Battle of Waterloo and the Great
     Commanders Who Fought It* (New York: Simon and Schuster, 2001), p. 16.
5   A. Briggs, *The Age of Improvement, 1783–1867* (London: Longman, 1979),
     p. 147.
6   B. Hilton, *A Mad, Bad and Dangerous People? England 1783–1846* (Oxford:
     Oxford University Press, 2006), p. 264.
7   Hilton, *Mad, Bad and Dangerous People*, p. 28.
8   *Report of the Proceedings in the House of Lords on the Bill of Pains and
     Penalties against the Queen*, vol. 1 (Edinburgh: Bell & Bradfute, 1820),
     p. 25.
9   L. Woodward, *The Age of Reform, 1815–1870*, second edn. (Oxford:
     Clarendon Press, 1962), p. 53; B. Disraeli, *Coningsby*, ed. B.N. Langdon-
     Davies (London: R. Brimley Johnson, 1904), pp. 86–89.
10   A. Smith, *An Inquiry into the Nature and Causes of the Wealth of Nations*,
     vol. 2 (London: W. Strahan, 1776), p. 35.
11   A. Smith, 'Arthur Thistlewood: A Regency Republican', *History Today* 3,
     no. 12 (1953), p. 847.
12   G.H.L. Le May, *The Victorian Constitution: Conventions, Usages and
     Contingencies* (New York: St Martin's Press, 1979), p. 129.
13   Plumb, *The First Four Georges*, p. 159.
14   Boyd, *Mad, Bad and Dangerous People*, p. 418.
15   Seeley, *Expansion of England*, p. 10.

CHAPTER 14

1   A. Chernock, *The Right to Rule and the Rights of Women: Queen Victoria
     and the Women's Movement* (Cambridge: Cambridge University Press,
     2019), p. 1; T. Martin, *Queen Victoria as I Knew Her* (Edinburgh: William
     Blackwood, 1901), p. 70.
2   Hilton, *Mad, Bad and Dangerous People*, p. 500. The biographers were Lord
     David Cecil (1939 and 1954), Philip Ziegler (1976) and L.G. Mitchell (1997).
3   T.E. Kebbel, *Life of the Earl of Derby* (London: W.H. Allen, 1890), p. 150.
4   N. Gash, *Pillars of Government and Other Essays on State and Society,
     c.1770–c.1880* (London: Edward Arnold, 1986), p. 153.
5   Hilton, *Mad, Bad and Dangerous People*, p. 503.
6   M. Sanders, *The Poetry of Chartism: Aesthetics, Politics, History*
     (Cambridge: Cambridge University Press, 2009), p. 170.
7   Alfred, Lord Tennyson, 'The Charge of the Light Brigade', in *Maud, and
     Other Poems* (Boston: Ticknor and Fields, 1855), p. 157.
8   K.T. Hoppen, *The Mid-Victorian Generation, 1846–1886* (Oxford:
     Clarendon Press, 1998), p. 178.
9   C.C. Osborne, *Letters of Charles Dickens to the Baroness Burdett-Coutts*
     (London: John Murray, 1931), p. 189.
10   B. Disraeli, *Selected Speeches of the Late Right Honourable the Earl of
     Beaconsfield*, ed. T.E. Kebbel, vol. 2 (London: Longmans, Green, and Co.,
     1882), p. 406.
11   W.E. Gladstone, *Political Speeches in Scotland, November and December
     1879* (Edinburgh: Andrew Elliot, 1879), p. 114.

12   J.R. Jewell, 'Using Barbaric Methods in South Africa: The British
     Concentration Camp Policy during the Anglo-Boer War', *Scientia Militaria*
     31, no. 1 (2003), p. 1; A.F. Havighurst, *Britain in Transition: The Twentieth
     Century* (Chicago: University of Chicago Press, 1985), p. 57.

13   G.R. Searle, *A New England? Peace and War, 1886–1918* (Oxford: Oxford
     University Press, 2004), p. 329.

14   H.G. Wells, *Anticipations of the Reaction of Mechanical and Scientific
     Progress upon Human Life and Thought*, fourth edn. (London: Chapman,
     1904), pp. 99, 107.

15   P. Larkin, 'Church Going', in *Collected Poems*, ed. A. Thwaite (New York:
     Farrar, Straus and Giroux, 2004), p. 58.

CHAPTER 15

1   H. Nicholson, *King George the Fifth: His Life and Reign* (London: Constable
     & Co., 1952), p. 106.

2   A.J.P. Taylor, *War by Time-Table: How the First World War Began* (London:
     Macdonald & Co., 1969), p. 45.

3   *Treaty of Peace with Germany* (Washington DC: Government Printing Office,
     1921), p. 32; Havighurst, *Britain in Transition*, p. 148.

4   A.J.P. Taylor, *English History 1914–1945* (Oxford: Oxford University Press,
     1975), p. 155.

5   Havighurst, *Britain in Transition*, p. 242; S. Jenkins, *A Short History of
     England* (London: Profile Books, 2011), p. 234.

6   S. Ball, 'Baldwin, Stanley, first Earl Baldwin of Bewdley (1867–1947)',
     Oxford Dictionary of National Biography; Havighurst, *Britain in Transition*,
     p. 200.

7   Gladstone, *Speeches*, p. 108.

8   J. Betjeman, 'Death of King George V', in *Collected Poems*, enlarged edn.
     (London: John Murray, 1970), p. 45.

9   F. Donaldson, *Edward VIII* (Philadelphia: Lippincott, 1975), p. 349.

10   B. Harrison, *Seeking a Role: The United Kingdom 1951–1970* (Oxford:
     Clarendon Press, 2009), p. 406.

11   N. Chamberlain, *The Struggle for Peace* (London: Hutchinson, 1937),
     p. 302.

12   I. Kershaw, *To Hell and Back: Europe 1914–1949* (New York: Viking, 2016),
     p. 343.

13   Hansard, House of Commons Debate 4 June 1940, vol. 361, *cc*. 796, 7890.

14   N. Stone, *World War Two: A Short History* (London: Allen Lane, 2013),
     p. 118.

15   N. Stone, *World War One: A Short History* (London: Allen Lane, 2007),
     p. xi.

16   Harrison, *Seeking a Role*, p. 532.

CHAPTER 16

1   D.R. Thorpe, Eden: *The Life and Times of Anthony Eden, First Earl of Avon
    1897–1977* (London: Pimlico, 2004), p. 433.
2   D. Childs, *Britain Since 1945: A Political History*, fifth edn. (London:
    Routledge, 2001), p. 63.
3   P. Clarke, *Hope and Glory: Britain 1900–2000* (London: Penguin, 2004),
    p. 270; Childs, *Britain Since 1945*, p. 76.
4   Childs, *Britain Since 1945*, p. 94.
5   Hansard, House of Commons Debate 22 March 1963 (vol. 673, *c.* 810);
    House of Commons Debate 17 June 1963 (vol. 679, *c.* 35); House of
    Commons Debate 20 June 1963 (vol. 679, *c.* 665).
6   Childs, *Britain Since 1945*, p. 124.
7   H. Wilson, *A Personal Record: The Labour Government, 1964–1970*
    (London: Weidenfeld and Nicolson, 1971), pp. 84, 465.
8   Harrison, *Seeking a Role*, p. 221.
9   T.E. Utley, *Enoch Powell: The Man and His Thinking* (London: William
    Kimber, 1968), pp. 85–6, 190.
10 Childs, *Britain Since 1945*, pp. 143–144.
11 Wilson, *A Personal Record*, pp. 525–526, 528.
12 Childs, *Britain Since 1945*, p. 176.
13 Childs, *Britain Since 1945*, p. 233.
14 Childs, *Britain Since 1945*, p. 261.
15 Childs, *Britain Since 1945*, p. 285.
16 K. Stewart, 'Equality and Social Justice', in A. Selden, ed., *Blair's Britain,
    1997–2007* (Cambridge: Cambridge University Press, 2007), p. 410.
17 C. Malkasian, *The American War in Afghanistan: A History* (Oxford:
    Oxford University Press, 2021), p. 56.
18 J.H. Lebovic, *Planning to Fail: The US Wars in Vietnam, Iraq, and
    Afghanistan* (Oxford: Oxford University Press, 2019), p. 69.
19 M. Arnott, 'The Coalition's Impact on Scotland', in M. Beech and S. Lee,
    eds., *The Conservative–Liberal Coalition: Examining the Cameron–Clegg
    Coalition* (Basingstoke: Palgrave, 2015), p. 167.
20 T. Shipman, *All Out War: The Full Story of How Brexit Sank Britain's
    Political Class* (London: William Collins, 2016), p. 39.

SELECT BIBLIOGRAPHY

Ashton, N. and Lewis, S., 'Deserted Britain: Declining Populations in the British Late Middle Pleistocene', *Antiquity* 76, no. 292 (2002), pp. 388–396.

Bacon, F., *The History of the Reign of King Henry VII and Selected Works*, ed. Vickers, B. (Cambridge: Cambridge University Press, 1998).

Baker, J., *An Introduction to English Legal History*, fifth edn. (Oxford: Oxford University Press, 2019).

Bartlett, R., *England Under the Norman and Angevin Kings, 1075–1225* (Oxford: Clarendon Press, 2000).

Bennett, M., *The English Civil War, 1640–1649* (Harlow: Longman, 1995).

Bernard, G.W. and Gunn, S.J., eds., *Authority and Consent in Tudor England: Essays Presented to C.S.L. Davies* (Aldershot: Ashgate, 2002).

Bernard, G.W., *The King's Reformation: Henry VIII and the Remaking of the English Church* (New Haven: Yale University Press, 2005).

Blair, P.H., *An Introduction to Anglo-Saxon England* (Cambridge: Cambridge University Press, 1956).

Bonner, M., *Jihad in Islamic History: Doctrines and Practice* (Princeton: Princeton University Press, 2006).

Brace, S. et al., 'Ancient Genomes Indicate Population Replacement in Early Neolithic Britain', *Nature Ecology & Evolution* 3 (2019), pp. 765–771.

Bradbury, J., *The Battle of Hastings* (Stroud: The History Press, 2020).

Campbell, J., John, E. and Wormald, P., eds., *The Anglo-Saxons* (Ithaca: Cornell University Press, 1982).

Carpenter, D., *The Struggle for Mastery: Britain 1066–1284* (London: Penguin, 2004).

Childs, D., *Britain Since 1945: A Political History*, fifth edn. (London: Routledge, 2001).

Chrimes, S.B., *Henry VII*, new edn. (New Haven: Yale University Press, 1999).

Clanchy, M.T., *England and its Rulers, 1066–1307*, third edn. (Malden, MA: Blackwell, 2006).

Clark, G., *The Later Stuarts, 1660–1714*, second edn. (Oxford: Clarendon Press, 1955).

Clarke, P., *Hope and Glory: Britain 1900–2000* (London: Penguin, 2004).

Cunningham, S., *Henry VII* (London: Routledge, 2007).

Curry, A., *Agincourt* (Oxford: Oxford University Press, 2015).

Dangerfield, G., *The Strange Death of Liberal England* (London: Constable & Co., 1936).

Darvill, T., *Prehistoric Britain*, second edn. (London: Routledge, 1996).

Davies, G., *The Early Stuarts, 1603–1660*, second edn. (Oxford: Clarendon Press, 1959).

Davies, J.A., *The Little History of Norfolk* (Cheltenham: The History Press, 2020).

Dickinson, H.T., *Walpole and the Whig Supremacy* (London: English Universities Press, 1973).

Dobson, R.B., *The Peasants' Revolt of 1381*, second edn. (London: Macmillan, 1983).

Dodd, G. and Musson, A., eds., *The Reign of Edward II: New Perspectives* (Woodbridge: York Medieval Press, 2006).

Doran, S. and Freeman, T.S., eds., *Mary Tudor: Old and New Perspectives* (Basingstoke: Palgrave, 2011).

Douglas, D.C., *William the Conqueror: The Norman Impact upon England* (Berkeley: University of California Press, 1966).

Dyer, C., *A Country Merchant, 1495–1520: Trading and Farming at the End of the Middle Ages* (Oxford: Oxford University Press, 2012).

Elton, G.R., *England under the Tudors*, second edn. (London: Methuen, 1974).

Elton, G.R., *The Tudor Revolution in Government: Administrative Changes in the Reign of Henry VIII* (Cambridge: Cambridge University Press, 1969).

Encyclopaedia Britannica (online).

F., J.R., 'Black Prince: Origin of Name', *Notes & Queries* 165 (1933), p. 266.

Feiling, K.G., *The Second Tory Party, 1714–1832* (London: Macmillan, 1959).

Finer, S.E., *The History of Government*, 3 vols. (Oxford: Oxford University Press, 1997).

Fowler, P.J., *The Farming of Prehistoric Britain* (Cambridge: Cambridge University Press, 1983).

Fremont-Barnes, G. and Fisher, T., *The Napoleonic Wars: The Rise and Fall of an Emperor* (Oxford: Osprey, 2007).

Frere, S., *Britannia: A History of Roman Britain*, third edn. (London: Pimlico, 1987).

Gillespie, C.C., *Boudica: Warrior Woman of Roman Britain* (Oxford: Oxford University Press, 2018).

Gillingham, J., *The Angevin Empire*, new edn. (London: Bloomsbury Academic, 2000).

Given-Wilson, C., *Henry IV* (New Haven: Yale University Press, 2016),

Gretzinger, J. et al., 'The Anglo-Saxon Migration and the Formation of the Early English Gene Pool', *Nature* 610 (2022), pp. 112–119.

Griffiths, R.A., *The Reign of King Henry VI: The Exercise of Royal Authority, 1422–1461* (London: Benn, 1981).

Grummitt, D., *A Short History of the Wars of the Roses* (London: I.B. Tauris, 2013).

Guy, J., *Tudor England* (Oxford: Oxford University Press, 1988).

Hallifax, S., '"Over by Christmas": British Popular Opinion and the Short War in 1914', *First World War Studies* 1, no. 2 (2010), 103–121.

Harper-Bill, C. and Vincent, N., eds., *Henry II: New Interpretations* (Woodbridge: The Boydell Press, 2007).

Harrison, B., *Finding a Role? The United Kingdom 1970–1990* (Oxford: Clarendon Press, 2011).

Harrison, B., *Seeking a Role: The United Kingdom 1951–1970* (Oxford: Clarendon Press, 2009).

Harriss, G.L., *Shaping the Nation: England 1360–1461* (Oxford: Clarendon Press, 2005).

Havighurst, A.F., *Britain in Transition: The Twentieth Century* (Chicago: University of Chicago Press, 1985).

Hawes, J., *The Shortest History of England* (London: Old Street Publishing, 2020).

Hicks, M., *The Wars of the Roses 1455–1485* (Oxford: Osprey, 2003).

Higham, N.J. and Ryan, M.J., *The Anglo-Saxon World* (New Haven: Yale University Press, 2013).

Higham, T. et al., 'The Earliest Evidence for Anatomically Modern Humans in Northwestern Europe', *Nature* 479 (2011), pp. 521–524.

Hilton, B., *A Mad, Bad and Dangerous People? England 1783–1846* (Oxford: Oxford University Press, 2006).

Hollister, W.C., *The Making of England to 1399*, eighth edn. (Boston: Houghton Mifflin, 2001).

Holmes, M., *The Failure of the Heath Government* (Basingstoke: Macmillan, 1997).

Hoppen, K.T., *The Mid-Victorian Generation, 1846–1886* (Oxford: Clarendon Press, 1998).

Hoppit, Julian., *A Land of Liberty? England 1689–1727* (Oxford: Clarendon Press, 2002),

Horrox, R., *The Black Death* (Manchester: Manchester Universit y Press, 1994).

Ireland, S., *Roman Britain: A Sourcebook*, third edn. (Abingdon: Routledge, 2008).

Jenkins, S., *A Short History of England* (London: Profile Books, 2011).

Jordan, W.K., *Edward VI: The Threshold of Power: The Dominance of the Duke of Northumberland* (London: George Allen & Unwin, 1970).

Kaye, J., *Kaye's and Malleson's History of the Indian Mutiny*, 6 vols. (New York: Longmans, 1914).

Kershaw, I., *To Hell and Back: Europe 1914–1949* (New York: Viking, 2016).

King, E., ed., *The Anarchy of King Stephen's Reign* (Oxford: Oxford University Press, 1994).

King, E., 'King Stephen and the Anglo-Norman Aristocracy', *History* 59, no. 196 (1974), 180–194.

Kishlansky, M.A., *A Monarchy Transformed: Britain 1603–1714* (London: Penguin, 1997).

Langford, P., *A Polite and Commercial People: England 1727–1783* (Oxford: Clarendon Press, 1989).

Lapidge, M., Blair, J., Keynes, S. and Scragg, D., eds., *The Wiley Blackwell Encyclopedia of Anglo-Saxon England*, second edn. (Chichester: Wiley Blackwell, 2014).

Leslie, S. et al., 'The Fine-scale Genetic Structure of the British Population', *Nature* 519 (2015), pp. 309–314.

Loades, D.M., *Two Tudor Conspiracies* (Cambridge: Cambridge University Press, 1965).

Loades, D.M., ed., *The Papers of George Wyatt Esquire of Boxley Abbey in the County of Kent, Son and Heir of Sir Thomas Wyatt the Younger.* Camden Fourth Series (London: Royal Historical Society, 1968).

Macaulay, T.B., *The History of England*, ed. Trevor-Roper, H., (London: Penguin, 1986).

MacCulloch, D., *Thomas Cranmer: A Life* (New Haven: Yale University Press, 1996).

Maddicott, J.R., *The Origins of the English Parliament, 924–1327* (Oxford: Oxford University Press, 2010).

Mattingly, D., *An Imperial Possession: Britain in the Roman Empire, 54 BC–AD 409* (London: Penguin, 2007).

Neidorf, L, ed., *The Dating of Beowulf: A Reassessment* (Woodbridge: Boydell & Brewer, 2014).

Nielson, J., and Skousen, R., 'How Much of the King James Bible is William Tyndale's? An Estimation Based on Sampling', *Reformation* 3, no. 1 (1998), pp. 49–74.

O'Day, A., ed., *The Edwardian Age: Conflict and Stability, 1900–1914* (London: Macmillan, 1979).

Olalde, I. et al., 'The Beaker Phenomenon and the Genomic Transformation of Northwest Europe', *Nature* 555 (2018), pp. 190–196.

Oliver, N., *A History of Ancient Britain* (London: Weidenfeld and Nicolson, 2011).

Ormrod, W. M., *Edward III* (New Haven: Yale University Press, 2011).

Oxford Dictionary of National Biography (online).

Parfitt, S.A. et al., 'Early Pleistocene Human Occupation at the Edge of the Boreal Zone in Northwest Europe', *Nature* 466 (2010), pp. 229–233.

Parfitt, S.A. et al., 'The Earliest Record of Human Activity in Northern Europe', *Nature* 438 (2005), pp. 1008–1012.

Patterson, N. et al., 'Large-scale Migration into Britain during the Middle to Late Bronze Age', *Nature* 601 (2022), pp. 588–594.

Paul, H.J., *The South Sea Bubble: An Economic History of its Origins and Consequences* (Abingdon: Routledge, 2011).

Pearson, M.P. et al., 'The Age of Stonehenge', *Antiquity* 81, no. 313 (2007), pp. 617–639.

Phillips, G., *The Rise of the Labour Party, 1893–1931* (London: Routledge, 1992).

Phillips, S., *Edward II: The Chameleon* (New Haven: Yale University Press, 2010).

Plumb, J.H., *The First Four Georges* (New York: Macmillan, 1957).

Poole, R., *Peterloo: The English Uprising* (Oxford: Oxford University Press, 2019).

Powicke, M., *The Thirteenth Century, 1216–1307* (Oxford: Clarendon Press, 1953).

Prestwich, M., *Edward I* (London: Methuen, 1988).

Prestwich, M., *Plantagenet England, 1225–1360* (Oxford: Clarendon Press, 2005).

Rappaport, M., *The Napoleonic Wars: A Very Short Introduction* (Oxford: Oxford University Press, 2013).

Rex, R., *The Tudors* (Stroud: Tempus, 2003).

Richardson, H.G., *The English Jewry under Angevin Kings* (London: Methuen, 1960).

Roebroeks, W., Hublin, JJ. and MacDonald, K., 'Continuities and Discontinuities in Neandertal Presence: A Closer Look at Northwestern Europe', *Developments in Quaternary Sciences* 14 (2011), pp. 113–123.

Ross, C., *Edward IV* (Berkeley: University of California Press, 1974).

Salway, P., *Roman Britain* (Oxford: Clarendon Press, 1981).

Salway, P., *Roman Britain: A Very Short Introduction* (Oxford: Oxford University Press, 2015).

Schama, S., *A History of Britain*, 3 vols. (London: BBC, 2000–2002).

Searle, G.R., *A New England? Peace and War, 1886–1918* (Oxford: Oxford University Press, 2004).

Selden, A., and Collings, D., *Britain under Thatcher* (Harlow: Pearson, 2000).

Smith, G., *England: A Short History* (New York: Charles Scribner's Sons, 1971).

Staunton, M., *The Historians of Angevin England* (Oxford: Oxford University Press, 2017).

Stenton, F.M., *Anglo-Saxon England*, third edn. (Oxford: Oxford University Press, 1971).

Stone, N., *World War One: A Short History* (London: Allen Lane, 2007).

Stone, N., *World War Two: A Short History* (London: Allen Lane, 2013).

Sweetman, J., *The Crimean War* (Oxford: Osprey, 2001).

Taylor, S.E., 'The Crown and the North of England, 1559–70: A Study of the Rebellion of the Northern Earls, 1569–70 and its Causes', PhD thesis (University of Manchester, 1981).

Thomas, R.P., 'The Sugar Colonies of the Old Empire: Profit or Loss for Great Britain?', *The Economic History Review* 21, no. 1 (1968) pp. 30–45.

Thornton, T., 'More on a Murder: The Deaths of the "Princes in the Tower", and Historiographical Implications for the Regimes of Henry VII and Henry VIII', *History* 106, no. 369 (2021), pp. 4–25.

Todd, M. ed., *A Companion to Roman Britain* (Malden, MA: Blackwell, 2004).

Toghill, P., *The Geology of Britain: An Introduction* (Shrewsbury: Swan Hill, 1999).

Turner, R.V., 'King John's Military Reputation Reconsidered', *Journal of Medieval History* 19, no. 3 (1993), pp. 171–200.

Turner, R.V. and Heiser, R.R., *The Reign of Richard the Lionheart: Ruler of the Angevin Empire, 1189–99* (Abingdon: Routledge, 2000).

Ward, J.H., 'Vortigern and the End of Roman Britain', *Britannia* 3 (1972), pp. 277–289.

Watkins, C., *Stephen: The Reign of Anarchy* (London: Allen Lane, 2015).

White, R.J., *A Short History of England* (Cambridge: Cambridge University Press, 1967).

Whitehead, B.T., *Brags and Boasts: Propaganda in the Year of the Armada* (Stroud: Sutton, 1994).

Whitley, C.B. and Kramer, K., 'A New Explanation for the Reproductive Woes and Midlife Decline of Henry VIII', *The Historical Journal* 53, no. 4 (2010), pp. 827–848.

Wilkinson, B., *The Constitutional History of England, 1216–1399: With Select Documents*, vol. 2 (London: Longmans, 1958).

Wilkinson, B., *The Later Middle Ages in England 1216–1485* (London: Longmans, 1969).

Williams, B., *The Whig Supremacy 1714–1760*, second edn. (Oxford: Clarendon Press, 1962).

Wilson, H., *A Personal Record: The Labour Government, 1964–1970* (London: Weidenfeld and Nicolson, 1971).

Wolffe, B., *Henry VI*, new edn. (New Haven: Yale University Press, 2001).

Wooding, L., *Tudor England: A History.* (New Haven: Yale University Press, 2023).

Woodward, L., *The Age of Reform, 1815–1870*, second edn. (Oxford: Clarendon Press, 1962).

Wrigley, E.A. and Schofield, R.S., *The Population History of England, 1541–1871: A Reconstruction* (Cambridge, MA: Harvard University Press, 1981).

ACKNOWLEDGEMENTS

My father offered valuable suggestions on an earlier draft of this book, for which I am glad to record my gratitude. My students at Nanjing University listened to much of the material in an earlier form; their smart questions helped me to perfect the narrative. I am grateful to my wife for her constant love and encouragement, and to my baby daughter for giving me a reason to get away from my books and laptop every once in a while.

The map of ninth-century England was drawn by Damian Dobrew, based on a map by R. Botev available in the public domain. The Sutton Hoo helmet in Chapter 2 and the scene from the Bayeux Tapestry in Chapter 3 were drawn by Nishani Sanjeewani. Dr Francis Young prepared the index and spotted a few errors into the bargain. Any book like this is a work of synthesis, so I would like to pay tribute to all the historians past and present whose work I have benefitted from in preparing it.

ABOUT THE AUTHOR

Jonathan McGovern was born and raised in Derby. He read History and English at St Peter's College, Oxford, and received his PhD from the University of York. He is author of *The Tudor Sheriff: A Study in Early Modern Administration* (Oxford University Press, 2022), as well as numerous scholarly articles. He was appointed a Fellow of the Royal Historical Society in 2022.

INDEX